A T. S. ELIOT COMPANION

A T. S. ELIOT COMPANION

Life and Works

F. B. PINION

BARNES & NOBLE BOOKS
TOTOWA, NEW JERSEY

First published in Great Britain 1986 by
The Macmillan Press Ltd

First published in the USA 1986 by
BARNES & NOBLE BOOKS
81 ADAMS DRIVE
TOTOWA, NEW JERSEY, 07512

ISBN 0–389–20620–2

Typeset by Wessex Typesetters
(Division of The Eastern Press Ltd)
Frome, Somerset

Printed in Hong Kong

Library of Congress Cataloging-in-Publication Data
Pinion, F. B.
A T. S. Eliot companion.
Bibliography: p.
Includes index.
1. Eliot, T. S. (Thomas Stearns), 1888–1965.   2. Authors,
American—20th century—Biography.   I. Title.
PS3509.L43Z8138   1986   821'.912 [B]   85–1255
ISBN 0–389–20620–2

For T. M. Farmiloe

Contents

List of Illustrations

Acknowledgments

The biographical sketch which introduces this work owes much to R. Sencourt, *T. S. Eliot: A Memoir*, London, 1971; T. S. Matthews, *Great Tom*, London, 1974; and Allen Tate's edition of *T. S. Eliot: The Man and His Work*, London, 1967. It draws also from the letters, diaries, and memoirs of a number of writers, as well as from H. Howarth, *Notes on Some Figures Behind T. S. Eliot*, Boston (Mass.), 1964, and London, 1965; W. T. Levy and V. Scherle, *Yours Affectionately, T. S. Eliot*, London, 1969; Joseph Chiari, *T. S. Eliot: A Memoir*, London, 1982; and the introductions to Valerie Eliot's facsimile edition of *The Waste Land* and Helen Gardner's *The Composition of 'Four Quartets'*. I am especially indebted to the Bodleian Library for permission to study the diaries and papers of Vivienne Haigh-Wood. Apart from some slight chronological adjustments and additions which have been made in the light of Peter Ackroyd's massive research, this section remains substantially as it was when completed in the summer of 1984.

It is impossible to assess my obligations to writers on Eliot over a long period. I have discarded many interpretations in the course of time, but I am sure I must be indebted to Grover Smith and others for whom I have not made room in my short list of bibliographical recommendations. No study has done more to reawaken, deepen, and intensify my interest in Eliot, particularly his poetry, than Lyndall Gordon's *Eliot's Early Years*.

My main indebtedness in the preparation of this book has been to my wife, who has closely scrutinized the text at two or three stages in its development, and thereby done much to eliminate obscurities and imprecisions. The benefit of such co-operation is incalculable, but it is undoubtedly high, as it has been for my previous publications.

I wish to express gratitude for assistance from many sources: to the Inter-Library Loan Department of the University Library,

Sheffield; to my brother Tom for generously giving up days to photograph places of Eliot interest in London and the provinces; to Professor Charlotte Lindgren of Emerson College, Boston, for most ready help and advice, particularly on illustrations and on Cape Ann; to Lord Harrowby's family for access to Burnt Norton and information on T. S. Eliot's visit; to J. W. Fisher for his most thorough preliminary investigations at the Bodleian; to Dr C. J. P. Beatty of the University of Oslo for calling attention to a passage in *Bubu de Montparnasse*, with reference to the last section of 'Preludes'; to Professor Charles Larson of the University of Missouri, St Louis, for making helpful inquiries; to Professor Harold Orel of the University of Kansas for a supply of relevant biographical articles from American journals; and to Roy Wilson of the Sheffield University Library photographic department for preparing a large selection of prints. For help at various times I am grateful also to other members of the Sheffield University staff: Angus Hulton of the Department of Classical Studies, Geoffrey Mitchell of the Department of Continuing Education, and Peter Morley of the Geography Department.

Illustrations 1, 2 left, 3 right, 4 above, 5 above and below, 7 right, 9 right, and 10 left are included by permission of the Houghton Library, Harvard University; 2 right, 3 left, and 4 below by permission of the Sawyer Free Library, Gloucester, Massachusetts; 8 left and 14 above by permission of the National Portrait Gallery; 9 left and 14 below by permission of the BBC Hulton Picture Library; 15 above and below by permission of both Sheffield Newspapers Ltd and the University Library, Sheffield. The portraits of J. M. Murry and Wyndham Lewis are from *The Bookman*, April and August 1932. The copyright of all the other illustrations – 6 left and right, 10 right, 11 left and right, 12 left and right (upper and lower), 13 above and below, 16 above and below – belongs to J. T. Pinion. Permissions to include the Burnt Norton photographs, that of the Eliot memorial plaque, and that of 'Uncle Tom's Cabin', are gratefully acknowledged respectively to the Earl of Harrowby, the vicar and churchwardens of St Michael's, East Coker, and the production director of Redland Bricks Ltd, Horsham.

The work of Frances Arnold on behalf of the publishers has helped me very considerably, and I wish to acknowledge my special indebtedness to her, as well as to my copy-editor, Mrs Valery Rose.

The author and publishers wish to thank the following who have kindly given permission for the use of copyright material:

Faber & Faber Ltd and Harcourt Brace Jovanovich Inc., for the extracts from *Collected Poems 1909–1962*, *Four Quartets*, *The Confidential Clerk*, *The Family Reunion*, *The Cocktail Party*, *Murder in the Cathedral*, and *The Rock*, all by T. S. Eliot, copyright 1934, 1939, 1943, 1950, © 1963, 1964 by T. S. Eliot, copyright 1935 by Harcourt Brace Jovanovich Inc., renewed 1962, 1963 by T. S. Eliot, 1967, 1971, 1978 by Esme Valerie Eliot; the extracts from the Notes to *The Waste Land: A Facsimile and Transcript*, edited by Valerie Eliot, with notes by Ezra Pound; and the extracts from *Selected Essays* and *The Idea of a Christian Society*, both by T. S. Eliot.

Faber & Faber Ltd and Farrar, Straus and Giroux Inc., for the extracts from *The Elder Statesman* by T. S. Eliot, copyright © 1959 by T. S. Eliot; the extracts from *On Poetry and Poets* by T. S. Eliot, copyright © 1943, 1945, 1951, 1954, 1966, 1967 by T. S. Eliot; the extracts from *To Criticize the Critic* by T. S. Eliot, copyright © 1965 by Valerie Eliot; the extracts from *Knowledge and Experience in the Philosophy of F. H. Bradley*, copyright © 1964 by T. S. Eliot; and the extracts from *Humouresque* by T. S. Eliot.

Faber & Faber Ltd and Harvard University Press for the extracts from *The Use of Poetry and the Use of Criticism* by T. S. Eliot.

Faber & Faber Ltd for the extracts from *After Strange Gods*, *Notes Towards the Definition of Culture*, and *For Lancelot Andrewes*, all by T. S. Eliot, and the various extracts from articles by T. S. Eliot in *The Times Literary Supplement*, *The Listener*, *The Athenaeum*, *The Egoist*, and *The Criterion*.

PART ONE

Eliot's Life

Valerie Eliot to Timothy Wilson, *Observer Review*, 20 February 1972:

> Tom often used to say his life was a Dostoevsky novel written by Middleton Murry.

Lines often quoted by T. S. Eliot from E. B. Browning's 'A Musical Instrument':

> The true gods sigh for the cost and pain –
> For the reed which grows never more again . . . .

Chronology

Titles are placed according to the dates of publication.

1888 26 September: birth of Thomas Stearns Eliot.
1898 Enters Smith Academy, St Louis.
1905 Sent to Milton Academy.
1906 Begins his graduate studies at Harvard University.
1910 Graduates and, after his summer vacation at Gloucester, Cape Ann, travels to Paris for a year at the Sorbonne.
1911 Returns to Harvard for postgraduate studies, after a visit to Munich (and probably to the Bavarian Alps).
1914 Awarded a Sheldonian Travelling Scholarship to pursue philosophical studies for one year at Oxford. After visits to Belgium and northern Italy, he reaches Marburg to attend lectures in philosophy. Leaves hurriedly when war is threatened, and reaches London just before its outbreak. Work at Oxford begins in October.
1915 Dardanelles (Gallipoli) campaign.   26 June: marries Vivienne Haigh-Wood.
1917 Joins Lloyds Bank in March. America enters the First World War, and Eliot volunteers for service in the Navy. *Prufrock and Other Observations*.
1918 Renewed attempts to enlist in the summer. War ends in November.
1919 Death of Eliot's father in January. *Poems*. Holiday in the Dordogne with Ezra Pound.
1920 *Ara Vos Prec*. Holiday with Wyndham Lewis in France: meets Joyce in Paris. *The Sacred Wood*.
1921 Eliot's mother visits England. October: to Cliftonville, near Margate.   November: to Lausanne.
1922 Editing of *The Criterion*; the first issue (October) contains *The Waste Land*. In America, after the appearance of the poem in *The Dial* (November), it is published for the first time in book form, with notes.

1923 The first British edition of *The Waste Land* in book form (September).

1924 Eliot's mother visits England again. He wishes to write modern drama to drum-beat rhythms. *Homage to John Dryden.*

1925 Eliot appointed to a directorship with the publishers Faber and Gwyer. 'The Hollow Men' completed and included in *Poems, 1909–1925.*

1926 *Savonarola*, his mother's long dramatic poem, published with an introduction by Eliot. Sweeney dramatic fragments published in October and the following January.

1927 Eliot becomes a convert to the Church of England. 'Journey of the Magi'. Introduction to *Seneca His Tenne Tragedies*. Eliot becomes a British citizen.

1928 Second edition of *The Sacred Wood*, with an important new preface. *For Lancelot Andrewes.*

1929 March: Faber and Gwyer becomes Faber and Faber. Essay on Dante.

1930 *Ash-Wednesday*, Eliot's translation of St-John Perse's *Anabase*, and 'Marina', are published. He meets Bishop Bell and Martin Browne.

1931 'Thoughts after Lambeth'; 'Triumphal March'.

1932 Leaves England in September to give the Charles Eliot Norton lectures at Harvard.

1933 Returns to England in June, having decided not to live with his wife again. *The Use of Poetry and the Use of Criticism.*

1934 *After Strange Gods*; *The Rock.*

1935 *Murder in the Cathedral.*

1936 *Collected Poems, 1909–1935*, including 'Difficulties of a Statesman' and 'Burnt Norton'.

1938 Awarded an honorary degree at Cambridge (June). 29 September: France and Britain sign pact on Czechoslovakia with Hitler at Munich.

1939 *The Criterion* discontinued. *The Family Reunion. Old Possum's Book of Practical Cats* published in October, about a month after the outbreak of the Second World War. *The Idea of a Christian Society.*

1940 'East Coker'. British troops evacuated from Dunkirk beaches from 29 May to 3 June.

1941 'Burnt Norton' (*see* 1936); 'The Dry Salvages'.
1942 Visit to Sweden. 'Little Gidding'.
1943 *Four Quartets* (New York edition; London edition, 1944).
1945 In May, at the end of war in western Europe, Eliot visits Paris; in December he sees Ezra Pound in Washington.
1947 23 January: death of Vivienne. Eliot receives an honorary degree at Harvard.
1948 Awarded the Order of Merit. *Notes towards the Definition of Culture*. Receives the Nobel Prize in Stockholm.
1949 Appoints Valerie Fletcher as his secretary (August). Lecture tour in Germany with Arnold Toynbee.
1950 *The Cocktail Party*. Lectures at the University of Chicago on education.
1951 Enlarged edition of *Selected Essays* (first published in 1932).
1953 Address at Washington University, to mark the centenary of its foundation by Eliot's grandfather.
1954 *The Confidential Clerk*.
1957 10 January: Eliot marries Valerie Fletcher. *On Poetry and Poets*.
1959 *The Elder Statesman*.
1962 *Collected Plays*; *George Herbert*.
1963 *Collected Poems, 1909–1962*.
1964 *Knowledge and Experience in the Philosophy of F. H. Bradley*.
1965 4 January: death of Eliot. *To Criticize the Critic* (and other writings).
1967 Memorial unveiled in Poets' Corner, Westminster Abbey, on the second anniversary of Eliot's death. *Poems Written in Early Youth*.
1969 *The Complete Poems and Plays of T. S. Eliot*.

1

St Louis to England

Thomas Stearns Eliot was born on 26 September 1888 in the mid-west frontier town of St Louis, near the confluence of the broad Missouri and Mississippi rivers. His parents were of New England descent. On the paternal side, several of his ancestors had been Boston merchants; one, a Congregationalist, declined to leave his ministerial post after being elected President of Harvard University. They were the descendants of Andrew Eliot, who emigrated to America in 1669 from his home in the village of East Coker, near Yeovil, Somerset. The ashes of T. S. Eliot were buried, about three months after his death in January 1965, in the church of his ancestral parish, and there, in the north-west corner of St Michael's, East Coker, a plaque was unveiled to his memory the following September. 'In my end is my beginning.'

The first of the Eliots to reside in St Louis was the writer's grandfather William Greenleaf Eliot, who left Harvard Divinity School to complete his education in Washington, where he fell in love with a beautiful girl who shared his missionary zeal. They decided they could be most useful at St Louis, which had become the chief transport centre for the western states, and was to increase in importance with the extension of the railways until the development of Chicago on the Great Lakes. Originally a French eighteenth-century trading-post, St Louis now had a considerable German immigrant population, and was largely Catholic, with a growing influx of southerners and New Englanders. Drinking, gambling, slave-ownership, and even duelling were common. From Washington, after his marriage in 1837, W. G. Eliot returned with his bride to this conglomerate centre on the edge of the wild west, intent on fulfilling his

6

Unitarian and civilizing mission. He had the personality, organizing ability, and integrity to achieve great things; an able business man later claimed that, had he and Dr Eliot been in partnership, they would have gained financial control of all the great enterprises west of the Alleghenies.

Philanthropy came foremost, however. Eliot's grandfather was a leading figure when flood and fire disasters, followed by cholera, had to be coped with; even with a growing family he and his wife found time and room at home to provide for twenty-six orphans. A strong Union supporter, he was active in preventing the secession of Missouri and abolishing slavery in the State. During the Civil War his administrative talents ensured the building and maintenance of several military hospitals. He fought for prohibition and women's franchise, opposed the legalizing of prostitution, and did all he could to promote education. He set up a free mission school, founded Washington University (St Louis), with Smith Academy as its preparatory school, and Mary Institute as a school for girls; from 1872 until his death in 1887 he was President of Washington University.

Only five of his fourteen children survived. Of the four sons, two became Unitarian ministers; the second, Henry Ware Eliot, a graduate of Washington University, went into a wholesale grocery business, then joined a brickmaking firm, of which he became secretary and ultimately chairman. In 1869 he married Charlotte Champe Stearns, a St Louis teacher; she was a Bostonian, whose maternal ancestors included a seventeenth-century judge in the infamous Salem witch trials (at one of which Andrew Eliot is said to have served on the jury); another ancestor was the second President of Harvard. Unusually intelligent and cultured, she resented women's lack of opportunity for university education, wrote poetry, and exerted a strong but kindly moral and spiritual influence in the home. Her seven children were all born at 2635 Locust Street; of the six who survived, the first four were girls; an interval of nine years separated Thomas, the youngest, from his brother Henry. Like Tennyson, Thomas Stearns Eliot owed much to his mother; his poetry, like hers, shows the appeal of sainthood and regeneration. (Such was her admiration for her father-in-law that she worked arduously on his biography, which appeared in 1904; her longest poem, on Savonarola, was published in 1926, with a preface by T. S. Eliot.) Her husband was interested in art and music; he had been a member of philharmonic and choral societies. He loved chess, and delighted his children in many ways, not least in sketching faces on egg-shells and drawing cats to the life. He gave generously to charities, Washington University, the Academy of Science which his father had founded, and the Missouri Botanical Garden. The Eliot home was happy and cultured.

Handicapped by congenital hernia, Tom was not allowed to take part in strenuous games, nor did he attend school until he was seven or eight. An early photograph suggests that he was mischievous and engaging, and he may have been spoilt at times. When his mother was engaged in social work, particularly with juvenile offenders, he was supervised by an elder sister, or by his Irish nursemaid Annie Dunne, for whom he conceived a genuine affection; she talked to him about God, and took him to her Catholic church. Some of his earliest pleasures are recalled in the poem 'Animula'. He remembered the sound of steamboats 'blowing in' the New Year, and expeditions to gather fossil shellfish on limestone bluffs above the Mississippi. It was more exciting and alarming to see the great river in flood, bearing its cargo of devastation and wreckage, with corpses of negroes and cattle, as an unforgettable testimony of nature's terrible ravages. He had acquired a taste for good food, and could remember late in life how, after enjoying his dessert when he was a child, he would feign astonishment at its disappearance, and exclaim 'There it isn't!' Far from being pampered, he was taught to be self-denyingly concerned for the wants of others, so much so that he grew up thinking it a sin to eat sweets, and unable to allow himself such an indulgence until he gave up smoking in his sixties. During his early years, his grandmother lived near, an embodiment of her departed husband's principles, which seemed like the Mosaic tables of God's testimony.

Henry Ware Eliot, who had prospered from railroad and other industrial investments, took his family to New England for seaside holidays; eventually to Gloucester, a deep-sea port on the sheltered side of Cape Ann. From 1896 they stayed at the shingled, high-chimneyed villa built for him at Eastern Point, a small rocky moorland peninsula overlooking the Atlantic and Gloucester harbour. Here Tom became friendly with fishermen of strong religious outlook, from whom he heard tales of storm and shipwreck. To the north-east of Cape Ann could be seen a rocky reef known as the Dry Salvages (a corruption, Eliot thought, of 'les trois sauvages', though 'Dry' is usually interpreted as non-submerged); lost in seething foam and spray, or in thick far-flung mist, this barrier had proved fatal to many vessels. During his adolescence Eliot became a proficient sailor; he learnt much from his brother Henry, more from local fishermen, and became habituated to varying voices of the sea, its howl and yelp, the wailing warning on Thacher Island or at Eastern Point lighthouse, the clanging bell, and the whistling buoy. With further experience, he participated in sailings as far north as Maine, becoming familiar with coast and islands; at times, when befogged close inshore, he could scent the pines or hear the song of the woodthrush; on returning, there were the rocky hazards of the Dry Salvages, the Little Salvages (visible only at low tide), and the intervening Flat Ground, which was always submerged.

It is no wonder that, probably after reading Melville, he wrote two nautically informed, incident-packed, fantastically sensational stories, 'A Tale of a Whale' and 'The Man who was King', both set in the South Pacific (to which he was to return in a Sweeney fragment). They were composed while he was a student at Smith Academy, which he had attended from 1898. Here he proved to be an outstanding scholar, taking the Greek prize and excelling in English; he remembered being introduced to the *Iliad* and the *Aeneid* in the same year. At the age of fourteen he came under the spell of Omar Khayyám's *Rubáiyát*, and wrote gloomy atheistical quatrains in the style of its 'translator' Edward FitzGerald. He enjoyed reading and re-reading *The Light of Asia*, a long epic poem by Sir Edwin Arnold on the life of Buddha. His poems in the *Smith Academy Record* reveal the influence of anthology lyrics by Jonson and Herrick, of *The Ingoldsby Legends*, Byron, and other Romantic poets, and of Victorians such as Tennyson and Swinburne. The ode written to express the feelings of graduands such as he on leaving their *alma mater* in 1905 would have pleased his grandfather: the new century would be great only if her sons proved to be heroic in the fight against pain and misery.

From Smith Academy Eliot proceeded to Milton Academy, a select New England preparatory school, where he concentrated on Latin, history, and physics. The transfer was intended to ease his way into Harvard University, which he entered a year later, following his brother Henry. Harvard was a Protestant centre, with a strong Unitarian bias. Reacting against puritanical extremism, Emerson (a strong influence on Eliot's mother) had sanctioned the authority of the inner light. Such democratic individualism had given assurance to entrepreneurial commerce bolstered by humanistic ideals which were to be attained through education, philanthropy, and goodwill. In promoting this 'religion of the future', the President of Harvard, Charles William Eliot, played a leading role. Wealth contributed to the growing conviction that the Christian concept of sin was antiquated. Familiar with the unscrupulous profiteering and corruption which had been exposed at St Louis, T. S. Eliot grew restive in the complacent atmosphere which emanated from such a material philosophy. He had only to walk in the lower quarters of Cambridge to see for himself that all was not well in the Bostonian ambience, or with the worldly certitudes of its eminently respectable citizens, their dull conventionality, and their cultural pretentiousness. In retrospect he realized that, though he had relatives to turn to, there were other reasons for his unsettled feelings; he had not lost his southern accent, and felt that he was a south-westerner in New England, just as he was a New Englander in St Louis. In one place he missed the long, dark Mississippi, the high limestone bluffs, the ailanthus trees, and the flaming cardinal birds; in the other, the fir trees, the golden-rod, the birdsong, the red granite, and the blue sea off Massachusetts.

The elective studies Eliot pursued for his first degree show a bias towards classical subjects, philosophy, and English literature with reference to European. During his first year he was introduced to the poetry of Donne; there was already a reaction against Tennysonian poetry, and Eliot subsequently became interested in the realistic verse of W. E. Henley and John Davidson, particularly the latter's 'Thirty Bob a Week'. His graduate courses in 1909 included allegory, English drama, poets of the Romantic period, French literary criticism related to nineteenth-century philosophy, and the philosophy of history. The deepest and most lasting cultural influence of this first Harvard period was that of Dante, whom he learned to read from an English–Italian edition. At the end of 1908 Arthur

Symons' *The Symbolist Movement in Literature* made an instant appeal to his poetic instinct. He was impressed by Verlaine's insistence that poetry could dispense with rhetoric ('Take eloquence, and wring its neck!'), and that it depends on utter sincerity, on expressing how one feels, not on how one thinks one should feel. Symons' stress on the need for vision which would link the everyday world with the spiritual, releasing the poet from the 'bondage of exteriority' to express 'the soul of things', affected him even more. Eliot was convinced that awareness of life, known, apprehended, or hinted at, could be more fully expressed by following the techniques of symbolist writers, especially French poets of the later nineteenth century. Of these Jules Laforgue appealed so strongly that he ordered his works in three volumes, poetry and prose. He received them in the spring of 1909, and discovered such an affinity that he not only wrote poems in the style of Laforgue but adopted his dandyism, even to the umbrella. No great change was required, for the tall, handsome, self-conscious Harvard scholar had already assumed a studied elegance in dress and deportment. He was already familiar with the poetry of Baudelaire, but for the discovery of which, and of the French poets most influenced by him, he believed in 1944 that he himself would never have become a literary figure.

Interest in French poetry, and in the progress of his own, made Eliot decide in 1910 to spend a year at the Sorbonne. Parental alarm for his moral welfare was more than offset by his zeal to participate in the intellectual and literary *avant-gardisme* of Paris. Here he was taught French by Alain-Fournier, who introduced him to his brother-in-law Jacques Rivière, one of the editors of *La Nouvelle Revue Française*, which he read regularly; he attended classes on Dante, and heard Bergson lecture each week. During the summer of 1910 he enjoyed the stimulating company of two of his Harvard acquaintances, Conrad Aiken and Frederic Schenck. The friendship which lingered most in his memory was that between him and Jean Verdenal, a medical student who lived at the same pension as Eliot, on the Left Bank. It is commemorated in the dedication of *Prufrock and Other Observations* (1917), where the Dantean warmth of sentiment reflects grief for the loss of one whose lively expression of feeling lived in a memory of the Luxembourg Gardens; the companion who waved a greeting with a branch of flowering lilac died at Gallipoli in 1915. Believing that a genuine poet needed to realize all aspects of life, and that American civilization was too 'thin' for this, Eliot made it his business to extend his explorations to the less savoury purlieus of Baudelaire's city, where he soon sensed the horror and boredom of worldliness in pursuit of sensual pleasure. One of the contemporary books which impressed him was Charles-Louis Philippe's *Bubu de Montparnasse*, a novel on prostitution, to an English translation of which he later wrote a preface, advocating the moral value of knowing to what depths human behaviour can sink. He even thought of settling in Paris, and becoming a French writer.

After a visit to Munich, where he finished 'The Love Song of J. Alfred Prufrock', and before returning to America, he met Conrad Aiken, who noticed the change in him: he was more tolerant, more anxious to know the truth not only of the age but of life as a whole. For this reason he concentrated on philosophy when he resumed his studies at Harvard. The nude *Yellow Christ* by Gauguin which he brought from Paris created a stir, as did his appearance in Left Bank clothes, with a malacca cane and, it is said, hair parted behind. Studying for his doctorate, he read French and German philosophy, and chose to write his dissertation on the English philosopher F. H. Bradley; for two years this led additionally to the study of Hindoo and Buddhist philosophies. During his undergraduate period he had enjoyed the lively lectures of Irving Babbitt, a scholar whose humanistic proselytizing was directed against writers of the Romantic period who based their philosophy chiefly on feeling; such individualism tended to anarchic assumptions, whereas social stability and progress depended on the more disciplined thought of classicism and tradition. Although Eliot accepted this conclusion, he found less basic reality in Babbitt's humanism than in Bradley's philosophy.

In *Appearance and Reality* Bradley maintains that perception is bounded by the circumference of the individual's experience; he holds that the Absolute inhabits every part of the universe, and feels, as Eliot did, the infection of earthly things compared with the perfection of a higher reality, which the mind can sense without being able to enter or explain. Bradley's philosophy was based on the conviction of an Absolute towards which this finite world is tending, and it was with the elucidation of this overwhelming question that Eliot struggled from the psychological basis of solipsism. Bradley had recognised the limitations of human experience and thought, but Eliot clung to the conviction that visionary hints of a higher world would come to the individual; even if they were illusory, they merited philosophical inquiry. His dissertation, *Knowledge and Experience in the Philosophy of F. H. Bradley*, never reached the coherence and finality after which he strained; it was published the year before his death, although he then found much of it unintelligible.

Eliot enjoyed a more sociable life than he had done in his undergraduate period. He took lessons in skating and dancing, exercised in the gymnasium, and received boxing-lessons from an Irishman who, to some extent, it is said, was the prototype of Sweeney. For the private entertainment of male friends and the satisfaction of his libido, Eliot wrote instalments of ribald verse on King Bolo and his big black queen, a practice he was to continue during the frustrating period of his first marriage and at intervals years after his religious conversion. He attended many concerts and operas (including *Tristan*), and made numerous social visits to Bostonian relatives and friends. From 1911 to 1913 he taught philosophy to undergraduate classes; the following year he presided over the Harvard Philosophical Society. He had become sceptical of the idea of progress, which he associated with evolutionary theory and Bergson. He memorized passages of Dante, studied books on the Hindoo *Upanishads*, and was delighted to find in the *Bhagavad-Gita* what was almost wholly lacking, he thought, in his Harvard courses, the fusion of philosophy and religion. The anthropological writings of J. G. Frazer and others struck him as inadequate, because they made no attempt to indicate what religious ritualism signified in terms of human need; he kept returning to the importance of intuition and the psychological basis for what is usually dismissed as illusion. How active was his religious spur is clear not only from the poetry he wrote at this time but also from the magnetism which the lives and visions of saints, including Dame Julian of Norwich, Jacob Boehme, and Saint Teresa, exerted on him; he made copious notes from Evelyn Underhill's *Mysticism* (1911). Bertrand Russell, a visiting professor in the spring of 1914, who remembered his 'pupil' Eliot as ultra-civilized, was most impressed by his knowledge of the classics and French poetry, but thought he lacked vigour and enthusiasm.

Eliot's doctoral thesis was far from finished when, in 1914, he was awarded a travelling fellowship to study Aristotle for one year under Harold Joachim at Merton College, Oxford; (Bradley was a Fellow of Merton, but it seems likely that Eliot never met the sexagenarian philospher, who had no time for students). First, however, he made a short European tour, visiting galleries and 'sights' in Belgium and Italy, before attending lectures by Rudolf Eucken at Marburg University. The course had hardly begun before it became evident that the assassination of Archduke Ferdinand of Austria had become a German pretext for open conflict between European colonial powers. Eliot withdrew just in time, reaching London on 3 August, the day before England became involved in the catastrophic First World War. An introduction from Aiken led to his meeting the American poet Ezra Pound, who, after a period in Spain, Italy, and Provence, had married and had settled in Kensington. Pound undoubtedly influenced Eliot's poetry by insisting on the importance of reading Dante. He became immensely enthusiastic about 'The Love Song of J. Alfred Prufrock', and it was through his agency that the poem was first published in a Chicago magazine the following year. He introduced Eliot to three important figures in the furtherance of *avant-garde* literature, Ford Madox Ford, Wyndham Lewis, and Harriet Weaver. Artist and writer, Lewis was responsible for the periodical *Blast*; the demure-looking Quakeress Miss Weaver controlled *The Egoist*. Pound acted as co-editor to Lewis, who later described Eliot as a Prufrock, bashfully ironic, with a Giaconda smile and a precisely articulated drawl.

Life at Oxford was not very exciting during the war, and the antique splendour of its buildings did little to compensate for lack of college amenities, especially in the winter. Most of Eliot's Christmas vacation at Swanage was spent in the study of Bertrand Russell and A. N. Whitehead's *Principia Mathematica*. He worked industriously for Joachim, Bradley's most distinguished disciple, his studies helping him not only with his dissertation but also in widening his knowledge of classical literature. So punctilious was his tutor in expression and punctuation that Eliot felt he owed more to him on the writing of English than to any other teacher. For exercise he took to rowing, and had the minor distinction of stroking his college four to victory when the majority of good oarsmen were fighting in France. He could have continued his work at Oxford another year, but unforeseen events had complicated his career, and there was more life and opportunity in London.

It is not known whether Eliot was ever in love before he came to England in 1914. He had taken part in scenes from Jane Austen at the home of a Cambridge aunt, playing the part of Mr Woodhouse, with Emily Hale as Mrs Elton. Emily subsequently taught drama at a number of American colleges, and exchanged about two thousand letters with Tom. At Oxford in the spring of 1915, possibly in the rooms of his Milton Academy and Harvard friend Scofield Thayer, Eliot met Vivienne Haigh-Wood, who was visiting Scofield's sister Lucy, after meeting her in Switzerland. The diary of Vivienne for 1914 suggests that she was engaging but highly neurotic. Eliot was attracted by her personality and intelligence; she was sensitive, witty, modern to the point of disillusionment at times, and lively in expression. She was good-looking, colourfully original in dress, and a stylish dancer who had received lessons in ballet. She seemed the type Eliot had yearned for in a Harvard poem which conveys his preference for the woman who bore tropical flowers bright with scarlet life. So exhilarated was he by the stimulating release she brought him from the prolonged fret of philosophic research and analysis that, encouraged by Pound, he committed the most incautious and disastrous act of his life. Without confiding in anyone or informing his parents, he married Vivienne on 26 June at a register office near her home in Hampstead; they spent their honeymoon at Eastbourne. Her mother and father (a landscape-artist and portrait-painter) were staying near her brother Maurice's regiment in Lincolnshire when they were informed by telegram. Maurice was eight years her junior; he had left Malvern School soon after the outbreak of war, and was now a subaltern in the Manchester Regiment. He and Tom became lifelong friends, and the Haigh-Woods soon took to their son-in-law. When Eliot's parents heard the news, he was summoned to Gloucester. Vivienne would not accompany him, principally because she dreaded the submarine-menace. Eliot could not convince his father of the wisdom of staying in England and forfeiting his chance of becoming a Harvard professor, but he promised to complete his doctoral thesis. Henry Ware Eliot (whom he never saw again) sent him the financial assistance he requested, but remained convinced that his youngest son's prospects had been jeopardized for life.

2

To *The Waste Land*

Vivienne appreciated Tom's genius and encouraged his enjoyment of what gaiety they could afford in war-stressed London. Eliot, for whom Beethoven's sonatas had a special attraction, played the piano occasionally, when mood and opportunity were favourable; once, in Pound's flat, he took part in the playing of his host's compositions. For a time he and Vivienne lived with her parents at Hampstead. Then, after a chance meeting with Bertrand Russell, they occupied a room in his London flat, and were introduced to a number of the artistic intellectuals who made a habit of staying at Garsington Manor, the home of Russell's current mistress, the flamboyant hostess Lady Ottoline Morrell. He thought Mrs Eliot a trifle vulgar (as did Aldous Huxley) but adventurous and likely to tire of her 'exquisite and listless' husband, who seemed ashamed of his marriage, and grateful if one was kind to her. With diminishing resources, Eliot had little difficulty, as war losses and recruiting increased, in finding a teaching-post; for one term, at the end of 1915, he taught French, German, and history at High Wycombe Grammar School. Russell liked Tom more and more, noting his unselfish devotion to his wife, but could not help sympathizing with her, though he detected cruel, Dostoevskyan impulses in her teasing, as he became more interested in their complex marital relationship. 'She is a person who lives on a knife-edge, and will end as a criminal or a saint', he wrote. At the end of the year she was very ill, and he took her to Torquay for a holiday, Eliot joining her after a few days.

His wife's physical disorders and neurotic temperament imposed a marital strain, Eliot's tormented sense of repulsion and inadequacy ultimately finding cryptic expression in 'Ode'.

In a letter to Conrad Aiken which reported the death of Jean Verdenal at the Dardanelles, he claimed that his experiences during the six months after his marriage gave him enough material for twenty long poems. Vivienne's illnesses and instability may help to explain his resignation from High Wycombe; he had little leisure, and probably found travel too tiring and time-consuming. Through 1916 he taught at Highgate Junior School, where the young pupil and versifier John Betjeman, who remembered him as the tall, quiet 'American master', was emboldened to favour Eliot with a colourfully bound copy of his best poems. Eliot's financial position had improved: from £140 per annum with free dinners at High Wycombe Grammar School he had advanced to £160 plus free dinners and teas; he benefited also from the interest on £3000 of stock which Russell had given him, because the firm in which he held these shares had undertaken the manufacture of munitions during the war. Eliot, who had informed his benefactor soon after they met that he was no pacifist, returned the debentures in 1927. He and Vivienne now tenanted a flat in Crawford Street, off Edgware Road, and it was their charwoman's disclosure on working-class sex and abortion that led years later to the writing of a dramatic pub-scene for *The Waste Land*.

Eliot managed to complete his Bradley dissertation by March 1916, and was ready to sail on 1 April, and present himself at Harvard for his oral examination, when the voyage was cancelled. The thesis was sent and accepted, but its author never thought it worth while to follow and present himself for his doctorate. He wrote articles for journals and newspapers, but was poorly remunerated. After a summer holiday with Vivienne at Bosham near Portsmouth, he began teaching at Southall a three-year university extension course of two-hour sessions on modern literature, the first series being on later nineteenth-century writers. Richard Aldington's impression that he was a brilliant lecturer does not seem to apply to this evening work, for his classes declined. He found more life in literature than in his final philosophical pursuits, nonetheless, though they were to prove indivisible.

Exhausted by his junior-school work at Highgate, in conjunction with his other responsibilities, Eliot resigned at the end of 1916, hoping to make ends meet by literary journalism, mainly book-reviewing. Payment rates were so low that it soon

became apparent that he must find regular employment again.
Fortunately the Haigh-Woods had an influential banking friend,
through whose interest Eliot secured a post in the City, by the
middle of March, with the Colonial and Foreign Department of
Lloyds Bank at 17 Cornhill. Impressed though he was by
Eliot's knowledge of foreign languages, the manager could offer
an initial salary of no more than £120 a year for preparatory
work on the settlement of pre-war enemy debts. A further
income of £36 per annum came in June 1917 when, on Ezra
Pound's recommendation to Miss Weaver, Eliot became
assistant editor of *The Egoist*, succeeding Aldington, who had
joined the British army. With the writing of articles and
reviews, and preparation for extramural teaching, Eliot had
little spare time; he was 'haggard and ill-looking as usual',
Aldous Huxley reported at the end of the year. Creative
endeavours provided relief from marital worries, and his
continued efforts contributed in the long run to the poems and
critical essays which were to startle a jaded post-war western
world.

The appearance of 'The Love Song of J. Alfred Prufrock' and
other poems by Eliot in a 1915 anthology edited by Pound had
been the occasion for a traditional attack on the two American
poets by Arthur Waugh in *The Critical Quarterly* of October
1916. Poetry was threatened with anarchy by the 'unmetrical,
incoherent banalities' of these emancipated literary 'Cubists'.
Recalling the classic custom of safeguarding the behaviour of
household sons by exposing an inebriated slave when the feast
was at its height, he risked his feeble wit by branding Eliot a
'drunken helot' whose example would save Georgian poets
from catastrophe. The publication of *Prufrock and Other
Observations* by the Egoist Press in June 1917 gave Pound a
welcome opportunity to voice a scornful illustrative reply in
defence of Eliot; in a subsequent review he claimed that nothing
better could be found in 'anything written in French, English or
American since the death of Jules Laforgue'. Conformists
continued to express disapproval or bewilderment, but Pound
found notable allies in Conrad Aiken, who declared that Eliot's
psychology was keener and subtler than that of the professionals,
and in May Sinclair, who thought 'Prufrock' and 'Portrait of a
Lady' on a par with Browning's dramatic poetry, 'Preludes'
and 'Rhapsody on a Windy Night' superior to Henley's *London*

Voluntaries, and 'La Figlia che Piange' a masterpiece in its own right.

Eliot found himself much in agreement with the views of T. E. Hulme, a proponent of 'Imagism' in poetry, and a firm believer in original sin. Like Irving Babbitt, Hulme held there was little hope of progress if the human race accepted shallow, self-seeking Rousseauistic notions of individual freedom and natural goodness; there are higher laws, proved by experience and absorbed by tradition, which emanate from the eternal. He disagreed strongly with the emancipated permissiveness which Bertrand Russell would undoubtedly foster, and thought his philosophy specious. Hulme became an artillery officer and was killed on the western front in September 1917, but his influence on Eliot's outlook was strong and lasting.

Eliot's reviewing-programme from 1916 to 1918 was formidable, in philosophical as well as in literary magazines. Whatever his hostility to the Church in 'The Hippopotamus' and 'Mr Eliot's Sunday Morning Service', his interest in the Christian faith may be seen in his 1917 reviews of works by William Temple, R. G. Collingwood, and Cardinal Mercier. In a brief article which appeared in *The Egoist* at the opening of 1918, Eliot honours Henry James not only as the most intelligent writer of his generation but also as one with a European outlook and with a mind which no *idea* could violate; the English, less disciplined, allowed ideas to corrupt their feelings. In a lighter vein, to encourage correspondence on articles and poems in the same magazine, he wrote slyly provocative letters under assumed names; as the Revd Charles James Grimble, for example, he suggested the benefit for British readers of being informed about foreign ways and of keeping open minds. He assumed a playful Arnoldian role.

During May 1918 the Eliots lived at Marlow, in a cottage lent them by Russell (who informed his lady mistress that he had made love to Vivienne the previous autumn, and found the experience loathsome). Vivienne was an invalid, and Eliot, still employed at his London bank during the week, was nervously exhausted. Brigit Patmore thought him snappy and lacking in humility, though capable of winning cordiality; Vivienne, it seemed, 'shimmered with intelligence'. She recalled how the Eliots danced on Sunday afternoons at a hall in Queensway, but found they now took everything with 'a terrible seriousness'.

It explained, she thought, why Vivienne said with a sigh, 'The frightful time I have with Tom'. He was in his thirtieth year (much younger than Prufrock), and talked about how old he was; yet his wife could move him to gaiety at times, 'even with a schoolboy sense of humour'. The USA had joined the Allies against Germany, and Eliot made a number of efforts to join the American navy or army. Disqualified by hernia and tachydermia (which was induced by nervous strains), he volunteered to serve in Intelligence, but nothing came of it.

In September 1918 Eliot began an additional course of evening lectures, a long series on literature, at Sydenham. On 15 November, four days after the armistice which concluded war with Germany, he took some of his poems to Hogarth House, Richmond, where he met Virginia Woolf, who detected a degree of intolerance in him; it was agreed to publish in a small edition, and *Poems* appeared the following May. This new publication might have done something to vindicate him in his father's eyes, Eliot sadly reflected, after being upset by news of his death in January 1919. He had already written poems and fragments with a major work in mind, and he probably gave further thought to this at weekends with Vivienne, sometimes by the sea, particularly at Bosham, where boating was an attraction; and again during the summer holiday he spent in France, without her, part of it with Pound in the Dordogne. By this time he knew a number of social celebrities, including the Sitwells. As a result of meeting Katherine Mansfield at Lady Ottoline Morrell's, he had become acquainted with John Middleton Murry, editor of *The Athenaeum*, a literary weekly which he had revived. He wished to have Tom as his editorial assistant, but promising financial prospects at Lloyds Bank and the need for security made Eliot decline the invitation; he was content to contribute occasional articles and reviews. His first contribution to *The Times Literary Supplement*, a leading article on Ben Jonson, appeared on 13 November. His best-known work of the period, however, is 'Gerontion', completed some time after the signing of the Treaty of Versailles in July, and included in a short selection of Eliot's poems which appeared under the strange title of *Ara Vos Prec*.[1] Again the edition was small, and the tenor of the earliest reviews suggests that the number of appreciative readers was apparently insignificant.

Tom was anxious to see his mother, and urged her to come

over while she was able. His leave would allow him only ten or fourteen days with her in the States; Vivienne could not accompany him because of the cost of the fare, and (he added in his letter to his brother) his mother would not welcome her. It is true that severe economies were imposed in the immediate post-war era, but Eliot's salary had risen to £500 a year. He was now in charge of his department, his main business still being the settlement of pre-war German debts; it involved him in knotty problems arising from elucidation of 'that appalling document the Peace Treaty'. He was also very busy with his literary work, especially in the preparation of selected essays for publication at a time when reputable publishers had need to be very cautious. The selection appeared in September under the mythic title of *The Sacred Wood*. Though not received with acclaim, the book did much to establish Eliot's reputation, and was hailed by Bonamy Dobrée in 1922 as the most important critical work since Wordsworth's preface to *Lyrical Ballads*. Influenced by Rémy de Gourmont and Julien Benda, it startled by the clear-cut definition of its anti-Romanticism.

Ezra Pound, deeming it a crime that Eliot should waste eight hours a day in a bank, had tried to launch a fund to secure him for literature, but such schemes could come to nothing, for the Eliots needed a regular income, especially for medical contingencies. Anxious about Tom's health, Vivienne recommended a holiday in the summer, and he spent it with Wyndham Lewis, walking and cycling in the lower Loire valley, and spending a few days in Paris, one mission being to deliver a parcel from Pound to James Joyce. This charitable package contained no more than a small assortment of clothing and a pair of old brown shoes. The meeting was restrained but polite, though Joyce insisted on dining his guests at a restaurant. Eliot thought him arrogant, but, after being spell-bound by the end of *Ulysses* (which he read in manuscript the following year), he invested him with charm; when the novel was first published, he acclaimed it the greatest literary work of the age. By the end of 1920 Pound, who had proved too bumptious to retain some of his literary positions in England, had settled in Paris as the correspondent for Scofield Thayer's American magazine *The Dial*.

Unable to work because of the noise in his Crawford Street neighbourhood, and anxious to escape to congenial surroundings for the writing of something more important than *The Sacred Wood*, Eliot had spent much time looking for a new flat, a search which culminated in the move to 9 Clarence Gate Gardens near Regent's Park in October. During the weeks that followed Vivienne spent most of her time nursing her father; when he was out of danger she collapsed and had to be placed in a nursing-home. She returned to the flat in April, before convalescing at the seaside. During these early months of 1921 Eliot began *The Waste Land* in earnest; he seems to have made considerable progress before his mother's arrival with his sister Marian in June for their expected summer visit. (Whether Henry accompanied or preceded them is uncertain.) They occupied the Clarence Gate Gardens flat, while Tom and Vivienne stayed in Wigmore Street. The two brothers attended a performance of Stravinsky's *Le Sacre du Printemps*, Tom, unlike most of the audience, being exhilarated. Here was music which expressed the stark realism of both the primitive past and the modern city; his London letter on the subject, in *The Dial*, won him Stravinsky's friendship for life. The family reunion was a happy one, though he sometimes found it expedient to exercise tact in adapting the old assumptions to changed circumstances.

Eliot's resumption of the old arduous routine which began with literary work in the early hours soon proved to be exhausting, and once again it was Vivienne's turn to worry. He was dismayed by his utter incapacity to write; he knew he had material which waited for expression, but all he could show night after night was a blank sheet of paper and a sharpened pencil in readiness beside it. He mentioned his plight to Conrad Aiken, whom he met for lunch two or three times a week in the City, near his bank. Aiken, who noticed that Tom always carried his pocket edition of Dante, referred the matter to a friend, who volunteered to discuss it with the psycho-analyst Homer Lane. When Eliot visited a specialist on his wife's insistence, he was instructed to leave home immediately, remain unaccompanied for three months, follow prescribed rules strictly, and never exert his mind. The bank gave him paid leave, which, fearing a mental breakdown, he could not conscientiously take until he had trained an assistant to deputize for him. The prospect filled him with dread; he felt that, if he gave up his professional post, financial worry and journalistic toil would soon reduce him to a worse state. He did not comply with his doctor's orders, but invited Vivienne to remain with him as long as she could at the Albemarle Hotel, Cliftonville, near Margate, where they stayed three weeks. Then, in November, on the advice of Ottoline Morrell, with reassurances from Julian Huxley, he set off to Switzerland, Vivienne accompanying him as far as Paris, where she stayed for a time with the Pounds. During his six weeks at a sanatorium in Lausanne he learned that there was nothing mentally wrong with him, and found the quiet and relaxation he needed to revise, assemble, and expand sketches and jottings he had made towards the ill-defined poem he had contemplated for years. Whether the poetic release which came, with especial freedom and felicity in the final part of the poem,[2] was due, as Aiken believed, to Eliot's anger, before leaving England, on hearing Homer Lane's view that his inability to write was due to his fear of falling short of perfection, and that he (Eliot) thought he was God, seems very dubious, so far apart were the breaking of the log-jam (as Aiken described it) and its conjectural cause. At the time of writing *The Waste Land*, Eliot thought seriously of becoming a Buddhist.

After a few days in Paris, where Pound agreed to edit his manuscript, Eliot returned to London with Vivienne in January (1922). Pound was confronted with a loose assembly of pieces, some out of proportion or still in the rough; he excised about half the verse, and made many suggestions for minor revision, later (not very aptly) referring to his major surgery as a caesarian operation. Eliot's reference to him as *il miglio fabbro*, probably from its use as a title for the chapter on Arnaut Daniel in Pound's *The Spirit of Romance*, may be an acknowledgment of his friend's superior judgment in giving the work its final shape, though the Dantean context undoubtedly suggests 'the better poet'.[3] The poem was revised in January, and accepted by Scofield Thayer, before he saw it, for publication in *The Dial*, where it did not appear until November. It was first published in England, in the opening (October) number of *The Criterion*; in book form, it first appeared in America, with notes, near the end of the year. Eliot had supplied useful literary references; when more notes were requested to fill blank pages, he responded with a number of comments, largely expletory and sometimes parodic. The first English edition, with the notes, was published in September 1923 by Leonard and Virginia Woolf of the Hogarth Press.

By this time the Woolfs and Eliots were very friendly. After hearing Tom read *The Waste Land*, Virginia had written: 'He sang and chanted it and rhythmed it. It has great beauty and force of phrase; symmetry; and tensity. What connects it together, I'm not so sure.' Two months later, in August 1922, after becoming bored and irritated by a realistic passage in *Ulysses*, she wrote in her diary, 'And Tom, great Tom, thinks this on a par with *War and Peace*! An illiterate, underbred book it seems to me; the book of a self taught working-man. . . .' Conversing with her towards the end of September, he maintained that Joyce was purely a literary writer, 'founded upon Walter Pater with a dash of Newman' (she had finished *Ulysses*, and thought its author a he-goat); his book would be a landmark, he continued, because it destroyed the entire nineteenth century. English poets were lazy; none interested him since the time of Johnson. Influenced probably by Middleton Murry, Eliot went on to say that D. H. Lawrence had great moments, especially in *Aaron's Rod*, his latest publication.

Pound made a second effort to collect money which would release his friend for literature, and the scheme was taken up also by Ottoline Morrell and Virginia Woolf, with Eliot's knowledge and all to no purpose; he was still afraid of losing the security which banking gave him, and preferred, largely for Vivienne's sake, to be as independent as possible. His position improved with the award of $2000 by *The Dial* for the best work by a younger poet.

Another friendship which had developed was with I. A. Richards of Magdalene College, Cambridge, a lecturer whose main interests were English literature and the psychology of criticism. They first met in 1920, when Richards was full of admiration for *Ara Vos Prec*. He visited Eliot at the bank, and found him bending over a large table 'covered with all sorts and sizes of foreign correspondence', in a small basement room with a skylight of thick green glass squares in the pavement, over which the heels of passers-by seemed to be hammering without stop. Later Tom used to stay with the Richards on King's Parade, Cambridge. It was hoped that Eliot could be lured into joining the academic staff of the University, but he thought better of it, preferring no doubt the less provincial life and culture of London. Furthermore, his financial prospects, his heavy medical expenses, domestic circumstances, literary ambition, and editorial commitment, all weighed heavily against such a move.

He had become acquainted with Richard Cobden-Sanderson, a publisher who, when he discovered that Eliot would like to found a literary review, had introduced him to Lady Rothermere, wife of the great newspaper proprietor, the first Viscount Rothermere, who had established the King Edward VII Chair of English Literature at Cambridge. She was enthusiastic about the proposal, gave Eliot complete financial backing, and entrusted editorial policy to him. The new journal was to be a quarterly, published by Cobden-Sanderson and entitled *The Criterion*. It would be interesting to know what persuasion, if any, was brought to bear on Eliot to introduce *The Waste Land* to the British public in the first number. Eliot was just thirty-four; his health had declined, and he had many anxieties. It is not surprising that, thinking primarily of Vivienne's continued illness, her courage and persistence in diet and exercises despite relapses and loneliness, he wrote to his brother, on the last day of 1922, of the strain and tensions in their overworked life. It was too early to judge the effect of his latest and most important poem on British and American readers. More significantly, he had informed Richard Aldington that, as far as he, the author, was concerned, *The Waste Land* belonged to the past; he was now seeking a new poetic style and form.

3

Religious Commitment and Marriage Breakdown

The Waste Land created a stir, but was not received with rapturous applause. The criticism it provoked, whether favourable or denunciatory, could do nothing but call attention to a work which communicated its poetry, and was destined to attract new readers year by year, whatever difficulties it posed. Academic interest in it was to grow rapidly with the expansion of higher education; otherwise the reactions which followed its publication were not uncharacteristic of those which prevailed during the inter-war period which followed. Sympathetic elucidations soon flowed from Edmund Wilson; he doubted whether any contemporary American poem of equal length displayed 'so high and so varied a mastery of English verse', and he was confident that, despite 'its complicated correspondences and its recondite references and quotations', it was intelligible from the first by force of the emotion conveyed by its images. For Elinor Wylie *The Waste Land* presented with 'little less than miraculous' skill the 'power of suggesting intolerable tragedy at the heart of the trivial or the sordid'; she could sense that the poem was conceived in personal suffering. Despite his regret that much of its inspiration was drawn from literature, and that its 'allusive matter' remained 'not wholly annealed', Conrad Aiken thought the poem succeeded; 'a brilliant and kaleidoscopic confusion', it was one of the most moving and original poems of his time. Louis Untermeyer concluded it was 'a pompous parade of erudition', 'a kaleidoscopic movement in which the bright-coloured pieces fail to atone for the absence of an integrated design'. Discreteness of imagery led to the charge from critics as far apart as John Crowe Ransom and Clive Bell that the poem was unimaginative. Poets of the Georgian breed such as J. C. Squire and Harold Monro (the second of whom had refused to publish 'Prufrock' because it was unintelligible) did not know what to make of *The Waste Land*, and the scholarly traditionalist F. L. Lucas regretted that this 'unhappy composition' had not been left to sink itself, wryly acknowledging the appeal such a 'new masterpiece' would have for coteries, eccentrics, 'the blasé and the young'.

Eliot had more demanding matters to consider. With *The Dial* as his closest model, he aimed to make *The Criterion* a forum for the most significant thought relevant to western Europe, in literature, philosophy, religion, and politics. By March 1923 he wished he had never undertaken a task which had become too exhausting a drain on time and energy, with no financial reward. (Eliot's contract with Lloyds did not allow him to accept payment for any other form of regular employment; *The Criterion* remained unprofitable, and he received no emolument for editing it at any time.) Had he been free, he would have devoted the whole of his time to creative writing, criticism, and journalistic enterprise; Vivienne's health was precarious, however, and she was totally dependent on him. Her medical treatment, with periods of convalescence in the country or by the sea, was a continual expense; she was naturally alarmed, even to the point of resistance, at the suggestion that he should sacrifice security for the sake of literature. Severe illness in April, when she was living in a rented cottage at Fishbourne, between Bosham and Chichester, reduced her almost to a skeleton; two London specialists were called in, and time and time again she seemed to be dying. Eliot cabled his American friend John Quinn, on whom he could rely in times of need, telling him that his affairs were chaotic. He knew he must not resign from Lloyds, and that he must manage *The Criterion* and his own writing as best he could.

A friend with whom he was to work closely was Herbert Read. A civil servant after the war, Read had assisted Osbert Sitwell in editing *Art and Letters*, a quarterly to which Eliot had contributed some poems and critical essays not long before its discontinuation in 1920. Retrospectively Read distinguished four literary groupings in post-war London: poets who supported Harold Monro, owner of Poetry Bookshop; devotees of

Middleton Murry (and this meant of D. H. Lawrence; Murry had become editor of *The Adelphi* after the failure of *The Athenaeum* in 1923); the Bloomsbury group; and the Sitwells, who campaigned against the literary establishment or the Squirearchy, as it was sometimes called, after J. C. Squire. Eliot was wary; he neither committed himself to, nor broke with, any of them. Representatives of all four contributed to the earlier numbers of *The Criterion*. Since Eliot's time was more flexible than Read's, it was agreed to meet each week for lunch at the Grove, a tavern in Beauchamp Place, not far from the Victoria and Albert Museum, where Read worked. Some of the latter's colleagues joined *Criterion* regulars and any foreign visitors who might be interested. More serious meetings took place once a month, usually at the Ristorante Commercio in Soho, where ideas were exchanged, contributions discussed, and agreement sought on the more general lines of policy. Eliot could display a playful and even hilarious self on these occasions. Anxious to avoid coterie criticism, he made no attempt to dominate. He believed that dogma was necessary for the clear formulation of his own ideas, but he had no intention of imposing them on others. It was necessary nonetheless to avoid conflict of purpose, and to that end he welcomed a nucleus of supporters who held 'impersonal loyalty' to a faith which was not opposed to his own. His leadership was unquestioned, though the support of Richard Aldington, who soon became his assistant editor, was to be sapped by jealousy.[4]

The letter in which Eliot set out his aims for *The Criterion* was probably written in 1924, and significantly he mentions his interest in Arnold, Newman, Bradley, and Charles Maurras. He accepted the Arnoldian viewpoint that the critic's duty is to cultivate disinterestedly the best that is known and thought at home and abroad, especially in Europe, from the past to the present. The early numbers represent literature in France, Germany, Italy, and Spain, and range chronologically from the *Alcestis* of Euripides to Dostoevsky, Joyce's *Ulysses*, Pound's *Cantos*, and contemporary English writers. There are lengthy articles on Bolingbroke by Charles Whibley, whose earlier years among the poets of Paris earned Eliot's respect, others on poetic and dramatic versions of the Tristram story, a generalization of Freud's theories by Jacques Rivière in translation, and a brief obituary on the art superbly displayed

by the music-hall comedienne Marie Lloyd. Eliot, the author of
this challenging article, returns to the subject after hearing of
the death of Sarah Bernhardt. His main concern is the
revitalization of the theatre, and his conclusion is that 'stage
gesture' as a copy of reality is dead. He finds a clue to the key
for future success in the 'abstract gesture' of the ballet-dancer
Massine; it symbolizes emotion, and he urges the stage adoption
of a 'literal untruth' in ritual, such as he found in the film
rhythm of Chaplin.

As editor he appears almost self-effacing; his name did not
appear on the cover or title-page until January 1927 (after he
had left Lloyds). In the first number his editing is restricted to
a few notes; the practice of giving abstracts of foreign periodicals
(only French, German and American initially) began with the
third; and brief editorial notes (one from Aldington) concluded
the fourth. Eliot attempts to define the function of a literary
review; it is not 'to provide material for the chat of coteries' but
to 'maintain the application, in literature, of principles which
have their consequences also in politics and in private conduct',
and to do this without allowing any confusion between them.
Its function, he concluded, is 'to maintain the autonomy and
disinterestedness of literature' and, at the same time, to show its
relations to all those 'other activities' which are 'the components
of life'. Aldington's supporting note begins, 'Literature cannot
exist *in vacuo*. . . .' The practice of opening with a commentary
lasted from April 1924 to April 1925; the first draws attention
to T. E. Hulme ('the antipodes of the eclectic, tolerant, and
democratic mind of the end of the last century'), his affinity
with Maurras, and (after a debate with *The Adelphi* on the
'inner voice' or individual judgment of romanticism) the need
for a classical movement in literature; the second returns to the
disinterestedness of criticism, particularly to the danger of
confusing literature with religion, a heresy which had been very
ably exposed by Jacques Rivière in *La Nouvelle Revue Française*.
'Books of the Quarter' reviews did not begin until the eighth
number of July 1924.

It was fortunate that Eliot had colleagues who were willing
to share his more burdensome editorial tasks. They had a
common aim, but it was reinforced by his personality and
integrity. He combined unusual discretion with equally unusual
courtesy; Bonamy Dobrée was convinced that it was 'really

natural', though it might seem affected in others. Eliot's worries had deepened. Vivienne had helped whenever she qould, but now, as Russell had predicted ten years earlier, their⎮marriage was breaking down. Protracted illness, drugs, and haunting fears had reduced her to a helpless state of semi-paralysis from which she could rarely rouse herself; such was her condition that she continually needed someone to take care of her. Separation would ease the strain for both of them, Eliot sometimes thought, and he turned to religion for comfort. In the early years of his marriage, he had visited churches in the City during his lunch hours, sometimes to admire their beauty (notably that of St Magnus the Martyr by Chrisopher Wren), more and more often for the sake of peace, contemplation, and spiritual refreshment. Cobden-Sanderson introduced him to William Force Stead, an American who had become ordained in the Church of England; Stead interested him in Anglican writings of the seventeenth century, and he was particularly captivated by the sermons of Lancelot Andrewes. Ambition deepened his sense of marital guilt; the vital question, he reflected, is not so much whether people are good or bad, but how deep is their realization of sin.

Perhaps he encouraged his wife to write. Some of her work was included pseudonymously ('F. M.', 'Feiron Morris', 'Fanny Marlow', 'Felix Morrison') in *The Criterion* during 1924–5, no doubt as light relief. Eliot had good cause to think her original; she shows sharp observation, distinctive satirical humour, and a gift for harmonious selection and organization. One item purports to give a young woman's impressions of life on the Left Bank in Paris, where to post a letter after dinner would damn her for life. Three pieces relate to Sybilla: 'Thé Dansant', 'Night Club', and 'Fête Galante', evidently fictionalized recollections, the first perhaps of Eliot not responding animatedly to petulant coaching in the one-step. 'Letters of the Moment' are more personally rooted in actuality. The opening of the first shows that the woman who expressed her admiration in large capitals beside the passage on the psychotic woman in 'A Game of Chess' (formerly 'In the Cage') thought of boredom in terms of *The Waste Land*. The writer's hyacinths have burst clumsily out of their pots, and come to misshapen bloom; 'one begins to beat against the bars of the cage . . . but toward what spring?' The second includes a passage on Fresca from one of the discarded fragments of *The Waste Land*, echoes 'Prufrock', samples the reviews, and ends with an invigorating recollection of walking in the wind by the sea. The authenticity of 'Necesse est Perstare', a short scene in free verse, seems to be beyond question: a lunch party breaks up, ending (for a session) the interminable inanity of chatter on Aldous Huxley, Elizabeth Bibesco, and Clive Bell; the 'I' of the poem looks across at the 'you', who had stretched his arms wearily over his head as if he were an old monkey; they look at each other, and she wishes she could join him by the window, gaze at the 'fleering' cold sunshine, and ask if it is *necessary* to *go through* this sort of thing. There can be no doubt that Vivienne helped to quicken Eliot's sense of the boredom, the pity, and the horror, of life.

His inability to give much time to his own writing is indicated by the fact that, outside his relatively slight contributions to *The Criterion* during this period, his one publication, *Homage to John Dryden*, published by the Hogarth Press in 1924, consists of three critical essays on seventeenth-century subjects (Dryden, the 'metaphysical' poets, Andrew Marvell) which had appeared in *The Times Literary Supplement* during 1921. After being summoned by Lady Rothermere to Switzerland, where she announced her unwillingness to continue subsidizing *The Criterion* when her contract expired in 1925, Eliot consulted his friend Bruce Richmond, editor of *The Times Literary Supplement*, who discussed the question with a former colleague, Frank Morley, now employed by Faber and Gwyer, a new firm of publishers. At the time Geoffrey Faber was interested not so much in the quarterly as in the editor. At All Souls, where he was a Fellow, he had heard Charles Whibley speak highly of Eliot; another recommendation came from the novelist Arnold Bennett. Eliot joined Faber and Gwyer, at 24 Russell Square, as a director in November 1925; before the end of the year they had published his *Poems, 1909–1925*, including 'The Hollow Men' in its final form. *The Criterion* lapsed for a short period, but Richmond raised funds for its continuation, and it reappeared as *The New Criterion*, a Faber and Gwyer publication, in January 1926; (it reverted to its original title in June 1928 after being issued as a monthly from May 1927 to March 1928).

In the first of his new quarterlies Eliot attempts to formulate his idea of a literary review. He writes disparagingly of miscellanies, and holds that one should find in the bound volumes of a review for ten consecutive years the finest sensibility and the most perceptive thought of that period. This suggests remarkable assurance for a man of thirty-seven, particularly for one who believed in the Bradleyan limitations of certainty. His growing recognition that literary criticism extends beyond what is purely literary is clear: literature cannot be dissociated from significant knowledge and ideas, whatever their provenance. A literary review must represent 'the interests of any intelligent person with literary taste', and its catholicity in the choice of authors must be 'ordered and rational'. Works by Georges Sorel, Maurras, Julien Benda, T. E. Hulme, Jacques Maritain, and Irving Babbitt illustrate the tendency he sees in modern writing towards reason or classicism. Against these he lists works by Wells, Shaw (*Saint Joan*), and Russell; all three hold 'amateur' religions, and (Eliot adds) Murry's religion is unintelligible. His editorial direction becomes increasingly apparent in the articles and the choice of books for review.

Eliot had qualities which recommended him highly as a publishing-director; he had valuable business experience, in addition to the tact, shrewdness, and charm which were essential to cope with customers' individualities; he combined wide scholarship with conscientious application, and was a discerning judge of literature. Largely under his direction his firm (Faber and Faber from 1929) became by far the most eminent launcher of modern British poets. From January to March 1926 he gave the Clark Lectures at Trinity College, Cambridge, his subject being 'metaphysical' poetry in the light of developments from Dante to Laforgue and Corbière. They reveal a philosophical preference for poets such as Cavalcanti and Dante, whose way of regarding subjects ontologically (*sub specie aeternitatis*) is superior to Laforgue's immature glimpses of unintegrated truth or those limitations in the area of Donne's thought which result from his concentration on ingenuities of conceit for emotional effects. Geoffrey Faber recommended Eliot for a research fellowship at All Souls, but, after hearing reports on his poetry, its august representatives rejected his application, only A. L. Rowse voting in his favour. In keeping with his more elevated status, Tom and Vivienne moved to 57 Chester Terrace near Belgravia. Whatever domestic anxieties and illnesses he had suffered, he still looked surprisingly youthful; a photograph shows him bowler-hatted in Bloomsbury, leaning elegantly and cheerfully on his tightly rolled umbrella outside the premises of Faber and Gwyer.

In the summer of 1926, when funds were needed to save London churches from demolition, Eliot, with Bonamy and Mrs Dobrée, joined a protest procession which marched through the City singing 'Onward, Christian soldiers' and other hymns at intervals. He did not, he wrote to Dobrée, expect Canterbury to join Rome, but thought that if the Church of England were disestablished its more serious members would become Catholic; others would join nonconformist churches, while the majority would be content with civil marriages and individual gods such as dogs, pipes, golfing, and allotment gardens. Such thoughts on pleasant Sunday secular religion were to recur in *The Rock*.

Vivienne had received treatment at a French sanatorium in June; later she and Eliot moved from one near Paris to another, specializing in nervous disorders, at Divonne-les-Bains near Geneva. Here Eliot discussed with Robert Sencourt, another patient, points which needed settling before he could join the Church of England. Sencourt (who ascribes this meeting to June the following year) remembered Vivienne's vague expression of hopelessness, her dank hair, blotched face, and frail figure within a loosely hanging dress; the strain from which both suffered came, he thought, from living together in disunity.

The appearance of the two Sweeney dramatic fragments in the October 1926 and January 1927 issues of *The Criterion*, with the two epigraphs from the *Oresteia* and St John of the Cross, has a special interest. When Bonamy Dobrée disagreed with the attitude to life expressed in the second epigraph, Eliot tried to make himself clearer. To kill human affections would make one 'rather more a completely living corpse than most people are', he explained; human affections, he thought, cannot lead to the love of God, but the love of God is capable of elevating our affections, which otherwise would be little different from those of animals. When (the previous April) he and his brother Henry visited Rome with their wives, Tom had surprised and embarrassed the others by kneeling before Michelangelo's *Pietà*. Here was a spiritually humble, contrite man ritualizing his acceptance of a higher authority. From adolescence onwards he had become hypersensitively subject to a sense of sin; perhaps it was a hereditary characteristic. It may have been Calvinist;

he thought he was of Scottish ancestry. His sin-complex had increased in the post-war years, partly from what he knew of the moral laxity and decadence of the western world, partly from reflecting on his inner rather than outer private life in the light of authors such as Newman, St John of the Cross, English seventeenth-century religious writers, and Pascal. What he sought was purification of motive in all he did; it was the question he had raised at the end of *The Waste Land*. The kind of drama he was creatively interested in concerned conversion; he believed, as he had written in 1923, that art in its highest form is not antithetical to popular art, but a refinement of it; and he had experimented in a form that would appeal to a much larger audience than could be commanded by scholarly, allusive poetry, however intense. When he told Aldington that he was seeking a style and form unlike those of *The Waste Land*, he had drama in mind; it was primarily for this reason that he had made a close and prolonged study of those Elizabethan and Jacobean dramatists who had shown that popular appeal and fine art are not incompatible.

Some time after returning to England, Eliot stayed with Sencourt's friend Lord Halifax at Hickleton Hall near Doncaster, where he accompanied his host to Mass each day. Lord Halifax saw no reason why the Church of England should continue to be dissociated from Rome. Eliot's mind was made up; after periods of Unitarianism and agnosticism, he had been attracted more and more to Anglo-Catholicism, the orthodox traditional Christian faith. He now accepted its central tenet, that God (the Word or Logos) had become incarnate in Christ, and that, by prayer, observance, and the discipline of thought and action, one could be more receptive to the Holy Spirit. He was impressed less by Newman's eloquence or the sustained harmonies of Jeremy Taylor than by the concision, wit, and analytical discipline of Lancelot Andrewes' scholarship.

On his return to London, Eliot lost no time in getting into touch with his friend W. F. Stead, from whom he learned that as a Unitarian he needed to be baptized before he could be received into the Church of England. Stead lived at Finstock near Oxford, where he made arrangements for private baptism; the church was locked when the first stage of Eliot's conversion was registered on the afternoon of St Peter's Day, 29 June. The next day Stead drove him to the Bishop of Oxford's palace at

Cuddesdon, where he was confirmed. A final stage commenced about nine months later when, before Father Underhill, another of Robert Sencourt's friends, he made his first confession. About midway between these last two ecclesiastical advances, Eliot made an important secular change when he became a British citizen on 2 November 1927.

His commitment was an act of faith, and faith implies uncertainty; to this extent he remained agnostic. His subsequent poetry emphasizes the almost insuperable difficulty of attaining a sense of unity with God, that intersection of the timeless with time which he calls Incarnation. It is no inevitable sequitur of a course of devotion; it comes, if it comes at all, spontaneously. Eliot's acceptance of the infinite mystery does not imply mystical experience; he denied that he was a mystic. For him there were only hints and guesses; his reward, as he makes clear at the end of 'The Dry Salvages', was in the constant quest for holiness, and in the hope that dedication would fructify in his life and work. He did not believe that the way of holiness lay through any particular Church, and he thought the Catholic Church too rigid and exclusive. His new affiliation was a life-line in times of distress. Whether it improved his relations with his wife seems very doubtful, for she could be cruel and cutting, had very little sympathy with his new ways, and rarely accompanied him to church.

The vicissitudes of Eliot's new hope are the subject of a number of poems from 1927 to 1930. Until he began them, he thought he would be unable to write more poetry after 'The Hollow Men'. The first, 'Journey of the Magi', was issued as one of the series of 'Ariel' poems which were published singly for various authors. It sprang from a passage in one of Lancelot Andrewes' sermons, and helped to facilitate the refraction of Eliot's innermost thoughts in further poems in the same series, as well as in the group which was dedicated to Vivienne and published as *Ash-Wednesday* in 1930. Appearing in the same year, 'Marina', the last of his 'Ariel' poems, is unquestionably his happiest and most lyrical. In 1928 he had written less felicitously when, in response to Babbitt's advice that he should make his new position known, he announced in the preface to his essays *For Lancelot Andrewes* that he was a classicist in literature, a royalist in politics, and an Anglo-Catholic in religion. Inevitably such a terse, unqualified declaration (based on the description of Charles Maurras, in *La Nouvelle Revue Française* of March 1913, as representative of the 'classique, catholique, monarchique' traditions) sounded misleadingly reactionary, uncompromising, and intolerant; Herbert Read, self-confessedly 'a romanticist in literature, an anarchist in politics, and an agnostic in religion', had no difficulty in working with him. Nevertheless, Eliot's slogan reflected the tendency of *The Criterion*.

Reviewing popular theologians in the May 1927 number of *The New Criterion*, Eliot impugns 'the rosy tradition of Rousseau' which Murry upheld in *The Life of Jesus* with a denial of Original Sin and the assertion that man is not only the son of God but must *be* God; it is 'terribly hard', Eliot comments, to believe that man is the son of God. Accused of neo-classicism, he points out that it had always been his policy to print men of genius like D. H. Lawrence, and includes an article by Murry on the question. Later, in a review of Russell's *Why I Am Not a Christian*, which he considers 'pathetic', he maintains that atheism is often a form of Christianity, and that it will be found in its High Church form in Matthew Arnold, its Tin Chapel form in Lawrence, and its Low Church form in Russell. It might, of course, be argued that Eliot's intellectual tendencies at the time are equally open to this unsubtle kind of polemical labelling.

The most notable feature of *The Criterion* in the 1928–30 period is the scope given to discussion of fascism and communism. In December 1926 the Vatican had condemned Charles Maurras and his *Action française* political movement. Eliot must have remembered some of its violent manifestations in 1910, but he still sympathized with the ideals of Maurras on social order and enlightened government, while sharing his enthusiasm for Dante. Leo Ward's attempt in *The Criterion* to prove Maurras anti-Christian elicits textual correction from Eliot in support of his affirmation that he had studied Maurras for eighteen years and found just the opposite. Eliot believed that, with the expansion of the electorate, the value of the individual vote was diminishing, and that, as democratic government declined, the power of a few politicians, or financial groups, or the Civil Service, grew; as religion receded, the populace turned their religious feelings more and more into politics. Behind the increasing demand for authority and order he found a spiritual anaemia which made people only too willing to accept the political theory of new régimes. The French school of thought in *Action française* was superior to fascism in two respects: it would preserve royalty and a hereditary class to safeguard the interests of the ordinary citizen from ambitious politicians or dictatorship, and it insisted on decentralization to the uttermost possible, unlike the Napoleonic system, which had a number of parallels with fascism. Communism and fascism were completely sterile; they had no value for Britain, and appealed to thoughtless people. New political ideals were necessary, and something might be gained from foreign theory, but not from the political practices of Russian communism and Italian fascism. Such thinking was to find its unequivocal expression in *The Rock*.

How often Eliot and his paranoiac wife lived apart is impossible to judge. She visited one sanatorium after another, and there must have been times when it was essential for him to escape from her. Their uneasy marriage had suffered shipwreck so badly that it was doomed to founder. Stephen Spender remembered what happened when an undergraduate had the temerity to call on them: a lady answered the door and, on hearing that he wished to see Mr Eliot, slammed it in his face as she wailed, 'Why do they all wish to see my husband!' The Church discipline which Eliot imposed on himself was one refuge; it was hardly happiness, but something more terrifying, he wrote to Paul Elmer More; it was both the dark night and the desert, more searching than morals, and more real than the sweetness and light of Arnold's culture. Meeting close friends in London lightened his load; Herbert Read tells us that 'he relished good food and beer and wine, but his speciality was cheese, of which he had tasted a great many varieties'. In the summer he would visit the country home of the Fabers near Aberystwyth, where he could relax, picnic, enjoy swimming in the sea, and, when he felt so disposed, for he lacked proficiency in the game, try his hand at tennis. He was happy with parents and children.

Late in 1929, after a number of removals, he and Vivienne moved to another flat (68) in Clarence Gate Gardens, near a church where Eliot worshipped daily. Francis Underhill of Liddon House (an Anglican centre for the pastoral care of university students) still acted as his spiritual counsellor, and it was on his advice that Eliot started the habit of going into retreat at Kelham Theological College near Newark, Nottinghamshire. His friendship with George Bell, who had become Bishop of Chichester after holding the deanship of Canterbury, was to have momentous consequences. The conference of bishops which was held in 1930 for the discussion of current issues led to Eliot's writing 'Thoughts after Lambeth', an essay published the following year in the 'Criterion Miscellany' series. The attempt to form a civilized non-Christian outlook in the western world was, he predicted, doomed to failure.

In reminiscences of Eliot which emphasize the remarkably outward-looking nature of a man who was perpetually subject to self-inquisition, (*The Listener*, 28 April 1977), E. W. F. Tomlin recalls how, when Eliot had finished his lecture on John Marston at University College, London, in 1930, he summoned up courage to go up and ask him a question on the controversial preface to *For Lancelot Andrewes*. He noticed Vivienne, short, with a scarf covering the lower part of her face, standing restively by her husband's side. As Eliot replied with courtesy, she continually sought to gain his attention by plucking at his sleeve, but he took no notice, adding that he had given up the idea of writing the three books which he had promised in his preface, on Donne, royalism, and modern heresy. They looked, Tomlin thought, 'a forlorn pair' as they left together.

When Vivienne enjoyed better health, she and Tom entertained guests at home, and Robert Sencourt recalls an occasion in 1930 when she invited a number of literary friends to Clarence Gate Gardens to meet the poet Ralph Hodgson and read extracts from their latest writings. It was Lady Ottoline Morrell, however, who took command, in her customary manner. Eliot read his unpublished 'Coriolan' poem 'Difficulties of a Statesman'. One morning Sencourt heard him courteously refuse Lady Astor's invitation over the telephone to meet H. G. Wells and Bernard Shaw at lunch with her; he wished her ladyship to know that he did not accept invitations from ladies he had not met, nor from anyone who invited him without his wife, nor from one who was divorced. Sencourt could see that there was no real companionship between him and Vivienne; he had taken her recently to the Riviera in a desperate bid to find a cure and a happier relationship. Virginia Woolf regarded her as a 'torture', a 'bag of ferrets' around Tom's neck. Cigarette-smoking was his main relaxation, and he was already afflicted with emphysema. There were times when he could fully savour the tragic intensity of the quotation with which he concluded his 1931 essay on Thomas Heywood: 'O God! O God! that it were possible To undo things done; to call back yesterday.'

The state of England gave him cause for disquiet. Aggravation of inequality and injustice as a result of continued economic recession, with unemployment on an unprecedented scale, bore widespread witness to moral and spiritual apathy in high places. It was absurd to think that politics could be divorced from morals; education without moral purpose, and economics without regard to moral welfare, he insisted, are vain. 'Temporary and eternal problems press themselves upon the intelligent mind with an insistence which they did not seem to have in the reign of Edward VII', he wrote. Like Lawrence, he regarded over-industrialization as a potent factor in the decay of virtues he associated with agricultural communities; it would lead to instability, uprootedness, and lack of patriotism. In an artificial society people resorted to the daydreams of films and popular fiction; in a properly organized world they would have something better to do than to read novels, which had become the opium of the day. He thought there would always be a need for poetry, and that a revival in drama was possible.

An invitation to give the annual Charles Norton lectures at Harvard offered him an acceptable release from Vivienne, but he must have craved time for preparing them. On 4 March he sent her an officially worded letter, signed with conventional affection, indicating that his visit to America would not be sufficiently profitable to afford her a liberal allowance on his return. In August he drove her in his small Morris car to attend the christening of his god-daughter Susanna, the youngest of the Morley family, who lived at Pikes Farm near Crowhurst, Surrey. About the same time they paid a visit to the Woolfs at Rodmell, near Lewes, in Sussex, and a photograph shows Vivienne standing rather apart and woe-begone beside Virginia and Tom. Sencourt thought that the decision to leave her for several months pushed her further over the brink of sanity; a friend saw her remove the stones from her necklace, throw them to the floor, and imagine they were animals that Tom must drive to their stall. With her brother Maurice and his wife, she accompanied him to Southampton, whence he was to sail to Montreal. On the way to Waterloo, according to one report, he discovered that some of his papers were missing and that his wife had locked them in the bathroom. A boy had to climb through the bathroom window before they could be recovered and brought to the station, just in time for the party to catch the train as planned.

Vivienne had companions who stayed with her as long as they could during Tom's absence: a young girl left because she was frightened; even a friend found she could not endure very long the company of a patient who was mentally ill; Lucy Thayer, who had attended her wedding, remained until she had to leave for the States. Vivienne looked forward to Tom's return, and even had a little party to drink to his health. In the meantime, with a heavy weight on his conscience, he was enjoying himself as much as he could in Boston; his mother had died in 1929, but he had many relatives to whom he could turn, particularly Henry and his wife Theresa at Cambridge. He may have discussed his marital plight with them and others, perhaps with his friend and correspondent Emily Hale, whom he met several times. At Harvard he had rooms in Eliot House, founded in honour of one of his distant relatives who had been President of the University; he held open tea parties, met students once a week, and made a number of professorial friends, including Theodore Spencer and John Livingston Lowes. His eight lectures (most of which had to be on familiar subjects, as he had scant time for research) were delivered at intervals from the beginning of November to the end of March; they ranged from the Elizabethan era to the modern, and were published by Faber and Faber in 1933, with the title 'The Use of Poetry and the Use of Criticism', and with a dedication to the memory of his old friend Charles Whibley, who had died in 1930.

Eliot lectured at many universities and colleges in different parts of the States, in California, Minneapolis, and Baltimore, for example, but particularly in the east. He seems to have been ready to extend his time abroad. A course of three lectures delivered at the University of Virginia, Charlottesville, and published in 1934 as *After Strange Gods*, proved rather unfortunate for his reputation. At Johns Hopkins he lectured on a familiar subject, metaphysical poets, and read to the Poetry Society. He met Scott Fitzgerald, an admirer whose *Great Gatsby* he had described as the first step forward in American fiction since Henry James. At Princeton he met Paul Elmer More, a very different type of person, a shy elderly scholar with theological leanings who came from St Louis. They did not correspond frequently, but were not averse to discussing their spiritual lives; Eliot, who thought they had much in common, told him he believed in the existence of Hell, and (an addition which suggests a strange illogical arbitrariness) in hell on earth for those who do not believe in the after-life. How much he suffered, or how indifferent he had become, as he returned to England at the end of June 1933, is a matter for conjecture; he had made arrangement not to return to his wife and to avoid seeing her as completely as possible.

4

Years of Growing Fame

A long absence from Vivienne in a congenial social and academic environment must have strengthened Eliot's conviction that he could no longer sustain a tolerable career and continue to live with her. No doubt he had been told this more than once. His final decision could not have been an impulsive one, like that which he made when he married precipitately; otherwise he could not have maintained his inflexible policy never, if possible, to see her again. Either before leaving England, more probably during his prolonged stay in the States, he made up his mind, and began preparatory moves to cope with the situation. His lawyers drew up a deed of separation, and sent Vivienne the requisite papers with a letter of explanation from Tom. Mrs Enid Faber agreed to do everything she could, in concert with Maurice Haigh-Wood, to look after her welfare. As soon as he returned to England, Eliot spent one night at his club, and then took refuge, as arranged, at Pikes Farm, where he lived most of the time for several months. Vivienne remembered how, sitting by him when their separation was given its final legality a few weeks after his return, she held his hand, and he never looked at her.

He did not stay at the Morleys' old red farmhouse, but at a cottage a short distance away, where he could work with little disturbance and have meals supplied whenever he wished; the Morley children called his retreat 'Uncle Tom's Cabin'. Normally he would dine and spend his evenings at the farmhouse. Everything was at his disposal. When Frank Morley and his wife returned, after three weeks' holiday in Norway, Tom was sunburnt and busy planning *The Rock*. He had discussed this with Martin Browne, whom he first met while staying with George Bell, Bishop of Chichester. Bell had initiated a link between the Church and the arts when, as Dean of Canterbury, he invited John Masefield and Gustav Holst to prepare the first original drama to be performed in a cathedral since the Reformation; he set another precedent when he appointed Browne director of religious drama in his diocese. Martin Browne was now organizing a pageant to raise funds for the building of Anglican churches in expanding suburbs of London, and Eliot had agreed to supply choruses and dialogues for scenes in the history of the Church of England which had already been planned for performance by amateur groups from different parishes. On Sundays he walked by country lanes for early morning communion in the ancient church of St George's, Crowhurst, with its renowned yew tree, said to be 1500 years old. He joined in games with the children, participated in the invention of crosswords in various languages, and learned to make bread. In November he accompanied Morley and another American to Scotland, where they met George Blake, and drove over Rannoch Moor to Inverness. With the approach of winter, Eliot left Pikes Farm for lodgings at 33 Courtfield Road, South Kensington.

Here he lived with Anglo-Catholics, one of whom, Miss Bevan, was struck by his sadness; his affection for her cat elicited some playful verses. His most important friendship was with Father Eric Cheetham of St Stephen's Church in Gloucester Road, where he worshipped and became vicar's warden, a position he held about twenty-five years. After a period at Courtfield Road, where he worked on *The Rock*, he moved to Father Cheetham's presbytery at 9 Grenville Place; the two moved to a flat at 11 Emperor's Gate in 1937. For many years Eliot sought spiritual guidance at the St Simon's retreat in Kentish Town.

So impressed was George Bell by *The Rock*, which was performed from 28 May to 9 June 1934 at Sadler's Wells Theatre, that he invited Eliot to write a play for the 1935 Canterbury Festival. The success of the chorus in *The Rock* encouraged Eliot to give it a prominent role in *Murder in the Cathedral*, the first title of which, 'Fear in the Way', probably hinted at the rising menace of another European war. With Robert Speaight as Becket, the performance in the chapter house (not far from the spot where Becket was murdered) won such acclaim that the play was staged at the Mercury Theatre, Notting Hill Gate, where, after being hailed by the critic for *The Times* as 'the one great play by a contemporary dramatist now to be seen in England', it ran for seven months. For more than a year after this it ran successfully in London (at the Mercury, the Duchess, the Old Vic) and the provinces, before being taken to the States, where it was performed in Boston and New York.

Vivienne remained devoted to Tom's memory, and was proud of his successes; his Rothenstein portrait became her shrine. She remembered his birthday, and sent him the key of her flat, leaving it accessible in the hope of his return. She thought of him protectively, convinced that he was the victim of a conspiracy against her, and indulged fond recollections of nocturnal walks in London streets soon after their marriage. Her unhealed wound evoked bitterness in 1935; seven years earlier, she noted in February, dear Tom had brought her back from France, where he would have preferred to leave her. She remained busy despite her illnesses, driving a car, joining Mosley's fascist movement in the confidence that it would elevate English standards, taking lessons in pianoforte and singing, and plaguing at some time or other those who patiently attended to their responsibilities for her welfare.

Eliot could not shake off the guilt of abandoning her, but there was no alternative. His love for Vivienne must have withered before he left her, and he knew his sanity would be threatened if ever he returned. For two or three years at least she sought a reunion, writing and telephoning his office, and even preparing an advertisement for publication in the personal column of *The Times* on the second anniversary of his departure for the States, requesting him to return, if he were free to do so, to the home he had left at 68 Clarence Gate Gardens. She attended performances of *The Rock*, and another of *Murder in the Cathedral*, hoping to meet him. Having seen a notice that he was to speak at a book exhibition in Dorland Hall, Lower Regent Street, she put his three latest books (copies of the two plays and *After Strange Gods*) in a satchel, and set off in her fascist uniform and beret with her dog Polly under her arm. Arriving almost late at the crowded doorway, she greeted him as he came, and was delighted with his open recognition of her as he hurried in. As she stood during his address, she held Polly high in her arms, and nodded approvingly. At the end she went up to the table, took out her three books, and asked him quietly to return. He signed the books, said he could not talk to her then, and left with his chairman Richard Church. He probably never saw her again; in the summer of 1938 she was committed to a private mental hospital in Finsbury Park.

For their summer holidays from 1934 until the outbreak of war Emily Hale's uncle and aunt, Dr and Mrs Carroll Perkins, friends of Eliots in Boston, rented a house and adjoining cottage in Chipping Campden. Eliot was their guest on a number of occasions, and in 1934 and 1935, if not in later pre-war years, Emily stayed at the cottage. On one occasion Mrs Perkins took him to admire the gardens at Hidcote; with Emily, possibly in the summer of 1934, he visited the garden at Burnt Norton, not far from Chipping Campden. At the time this eighteenth-century manor (so called because the owner of the original had set fire to it and died in the burning) was empty. The route almost certainly taken by Tom and Emily in the light and shade revealed first the dry upper pool with its semicircular fringe of yew-trees in the background, then the dry lower pools, then the rose-garden. How mutually attached they were remains a matter for conjecture, which is heightened by the ban on reading his numerous letters to her (at Princeton University) before the year 2020. Further visits relative to *Four Quartets* were made by Eliot, in May 1936 to Little Gidding, and in August 1937 to East Coker. Conceived as an independent poem, without a sequel, 'Burnt Norton' was written in 1935.

Despite its direction in accordance with Eliot's thought, *The Criterion* had always appeared rather miscellaneous in its main articles; surveys or 'chronicles' of contemporary art, music, broadcasting, theatre, and fiction had been introduced, and book reviews and synopses of foreign periodicals had increased. During the fascist–communist Spanish civil war, Eliot regretted that the 'balance of mind which a few highly-civilized individuals, such as Arjuna, the hero of the *Bhagavad-Gita*, can maintain in action' was difficult for most observers, and rarely fostered by the press. He believed that the right life for the majority of any nation was 'the real and spontaneous country life'. By October 1938 he had lost all hope in contemporary politics, and in the creation of a 'European mind'; with the growth of dictatorships, the latter had almost disappeared. The failure of Britain and France to take effective action in the Munich crisis made Eliot lose heart, as he realized when the prospect of war involved him in hurried plans for suspending publication. With his resignation, *The Criterion* made its last appearance in January 1939. His consolation was that he had introduced writers such as Marcel Proust, leading authors such as Lawrence, Wyndham Lewis, Joyce, and Pound, and young poets such as Auden, MacNeice, and Spender.

During the 1930s Eliot had come to believe that the salvation of western Europe depended less on political and economic measures than on theology and ethics. It is significant that the last issue of *The Criterion*, in which he admits that this trend had led to 'emphases which somewhat stretched the original framework of a literary review', contains a review article on Maritain's vision of the Christian city which could ultimately arise from the ruins of war if its aims were kept alight in 'intense *nuclei*, like the monastic orders'. By subtle choice of contributors and subjects, Eliot's editing had enlisted aid for the furtherance of his own thought, without discouraging contrary views.

Eliot's main pre-war literary interest had been in drama. He had made a close study of Ibsen's plays before working on *The Family Reunion*, preoccupation with the subject of which undoubtedly arose with the need to find an 'objective correlative' for the sense of guilt which he had to face in the summer of 1938, when his wife was committed to a private mental home. It was the first of his plays to present a contemporary subject; with Michael Redgrave in the leading role, it was produced at the Westminster Theatre in March 1939, earning much praise for its versification and diction, with less assurance on its subject and stage effectiveness. The same month, at Corpus Christi, Cambridge, Eliot gave three lectures which appeared in October as *The Idea of a Christian Society*. Earlier, about the time the Second World War broke out, he was on another visit to East Coker, where he took photographs of the church and village. Five weeks or so later, on 5 October, *Old Possum's Book of Practical Cats*, previously announced as *Pollicle Dogs and Jellicle Cats*, was published, presenting Eliot as the poet of light entertaining verse which has kept its charm for young and old.

'East Coker', written with the design of *Four Quartets* in mind, first appeared in March 1940. Soon after the evacuation of

British troops from the beaches near Dunkirk, Eliot wrote 'Defence of the Islands' in response to a request from the Ministry of Information. At the New York World's Fair of 1940 it formed part of the text which accompanied photographs illustrating Britain's war effort; the following year it was published in *Great Britain at War* by the Museum of Modern Art, New York.

In November 1940, when heavy air-raids on London were expected, Eliot left Emperor's Gate and became the guest of an old friend, Mrs Mirrlees of Shamley Green, a village near Guildford in Surrey. There he did most of his work, spending two days of the week, Tuesday and Wednesday, in Russell Square, where he stayed the intervening night on fire-watch duty, with often an extra day in the office on Thursday. It was not a propitious time for writing, and Eliot had to content himself most of the time with shorter pieces and occasional lectures. His major poetry came from his concentration on the two poems which completed *Four Quartets*, 'The Dry Salvages' making its first appearance in February 1941, and 'Little Gidding' in October 1942. To meet a demand which had been stimulated by the war, Eliot had prepared a selection of Kipling's poems, with an introduction, which was published just before the Christmas of 1941. During the summer of 1942 he spent five weeks with George Bell in Sweden, ostensibly for religious discussions, when the bishop's secret mission was to hear proposals from delegates representing the German group who planned to overthrow Hitler as a preliminary to peace. During the latter part of the war Eliot attended many meetings and conferences on educational reforms at home, and on the political rehabilitation of Germany during the post-war period.

At the earliest opportunity, in May 1945, Eliot lectured in Paris, where he met Sylvia Beach, the first publisher of Joyce's *Ulysses*. In the post-war era he became a distinguished lecturer on contemporary social and cultural questions as well as on literary subjects. His visit to the United States in December 1945, the first after leaving Vivienne in 1932, and the precursor of several, was prompted by a sense of obligation to Ezra Pound, now incarcerated at St Elizabeth's Hospital, Washington. Pound, who had lived in Italy since 1924, had become so infected with fascist ideas and admiration for Mussolini's reforms that he had taken part in anti-democratic broadcasts during the war. He had been flown to Washington, tried for treason, and confined for psychiatric cure (he was not released until 1958). Eliot did not agree with his political extremism but, as he indicated in an article published in *Poetry* the following year, he was immensely indebted to him for his editorial part in the production of *The Waste Land*, and felt that modern English poetry (American included) owed much to one who eminently belonged to the European tradition. He admired his excellence as a judge of poetry, but thought him more fallible in his judgment of men.

Not long after his return to London, Eliot agreed to share a flat with John Hayward, a bibliophile of distinction who suffered from muscular dystrophy. Eliot had known him as a contributor to *The Criterion*, even more for the parties which were held at his home, 22 Bina Gardens, near Gloucester Road, and commemorated in *Noctes Binanianae*, a privately printed verse record of evenings attended by directors of Faber and Faber, all partial to Sherlock Holmes fiction. In these skittish memorials Hayward appears as Spider or Tarantula, with Eliot as Elephant (never forgetful) or Possum. Their new apartment (19 Carlyle Mansions) overlooked a stretch of the Thames often painted by Turner and Whistler. Eliot, preferring to live in almost monastic simplicity, with only a crucifix on the walls of his bedroom, chose a small room for his study; he could always join John Hayward in his bed-sitting room or the dining-room or drawing-room. His day began with devotion at St Stephen's, Gloucester Road, then breakfast in his flat before setting off to Russell Square. When it was fine in the evening he usually took John out in his wheelchair, and they often stopped to watch boys playing football in the grounds of the Royal Hospital, Chelsea.

One morning in January 1947 Hayward had to convey the news that Vivienne had died in the mental home to which her brother had committed her in 1938. More than thirty-one years had passed since Eliot married her, and for more than fourteen years he had avoided her. He had loved her, been devoted to her, and, when the strain created by her morbidity and hysteria had reached almost breaking-point, been tempted to leave her, only to stay on stoically without hope; when he could no longer think of returning to her after his American tour, he had neither the courage nor the heartlessness to see her again. No doubt he was stung many times by remorse, and even by a sense of treachery. When he heard the news, he buried his face in his hands and cried 'Oh God! Oh God!' He and Maurice Haigh-Wood, with whom he remained a firm friend, made arrangements for her exequies at Pinner, which they attended with the Fabers when the earth was frozen and snow-bound. On hearing news in April that his brother was dying, he flew to America, where he stayed two months, partly to wind up Henry's affairs, partly to offset expenses by lecturing, as he usually did. He was awarded an honorary degree by Harvard University.

Eliot was now reaching the height of fame and honour. He was still intent on drama, and both *Murder in the Cathedral* and *The Family Reunion* were performed at the 1947 Edinburgh Festival. As a result of their success he was invited to provide a new play for the 1948 Festival, but this proved to be impossible, though the first draft (then entitled 'One-Eyed Riley') was discussed with Martin Browne in June. In January 1948 Eliot received the Order of Merit, an award made by the British Sovereign, and a rare distinction, since it is untenable at any time by more than twenty-four holders. He dined with the King and Queen, and visited Pope Pius XII for a private audience. The following March he preached the one sermon of his life, at I. A. Richards' college, Magdalene, Cambridge, where soon afterwards he became an honorary Fellow. In the sermon he spoke about anti-religious influences he had experienced from Montaigne, George Eliot, Herbert Spencer, and Bertrand Russell; for most of us the great betrayals do not come, he said, only 'the constant, daily, petty pusillanimity' against which one must be fortified by penitence and humility.

In September, after completing at least two acts of *The Cocktail Party*, Eliot sailed on the *America* to take up a fellowship for study at Princeton, which gave him the opportunity to see both Emily Hale and Pound. He had not been in America long before he heard that he had been awarded the Nobel Prize for Literature. To receive this award he had to cut short his Princeton programme and present himself in December at Stockholm, where he dined with the Crown Prince and Princess of Sweden. He told Robert Giroux, a director of his American publishers Harcourt, Brace and Company, that he could remember only two things about this visit. Having to wear formal dress for the presentation ceremony, and being expected to crown the Swedish Snow Queen, he wished the two events could be combined on a skating-rink, so that he could appear with skates and tails. When he left Stockholm, and was asked by a reporter for which book he had received his prize, he said he believed that it was for the entire corpus; after being asked when he wrote that, he thought what an excellent title 'The Entire Corpus' would be for a mystery.

Eliot's allegiance to his friends was proved again when he refused to allow the staging of *The Cocktail Party* at the Edinburgh Festival without Martin Browne as its producer. Through Denis Saurat, Director of the French Institute, and Professor of French at London University, he had met Joseph Chiari, a Corsican admirer of his poetry who had been the political and cultural envoy of the Free French movement under General de Gaulle. Chiari was the French consul in the Scottish capital, and spent much time with Eliot, when *The Cocktail Party* was produced in August 1949 with Alec Guinness as principal. Eliot arrived with his sister Marian and a niece, and was astonished when the taxi-driver who drove them from the station to their hotel refused payment. 'No, thank you, Mr Eliot', he said; 'I have had the honour of driving you, and that is enough.' The next day he brought Chiari a copy of Eliot's play with a request for the author's signature, to which there could be no objection. Eliot was sensitive to kindness and courtesy, and Chiari supplies eloquent testimony to his generosity and lasting appreciation of friendly acts.[5] The French consul held a reception, at which Eliot could be seen chatting with Neil Gunn while a completely inebriated Dylan Thomas flattered the actress Eileen Herlie. With the pressure of meetings and introductions, a radio talk, and press interviews, Eliot was glad to have a day with Chiari on a memorable tour of the Tweed country which ended with a visit to Abbotsford. The success of the play moved Eliot to remark as they were walking to a late-night party organized by the Scottish PEN Club that he wished his mother could have been with them; 'she would have been so glad'.

Towards the end of the year Eliot was commissioned to spend a few weeks with the historian Arnold Toynbee on a lecture tour in Germany, his subject being the need for European unity and concord, with emphasis on cultural, particularly Christian, tradition and on freedom of expression. He could never forget the 'colossal folly' of President Roosevelt when, swayed by a superannuated American suspicion of British imperialism, he had trusted Stalin rather than Churchill, thereby surrendering eastern Europe to the Kremlin, and opening 'the way towards the Dark Ages' which seemed to menace the world. He met 'many wonderful individuals', he told William Turner Levy, including the Bishop of Hanover, but they were all of the same class; he wished to meet people from 'different walks of life', but he was continually on the move, and denied the opportunity. War had 'mutilated the face' of Germany, but the beer was as good as ever. In the winter he spent a few weeks with the Geoffrey Fabers in South Africa. T. S. Matthews reports the story of his misfortune at Cape Town, when his hostess Sarah Gertrude Millin, a Jewess, having occasion to look through his poems late at night, and coming across an anti-semitic line, rapped at his door and asked him to leave the next morning.

Eliot had at last found that he had more than adequate financial resources, though income tax had accounted for the greater part of his £29,000 receipts for *The Cocktail Party*. The Nobel Prize brought in £11,000; his annual salary was £1500; his royalties amounted to £2500; and he earned additional sums in lecture fees. During 1950 *The Cocktail Party* had long runs, first in New York, then in London. Following its production at the Edinburgh Festival, *The Confidential Clerk* ran for more than half a year from September 1953 in London, and, after successes in New Haven (Yale University), Boston, and Washington, from February to the summer of 1954 in New York.

Eliot's fame was reflected in the size of his lecture audiences; more than two and a half thousand assembled at Central Hall, Westminster, to hear 'The Three Voices of Poetry' in November 1953. In America there was no repetition of what happened at the University of Chicago in the autumn of 1950, when dwindling audiences attended Eliot's four lectures on education. He gave the centenary address at Washington University in 1953. In 1956, at the University of Minnesota in Minneapolis (where he was the guest of Allen Tate), he received $2000, the highest fee on record for a lecture on literature, for presenting 'The Frontiers of Criticism' to a stadium audience of well over thirteen thousand. (He was remembered at Marquette University for the amusing ambiguity of a telegram he sent declining an invitation to call on the way: 'Regret impossible stop writing'.) At the University of Texas, Austin, in 1958, he received tumultuous applause after addressing over seven thousand in the basket-ball building, to the accompaniment of thunder, lightning, and clattering hail.

European honours befell him. In 1951, with the President of France, the British ambassador, and many other dignitaries attending the ceremony, he opened 'Le Livre Anglais', a Paris exhibition orgar   onale to illustrate the history of]   gh the centuries. Eliot owed muc   aper to his friend John Hayward,   ie planning of the exhibition. In   Hanseatic Goethe Prize, which he   n Hamburg, at a stage of life wl   of humility, and proved better c   German sage than he had been in   on he received the Dante Gold Medal in Florence in 1959.

5

Final Happiness

In 1949 a momentous change had taken place in Eliot's office when he appointed a new secretary. This was Valerie Fletcher, whose interest in his poetry was awakened at the age of fourteen, when she first heard John Gielgud's recording of 'Journey of the Magi'. A friend of her family who knew Eliot persuaded him to autograph a copy of his poems for her, and her interest became such an obsession that her one ambition was to become his secretary. With this in mind she left her home in Leeds, against her parents' wishes, to train at a secretarial college. She disliked this so much that she left, and engaged an agency to find secretarial work with a writer; her second employer was Charles Morgan. She left him after a year, and this proved to be a recommendation when Eliot interviewed her. Before leaving her application she had walked about Russell Square for nearly two hours. During the interview he smoked hard; at the end he told her that no decision could be made until he had seen the other candidates. He pointed to her bandaged hand, and expressed the hope that she would be able to type again in ten days. Two days later she was offered the appointment. She proved to be devoted, unassuming but engaging, and unusually competent; she found Eliot attractive in person and manners. That he and she were falling in love in 1956 Eliot may have been slow to realize, for, as Robert Sencourt writes, 'he could hardly think that a handsome and healthy young lady of thirty would wish to espouse an invalid of sixty-eight'. Despite his fame he was becoming more lonely, and he had even thought of entering an abbey.

Eliot's health was deteriorating; he suffered from weakening lungs and a bronchial condition. Returning from the States on

54

the *Queen Mary* in 1956, he was confined to the sick bay for the remainder of the voyage after a severe attack of tachycardia. He gave up smoking cigarettes for a cigar a day, which he succeeded in reducing to one a week, but his emphysema steadily worsened. In his later years he avoided the cold and fog of London winters, usually for the warm sunshine of the West Indies.

But for his friend Mrs Behrens, Eliot's second marriage might never have taken place. After having Miss Fletcher stay two summers at her home in the south of France, she must have felt sure of her eligibilit.. f.. .. . .. ed to have both of them as her , he asked Valerie if she knew hi ever heard her use it; he told he she felt, he would have proposed : a gnawing sense of obligation to had been living for a long peri ews of his forthcoming marriage hat he did not do so until a day Hayward probably had his susp...., and resented Eliot's action and secrecy. His friendship had become rather dependent and possessive, and his jealousy did not allow him to be reconciled to the situation or to Tom. Thereafter they met rarely, and only by chance.

Eliot's second wedding took place on 10 January 1957, with greater privacy than Hardy's. As his solicitor Gordon Higginson had an obliging friend who was vicar of St Barnabas's Church, Addison Road, Kensington, arrangements to avoid publicity were facilitated. A licence had to be obtained from the Archbishop of Canterbury to omit the publishing of the banns and to hold the marriage service outside customary church hours. Tom and Valerie were married on a dark wintry morning at 6.30, and it was while waiting in the church with his best man Higginson for the arrival of Valerie and her father that Eliot discovered a remarkable coincidence: his wedding was to take place where Jules Laforgue, to whom he owed much of his early poetic development, had been married in 1886. Another followed, when it was found that the house where they breakfasted with the officiating priest had once been the home of Ezra Pound. The news of Eliot's marriage astonished most of his friends, disappointed at least one hopeful lady, and shocked Emily Hale.

After a honeymoon in Mentone, and his recovery from bronchitis at Brighton, the Eliots moved into a ground-floor flat in Kensington Court Gardens. What a pleasure it was to see them there, Chiari felt, Tom perfectly relaxed and 'quietly saying to me: "I don't deserve such happiness"', or to watch them arriving hand in hand at the Russell Hotel, or wherever he met them. One cannot imagine Eliot living in luxury at home, and his Kensington flat was described as dowdy and typically brownish, with walls bare except for bookshelves, which were to be found in the dining-room, where reference books were conveniently placed to settle points whenever the need arose in discussion. Subsequently the walls were graced with watercolours by Henry Moore and Ruskin, an Edward Lear landscape, Wyndham Lewis drawings, and sketches of cats by Eliot's father. Eliot described the Turneresque Ruskin as 'gradely', a Yorkshire word of approbation he probably caught from his father-in-law. *On Poetry and Poets*, a collection of his later critical essays, was dedicated to Valerie. Love had at last brought Eliot unprecedented happiness, which may be felt in the love scenes and closing serenity of *The Elder Statesman*, as well as in its dedication. Eliot's final play, first performed at the 1958 Edinburgh Festival, ran for only two months in London, where it excited little enthusiasm.

His health was uncertain, and he was very ill in 1958 while staying with Valerie in Morocco. Their visits to the States were timed to avoid wintry climates by sojourning in the Caribbean, where he loved to swim. The waters of Nassau, Bermuda, Barbados and Jamaica 'seemed to assuage his final illness as nothing else could', we are told, but he always looked forward to returning home. Whenever possible Valerie, though a poor sailor herself, insisted on accompanying him by sea, because she knew he enjoyed that form of travel. In Massachusetts they visited relatives, friends, and many places which memory had made dear. They stayed a number of times with the publisher Margot Cohn in New York. So foggy was it in the 1961 fall that Eliot had to leave her flat for hospital treatment; on one occasion the doctor, her brother-in-law, was shocked to see the deterioration of his lungs. Tom and Valerie revisited Nassau in 1963–4, a year after a serious illness which had kept him in Brompton Hospital five weeks, and from which he never recovered. Bent and hampered by breathing difficulties, seriously ill at times and often unable to help himself, he was sustained by spiritual strength and married happiness.

The New English Bible (the New Testament only) of 1961 excited a good deal of controversy, and Eliot's views on its style were sought by *The Sunday Telegraph*, which paid him a fee of £250, half of which he gave to his parish church. He regretted the ordinariness of the language, which had often been substituted for the more rhythmic and beautiful, and made much of the maladroitness of replacing 'neither cast ye your pearls before swine' with 'do not feed your pearls to swine'. Religion is enhanced by the music of language, he held, but the new translation bore ample testimony to the decline of English, and its use in religious services would contribute to its further deterioration.

From 1958 to 1963 Eliot was a member of the Commission for the Revised Psalter of *The Book of Common Prayer*, the object of which was to eliminate errors, archaisms, and obscurities from the psalms, with the least possible damage to Coverdale's translation of 1535. Meetings were usually held at Lambeth Palace, the London residence of the Archbishop of Canterbury, with C. S. Lewis playing an active part and Eliot ready to plead for the retention of the old familiar expressions which had been vitally significant in the religious life of the people; he would do this even when the words did not quite correspond to those of the original. Eliot and Valerie stayed with her parents at Leeds for the last conference, to which she drove him each day; it was held at Bishopsthorpe, home of Dr Coggan, Archbishop of York and Chairman of the Commission, who noticed Eliot's frailty and was afraid that he might collapse at any moment.

Religion had not narrowed his personality; he always responded to the popular artist. This kind of appreciation may be rare among cultured intellectuals, but Eliot's sympathies were always drawn to common, humble people, and to professionals adept in popular entertainment. In her old age, Virginia Woolf's housekeeper thought that there was no one to equal him among the visitors she had known at Rodmell. Kingsley Amis remembered seeing him in a long queue waiting for Charlie Chaplin's autograph. Eliot's admiration for Marie Lloyd is well known; it was the same with Groucho Marx, a 'master of nonsense' with whom he became friendly in New

York. In his office he kept a photograph of Groucho beside portraits of Goethe, W. B. Yeats, and Paul Valéry. Groucho Marx and his wife came to London in June 1964, and were entertained at Kensington Court Gardens, where Eliot was delighted to serve the wine and to discover that he shared the American comedian's relish for cats, puns, and cigars.

If contentedness seemed to make Tom Eliot dull, as his old admirer Aldous Huxley found when he returned to London in the autumn of 1958, nothing was more fortunate for him than his second marriage; during his invalid years with Valerie he experienced adult happiness and security such as he had never known. With her parents, who were of his own generation, he was very much at home; he enjoyed being with them and sharing their interests. Fittingly his last journey was to them; his emphysema made it impossible to spend the winter in the West Indies or to receive his last award, the Medal of Freedom, from the American President Lyndon Johnson. Father Jennings, Eric Cheetham's successor at St Stephen's, the church with which Eliot was longest associated, came regularly to administer the sacrament at Kensington Court Gardens. After Christmas, when Eliot was visited by Allen Tate, his strength waned rapidly; his breathing became difficult, and oxygen had to be supplied. He died on 4 January 1965. His body was cremated at Golders Green, and his ashes, after resting for a period on an altar at St Stephen's, were taken to St Michael's Church, East Coker, as he had directed.

A month after his death, a service to his memory was held at Westminster Abbey. The Queen and the Prime Minister were represented, as was the American President. Many distinguished authors and artists were present, and Sir Alec Guinness, who had played the leading role in *The Cocktail Party*, read from five of Eliot's poems. Significantly many young people were in attendance; among the elderly was Ezra Pound, who had flown over from Venice to pay homage to a friend who had not forsaken him at the time of his greatest need. Later he said, 'His was the true Dantescan voice – not honoured enough, and deserving more than I ever gave him. . . . Who is there now for me to share a joke with? . . . I can only repeat, but with the urgency of fifty years ago: READ HIM.' On the second anniversary of his death, a memorial to Thomas Stearns Eliot, O. M., was unveiled in Poets' Corner, Westminster Abbey.

PART TWO

Eliot's Works

Go, weak sad men, lost erring souls, homeless in earth or
   heaven. . . .
You still shall tramp and tread one endless round
Of thought, to justify your action to yourselves,
Weaving a fiction which unravels as you weave,
Pacing forever in the hell of make-believe
Which never is belief. . . .
Third Priest, Murder in the Cathedral

'It is the word of life', the parent cried;
– 'This is the life itself', the boy replied.
George Crabbe, 'Peter Grimes'

6

Early Verse

For better or worse ultimately, T. S. Eliot in his boyhood and adolescence did not enjoy such powers of expression as those which enabled Tennyson to write abundantly with unusual euphony in his early years. Nothing suggests that he lisped in numbers, or that he ever wrote freely except in abnormal circumstances. But for a small number of poems, most of which were preserved in academic journals, there appears to be no direct evidence of his poetical proclivities before he reached the age of twenty-one. In his introduction to Eliot's *Poems Written in Early Youth*, John Hayward refers to a few *jeux d'esprit* which did not survive in any recorded form.

Eliot was well on in his seventeenth year when 'A Fable for Feasters', the first of his surviving poems, appeared in the *Smith Academy Record*. Written in the stanza of *Don Juan*, it is conversational or prosaic in syntax and idiom, without Byron's ease of manner and rhyming ingenuity. Sometimes gauche but more often vigorous and compact in expression, it often coincides pleasingly with metrical demands, but lapses occasionally into awkward inversion. Whether its high-spiritedness derives as much from Byron's poem as from *The Ingoldsby Legends* by R. H. Barham is doubtful; it could have owed much to 'The Monk', which is written in the *ottava rima* of *Don Juan*. Eliot's story is simple rather than inventive. The epicureanism which it presents shows boyish delight in speculating on a luscious repast: the boar's head is brought in by four *pages*, its mouth holding an apple, and its skull, saus*ages*. As the monks doze over their Christmas wassail, the ghost against which they thought they had secured themselves steals in and whisks off the abbot; before one could say 'O jiminy!'

the pair had vanished up the chimney. A vain search having been made for their 'Bishop', the monks declared he had been carried up to heaven by St Peter; rumours that his destination had been underground were then scotched by his canonization. The monastery had learnt its lesson, however; the monks became devout and abstemious, and submitted to flagellation until they were reformed. The author ends by declaring that his record of their 'doings' came from an ancient manuscript discovered in the ruins.

It could be said that the poem points to the poet's love of good food and to his puritanism; above all, it indicates the gift of humour which Eliot was often to turn to verse, though he unfortunately thought little of it merited artistic refinement. It is worth remembering that most of his non-academic readers will think of him less as the poet of *The Waste Land* than as the writer of *Old Possum's Book of Practical Cats*.

A short lyric in the stanza of Ben Jonson's 'Drink to me only with thine eyes' appeared in the *Smith Academy Record* two months later than 'A Fable for Feasters'. The earliest of Eliot's poems to be preserved in manuscript, it was completed on 24 January 1905 for Roger Conant Hatch, his teacher of English, who awarded him an 'A', and expressed the hope that Eliot would make his name as a writer; his mother thought it more beautiful than any poetry she had ever written. The poem takes off from the philosophical assumption that time and space do not exist, and ends with thoughts of withering flowers and the transitoriness of love which are reminiscent of Herrick's 'Gather ye rosebuds while ye may'. Its revision for publication at Harvard more than two years later suggests that the poet had little verse in his locker. The changes made do not affect the melody; they modify the thought and make it more explicitly coherent. The opening supposition is no longer followed by the inference that the sun is no greater than we, but by one which is less scientifically objectionable: the ephemeral fly lives as long as we. With no change in the Jonsonian imagery ('. . . I sent thee . . . withered . . .') the poem concludes with a more subdued and general outlook; it is not the days of love but the flowers of life that are few. Tennyson probably wrote nothing quite as unoriginal as this in his youth, but its lyrical expression makes it the most Tennysonian poem Eliot ever wrote, despite the regularity of its movement.

More ambitious and laboured are the lines Eliot recited on Graduation Day at Smith Academy in 1905. The initial imagery owes a little to sailing-experience off Cape Ann, but quickly gives way to colonists embarking for a foreign shore, less happily to clouds fleeing after a summer storm, then (changing from simile to metaphor) to the tortuous slow path of the future which appears like a flowering lane to the hopeful eye of youth. To anyone familiar with the dramatic rhythms of the later Eliot, this will appear slow, old-fashioned poetry indeed. Destitute of imagery for a while, the sequel is more prosy, though dignified by high sentiments of tasks to be fulfilled by the departing alumni. The thought that the memory of the school will always be dear creates a misty image of purity, tautologically adjectival with reference to fanes within which altar fumes of incense rise in the sanctuaries of the soul. The final stanza on returning to Smith Academy, and on its future greatness, had an irony and pathos for their author, the school being closed a few years after he left.

While working for his first degree from 1906 to 1909, Eliot contributed six lyrics to *The Harvard Advocate*, the first appearing towards the end of his first year, to be quickly followed by the revised Smith Academy lyric 'If space and time, as sages say'. Before the publication of the next two, almost a year and a half passed. The last pair appeared on 26 January 1909. All these poems are brief and well finished. 'Song' suggests incipient but vague symbolism. One might assume that it conveys no more than nature's indifference to death, the faded wreath contrasting with a natural scene which is unchanged and still bright with flowers. It seems more likely, however, that the fading of the wild roses and the dying of the leaves in the wreath image a dying love, the poetical idea developing from Jonson's

> I sent thee late a rosy wreath,
>   Not so much honouring thee
> As giving it a hope that there
>   It could not withered be.

Unlike the earlier 'If Time and Space, as Sages say', it expresses a disillusionment with life to which students are prone, as does 'Before Morning', a poem of undoubted symbolical imagery, where the recurrence of reviving hope for young and old alike is expressed in the turning of fresh and withered flowers toward the mingled red and grey of the eastern sky at daybreak.

'Circe's Palace', ostensibly serious, derived from, and set seal to, a college joke; it points toward 'The Love Song of J. Alfred Prufrock', though in a different strain. The title was the name given by a coterie of Harvard students to the home of a Bostonian hostess who loved to invite them to tea; her conversational attempts to beguile may be imagined from Conrad Aiken's recollection of 'the oh so precious, the oh so exquisite, Madeleine, the Jamesian lady of ladies, the enchantress of the Beacon Hill drawing-room – who, like another Circe, had made strange shapes of Wild Michael and the Tsetse [T. S. Eliot]'.[6]

'On a Portrait' is a sonnet on Manet's *La Femme au Perroquet*. The pictured woman is not exactly a Mona Lisa, but for Eliot she presents woman's inscrutability, of which he is continually reminded; she remains alone in the room to which students return after a busy day. Nothing is definite about her as in a sculptured goddess; all is vague, dreamlike, and evanescent. Inevitably he is unequal to the task of expressing the subconscious evocations of his subject; it produces the insubstantial fancy of a meditative lamia in the seclusion of a wood, but, within the limited 'circle' of his thought or knowledge, he is left regarding her curiously, like the parrot. The image of the final couplet has the clean-cut objectivity or hard precision which Eliot aspired to, and was to enjoy finding in poets such as Marvell.

For the expression of feelings, he has recourse to symbolical imagery in 'Song', where the recurrent whiteness of flower and mist and bird is used rather in the Lawrentian manner, though with greater restraint and control, to imply a kind of social spirituality in the apparent conventions of love which the poet finds wearisome; he longs for the scarlet flowers of life. The poet in Eliot could not be subdued to the Bostonian conformity which he associated with the unalterable law of Arnold and Emerson.

Growing more segregated intellectually in a world of increasing complexity, Eliot could find no consolation for his questioning mind, his fleshly and spiritual torments, and a yearning for values which transcended the familiar bourgeois complacency of a materialistic world, until he found vicarious expression in the poetry of Jules Laforgue. Such was the affinity between these young poets that Eliot described it as a peculiar intimacy to which his poetry, at a critical stage in his literary development, owed more (as he stated late in life[7]) than to any other poet, particularly in realizing the poetic possibilities of speech idiom. In Laforgue, among other attractive idiosyncrasies, he found the combined appeal of wit, scholarly allusiveness, polished, conversational style with touches of lyricism, images of city life, ironical collocations, and the light-hearted pessimism of a balked idealist and religious spirit. It illuminated a recognisable area he could follow for himself, and hinted at dramatic styles in presenting his own perceptions of life. For Laforgue the pierrot came to typify the blend of the serious and comical, or the noble and sordid, those paradoxes of life which made Pope (and Hamlet) see man as the glory, jest, and riddle of the world. In *Derniers Vers*, the pierrot, 'pauvre, pâle et piètre, individu Qui ne croit à son Moi qu'à ses moments perdus', assumes overt Hamlet overtones, and in this respect at least is a progenitor of Eliot's Prufrock.

How many poems Eliot attempted or completed while under the spell of Laforgue in 1909–10 is not known. Poetry, it must be remembered, was no more than a pastime; his main pursuits were academic. Four poems influenced or suggested by Laforgue have been published, three in *The Harvard Advocate*; the fourth was reserved for ultimate inclusion in Eliot's *Collected Poems*. Whatever the merits of these verses, nothing in them indicates remarkable progress; poetically they are no more than exercises showing varying degrees of ingenuity or accomplishment. Though not altogether satisfactory as a composition, the sonnet 'Nocturne' is the most fascinating in the treatment of its subject. It is a fantasy which presents the Romeo and Juliet story in caricature or comical charade. Its tone is not so much of cynical amusement as of clinical delight in deflating popular romanticism. When the banal protestations of the '*grand sérieux*' Romeo fail, he plays a commonplace tune on his guitar. Out of pity for hero and heroine, the author has him stabbed. Juliet faints; and an effective finale is produced with moonlit blood, and the frenzied eye of the hero turning up to a bored Laforguian moon. Such a conclusion will drown female readers in tears; there is no need for the usual happy ending, or even an instalment of love next week. With obvious ironical ambivalence, the writer is satisfied that this is the perfect climax sought by all true lovers.

Laforgue's manner is conveyed to some extent in 'Humouresque', which is a development from a verse in the twelfth of the 'Locutions des Pierrots':

> Encore un de mes pierrots mort;
> Mort d'un chronique orphelinisme;
> C'était un coeur plein de dandysme
> Lunaire, en un drôle de corps.

Eliot's verse is snappy but, if it implies more than the original on the human predicament and the philosophical uncertainty of life, it fails, not least in the final quatrain, which confirms one of Arthur Symons' assessments of Laforgue: 'He will not permit, at any moment, the luxury of dropping the mask.'

'Spleen' is more real and interesting. The picture it presents recalls the Bostonians of Henry Adams' retrospect: 'that the most intelligent society, led by the most intelligent clergy, in the most moral conditions he ever knew, should have solved all the problems of the universe so thoroughly as to have quite ceased making itself anxious about past or future . . . seemed to him the most curious social phenomenon he had to account for in a long life'.[8] Eliot sees complacent Bostonian church-worshippers with Sunday faces on which certainty is writ large, declaring complete assurance in their own virtues and religious beliefs; the poem ends satirically with an image of a superannuated civilization, balding, grey, languid, but bland and punctiliously elegant, waiting rather impatiently (as if the social proprieties due to them are being infringed) at the door of the Absolute. Here we have a conventional religion and community which are outside the 'circle' of Eliot's thought. Like Laforgue in 'Dimanches' he is cut off, isolated:

> Et alors, eh! allez donc, carillonez,
> Toutes cloches des bons dimanches!
> Et passez layettes et collerettes et robes blanches
> Dans un frou-frou de lavande et de thym
> Vers l'encens et les brioches!
> Tout pour la famille, quoi! *Vae soli!* C'est certain.

The title 'Spleen' takes on more meaning from 'The First Debate between Body and Soul', a poem Eliot wrote about the same time, calling on the Absolute to save him from sensual stain; his shabby Boston surroundings reflect his self-depreciation and the Swiftian loathing he has for the body and its functions.[9]

'Conversation Galante' is comparable to Laforgue's 'Autre Complainte de Lord Pierrot', which Eliot first met in Symons' *The Symbolist Movement in Literature*. Eliot's anti-romantic young sophisticate is anything but gallant; like Pierrot, he parries the advances of the woman with banter. There is a difference: the woman in Eliot's poem is romantic but empty-headed; whereas Laforgue's hero is quick-witted and concise, Eliot's talks with ready fluency to avoid awkward silences. First he comments on the sentimental moon in mock poetics; then, more suavely and cuttingly (and the lady is *touchée*), on the practice of trying to express moonshine in terms of some nocturne when one has really nothing to say (this recalls the Romeo and Juliet farce of 'Nocturne'). Finally, in deliberately confusing turns of thought, he flatters her after making an ambivalent statement on woman, the full meaning of which she has not understood. She can only reply, 'Are we then so serious?' (Lord Pierrot ends defensively, 'C'était donc sérieux?'). Eliot had learned from Laforgue the value of a hero who could be used dramatically as a mask; his high-spirited prolocutor, rather in the style of Hamlet, expresses Eliot's feelings in camouflage. The glib furtherance of self-denigratory flattery which is quite inconsistent with the course of the conversation is an authorial ruse, a cover for insinuating what a young poet, harassed by the conflict of soul and body, had come to feel. Woman, it seemed, stands perpetually in the way of the Absolute.

The short ode Eliot wrote to commemorate his graduation and departure from Harvard in June 1910 is incredibly jejune, and one cannot believe that he devoted much time or thought to its jigging anapaests. It is unfortunate that they were ever printed or preserved.

7

From 'Preludes' to 'Prufrock'

Before leaving for France in 1910, Eliot had begun a number of poems, including 'Preludes', 'Portrait of a Lady', and possibly 'The Love Song of J. Alfred Prufrock'. As an earnest of his intentions he bought a notebook at Gloucester, entitling it, retrospectively rather than anticipatively, 'Inventions of the March Hare'. (Appropriate as this description may seem to such poems as 'Nocturne' and 'Conversation Galante', it applies also to poems of self-torment such as 'The First Debate between Body and Soul'.) After entering his unpublished verses from November 1909 onwards, he added to it at various times, notably in Paris and at Harvard, until he reached London in 1914. Among the most interesting entries are confessional poems, some of them remarkable for phantasmagoric and sustained images of martyrdom, heightened visions of an abnormally excited, sometimes fevered, imagination, expressive of the spiritual agony which for many years was never to be long quiescent, which was to give Eliot kinship with Baudelaire, and prove to be the mainspring of his best poetry.

The scenes in 'Preludes' have been ascribed to St Louis, Boston, and Paris; the third may have been suggested by *Bubu de Montparnasse*, Charles-Louis Philippe's novel of a Parisian world. What is certain is that most of them are American (probably derived from the Boston area), and that in whatever city the younger Eliot lived he found a strange fulfilment in exploring its slummier quarters. Disillusioned with the superficialities of the more conventional suburbia, he wished to see life. Like Leontius in Plato's *Republic*, whose curiosity to see the corpses of executed criminals overcame his disgust, he was both attracted and repelled by the squalid and sordid. From his general impression emerged images which reflect the meaninglessness of circumscribed life, with no vision beyond the human in its ordinariness and squalor. 'Caprices in North Cambridge', an unpublished poem rather like 'Preludes', after presenting bottles, broken glass, broken barrows, trampled mud interspersed with grass, dirty windows, and bedrabbled sparrows scratching in the gutter, dwells on vacant lots filled with rubbish.[10] The symbol of stony rubbish inimical to Life in *The Waste Land* is already emerging.

Like other poems by Eliot, 'Preludes' grew from fragments, and was not easily concluded. The first two parts belong to 1910; the remainder was written in 1911, the third section in July, after the conclusion of his courses at the Sorbonne, and the final towards the end of the year, when he was back at Harvard. The winter evening scene with the smell of steaks at six o'clock connotes a kind of living; a lonely steaming cab-horse stamps as it waits for it knows not what; a showery gust wraps grimy decaying leaves and newspapers from vacant lots around one's feet (anticipating the men and bits of paper that are whirled by the cold wind in the time-ridden world of 'Burnt Norton'); showers beat on broken blinds; and the lighting of the lamps at the 'burnt-out' end of another smoky day gives a sense of dim earth-bound illumination which accents the surrounding darkness. These 'Preludes' hint at the poetry to come; the deliberate disconnection of their imagery helps to emphasize the meaningless round of life, evening to evening, and points forward to the 'I can connect Nothing with nothing' of *The Waste Land*.

The morning is marked by the stale smell of beer from sawdust-trampled streets over which muddy feet hurry to coffee-stands. This resumption of life, with other masquerades of earthly time, reminds one of all the hands raising shades (or blinds) that have lost whatever brightness they had. The synecdochic use of 'feet' and 'hands' suggests a degree of depersonalization. The close-up of the female lying awake, conscious of the sordid working of her mind in darkness and, when sparrows are heard at daybreak in the gutter, of thoughts about humanity which the people of the street would hardly understand, accentuates the sordor which is finally imaged in the soiled hands clasping the yellow soles of her feet as she sits on the edge of her bed. The fourth prelude is syntactically defective. The soul that is stretched across the skies is not the conscience of the street which is impatient to renew its worldly activities, as if they were its dominion. It sees the skies fade behind the city block, feels trampled by the insistent feet, and is aware of a civilization which has the assurance of a limited range of certainties. Yet man, with this limited knowledge, and a history of evil (the conscience of a blackened street) thinks the future of the world is in his hands.

It would be a mistake to think that Eliot finds beauty in ugliness, as Hardy concluded a poet should, through associating the human lot with material conditions which are unattractive or degrading. He selects images to create a succession of scenes which underline spiritual darkness. The images have the effect of symbols; he cannot dissociate them from the fancy that there exists something beyond our ken, something 'infinitely gentle' upon which infinite suffering is inflicted by the ways of the world. His need for assurance in religious faith is marked in the stress on 'infinite'. It is no more than a suggestion which the wordly will scorn, as the poem indicates with a cynical rejoinder in bold vulgar idiom:

> Wipe your hand across your mouth, and laugh;
> The worlds revolve like ancient women
> Gathering fuel in vacant lots.

'Life is a pure flame, and we live by an invisible Sun within us', wrote Sir Thomas Browne; but here the flame is extinguished, and *The Waste Land* with its wintry mundane priorities is already in the offing. Individuals live in their own worlds, and people are like old women with an instinct for survival, an appetency foreshadowing that of those hollow men in 'East Coker' whose lot is vacancy.

The title of the poem 'Rhapsody on a Windy Night', which was written during Eliot's year in Paris, seems to be an autobiographical slip. The wind does not contribute to this ingenious series of sketches, which depend for their effects mainly on moonlight and gaslight, the street-lights combining with the moonshine in the 'synthesis' of the persona through whom we share a sequence of visual impressions and related memories. We can imagine their occurrence to Eliot on a windy night in the Paris of *Bubu de Montparnasse*, once he had been reminded of a Laforguian link: 'Your damned thin moonlight, worse than gas', he had written in 'Humouresque (after J. Laforgue)'. The moon in 'Rhapsody' is presented unromantically after Laforgue; her washed-out face is cracked with smallpox; she winks feebly, twisting a paper rose smelling of dust and eau-de-cologne. 'La lune ne garde aucune rancune' echoes Laforgue without quoting him, and illustrates, in conjunction with 'Regard the moon', the habit Eliot acquired of linking external with internal rhyme, and of recourse to syllabic reiteration to the same end. Anaphora, another kind of repetition which he frequently employed in his later poetry, particularly at the beginnings of lines, announces itself very strongly in this poem. The geranium image is another reminiscence from Laforgue, and the verse as a whole owes much to him, from the descriptive manner to the dramatic, from the more regular lines with which it begins to lines of great variety in length, with the fillip of interspersed end-rhyme at irregular intervals.

'Rhapsody on a Windy Night' offers a brilliant psychological whole, impressions being controlled by a sufficiently hinted narrative to provide a homogeneity of effect and a completion which 'Preludes' cannot attain. Eliot's memories are attributed to an inebriate whose visual observations are presented at intervals from midnight until he eventually reaches his home at four o'clock. His progression is punctuated by pauses at street-lamps, where he notes the time: half-past one, half-past two, half-past three. What he observes reflects his character and condition; the moon, for example, seems to wink at him, smile into corners, and smooth the hair of the grass; she has lost her memory. The incantations she whispers worry him because the floors of his memory have dissolved, letting him down when every street-lamp, after revealing something of interest, beats like a fatalistic drum in its insistence on the recall of parallels from the past which will not emerge from the dark spaces of oblivion; it is as if a madman were shaking a dead geranium.

As time passes the observer's memory improves. The first street-lamp by which he passes tells him to regard the woman who moves hesitatingly towards him as the light disclosed by her opening door silhouettes her mockingly, her dress torn and soiled, the corner of her eye twisting like a crooked pin. This look calls up memories of twisted things, a skeletal branch on a beach, and a broken rusted spring in a factory yard. Eliot conveys the reduction of its strength syntactically, the diminishing-effect being obtained through the qualification of one qualifying clause by another, with results that contract sharply in final brittle effectiveness.

At two-thirty the narrator watches a cat spread itself at full length to lap up a piece of rancid butter, and again his mind drifts, the feline tongue reminding him of a child's hand which seemed to slip out automatically and pocket a toy running along a quay. There follows a characteristic Eliot observation: nothing could be seen behind that child's eye. The eye makes his dramatic persona think of peeping Toms he had seen in the street, squinting through lighted shutters. The automatic action of the boy makes him consider life at a subhuman, instinctual level, as he recollects an afternoon experience when an old barnacled crab in a pool gripped the end of his stick.

The moon at half-past three recalls nocturnal smells such as those of dry geraniums, chestnuts in the streets, women in shuttered rooms, and cocktail bars. Eliot has succeeded dramatically in presenting images with sinister or distasteful associations which convey common life. The poem has the same connotations as 'Preludes'. At four o'clock our friend is pleased to recognise the number on his door. He finds his key and notices the ring of light which a small lamp casts on the stair. It indicates the circle of understanding in which one is imprisoned. 'Nothing is real, except experience present in finite centres', Eliot was to write; and his note on the Ugolino passage in *The Waste Land*, with its imprisoning key and broken Coriolanus, quotes the philosopher F. H. Bradley: 'my experience falls within my own circle, a circle closed on the outside'. Preparing, like the conscience of the street in 'Preludes', for the same round of life on the morrow, is the 'last twist of the knife' for the somnivolent refuge-seeker.

A more explicit development of Eliot's thought is revealed in the imagery of the most notable of his unpublished Paris poems, 'The Little Passion' (revised about 1914), where a drunk persistently seeks dark retreats; he knows that he is spiritually dead, and that the lines of street-lamps lead to a cross on which souls are crucified. Instead of following the lights, he lets them spin round him like a wheel.[11]

'Portrait of a Lady' and 'The Love Song of J. Alfred Prufrock' are dramatic monologues based on the hostess society Eliot knew too well in Boston. Both 'studies' are Jamesian to a degree, as the echoic title of the first suggests. This was begun in February 1910, and completed much later in the year: 'Prufrock' was resumed and copied up in the summer of 1911, in the interval between Eliot's year at the Sorbonne and his return to Boston. It marks the end of the first important period in his poetical career. While absent from Harvard, from the early summer of 1910 to September 1911, he achieved not only a higher output but also a more persistently high level of poetry than he was to reach in any comparable period over the next ten years.

The speaker's confidences in 'Portrait of a Lady' are the subject of three sessions with a friend. In the first he recalls a befogged and smoky December afternoon when his hostess's dimly illuminated room suggests death. The second is more immediate, in spring-time, when a bowl of lilacs makes her think of his quickly passing youth, of April sunsets and her 'buried life', and of Paris in the spring. Life seems youthful and wonderful again, though she affects to be near her 'journey's end', with nothing to look forward to but serving tea to friends. His final meeting takes place one dark October evening, just before he is due to go abroad (Eliot is probably introducing an autobiographical hint). Disinclination makes him feel that he has climbed the stairs on his hands and knees. When she says he will find much to learn, he sees his simulated smile subside heavily among the bric-à-brac. This psychologically loaded simile reflects a sudden access of guilt, as he realizes the unintended irony of a dull remark; consciously insincere, he feels like a dancing bear, or a parrot, or a gibbering ape, as he tries to maintain polite conversation.

He is no mere victim of the lady's attentions; as the epigraph implies, he is also a victimizer, having willingly and callously allowed himself to encourage them and excite her emotional hopes. The sudden impatience which makes him twice cut short his disclosures expresses as much disgust with himself as distaste for her. Echoing Laforgue's 'Allons, fumons une pipette de tabac' from 'Complainte de l'Automne Monotone', he suggests that he and his friend find other interests outdoors. '*Cauchemar*', the lady's rather affected description of life's emptiness without her friendships, is an expression from Laforgue. His influence is particularly noticeable in the repetitions she uses to increase her emotional appeal as she dwells with lingering emphasis on her friend's ignorance of what life has to offer or, more sentimentally, on how little the passing of life leaves her to offer. If lilac is the bloom of love, she does indeed twist its stalks; when her self-possessed visitor leaves, he has no more time for the scent of hyacinths across the garden than he has for the trite common song of yearning played by the street piano.

The portrait is of a lady of velleities, not of passion, and the series of monologues is primarily interesting as self-revelation. The speaker is fond of music, and apt to express his feelings in musical terms. He becomes almost frenetic when his hostess begins to exploit this partiality in soulful intimacies, so much so that a new kind of prelude begins a dull, hammering tom-tom in his brain. When she tells him in spring that youth is cruel and smiles at situations which it does not understand, he smiles and continues drinking the tea she habitually provides; to him her soul-seeking voice soon assumes the insistent tone of a broken violin on an August afternoon. He is bored, in short. His early, unshaken self-assurance is conveyed in a precision of language which forms a sharp contrast to the softness of her more common parlance. He can conjure up deftly the tones of violins or the picture of the pianist playing Chopin preludes through his hair and finger-tips, but his amusement has a hard, almost cynical vein. Nevertheless, his conscience begins to awaken; at first the young man who can be seen any morning in the park reading his comics or the sporting-page regards it as cowardly to make amends; in the end, when he thinks of the lady's death (recalling Laforgue's 'Autre Complainte de Lord Pierrot': 'Enfin, si, par un soir, elle meurt'), he wonders if, morally, she will not have the advantage over him. There has been something caddish in his behaviour. He and his friend have been listening to music; its 'dying fall' is successful, he observes, with witty but wry allusion to music which is the 'food of love' in Shakespeare.

The 'dying fall' applies to the lady, but it is by other literary allusions that the seriousness which offsets the principal impact of the poem is deepened. April sunsets recall both the hostess's buried life and, in conjunction with the gulf across which she sees the young man reaching his hand, Matthew Arnold's 'Isolation', which images individuals as islands separated by the 'unplumb'd, salt, estranging sea' of life; only on spring evenings, when nightingales sing by starlight, do they feel that they belong to one another. The reference to Arnold's 'Buried Life' is clearer and Eliot's poem, though largely its obverse, does not intend it to be minimized:

> Yes, yes, we know that we can jest,
> We know, we know that we can smile;
> But there's a something in this breast
> To which thy light words bring no rest,
> And thy gay words no anodyne.

The timid, indecisive hero of 'Prufrock' (the name taken from a prosperous furniture firm in St Louis) contrasts notably with the speaker in 'Portrait of a Lady'. A middle-aged intellectual, somewhat of a caricature, he is not without features of the younger Eliot, with his religious, philosophical seriousness, his fear of the opposite sex, and his boredom with Boston society. Prufrock is sure that he has reached the butt-end of his days. He is tired of measuring out his life with coffee spoons in social circles where, when he is most serious, he cannot sustain an intelligible conversation with the ladies, and where he imagines people staring at him, summing him up, pinning him, as it were, to wriggle on the wall. He has wept and prayed and fasted, and his recurring inability to resolve his thoughts has led him to the edge of nervous breakdown; it is as if a magic lantern throws his nerves in patterns on a screen. So introspective has he become that his reflections take the form of communion with the self of which he is psychotically conscious. The poem is an interior monologue, its 'you and I' or 'you and me' reflecting the introspective self and the self he imagines himself to be.

Having distanced some of his own prepossessions and peculiarities sufficiently to observe them with amused detachment, Eliot has created an original in a complex imaginative whole which is unusually lyrical for a dramatic piece in common speech, and which owes something to literary sources. The idea of a pathetic droll with a Hamlet complex is undoubtedly Laforguian, and one part of the subject, the aesthetic rhapsodies of Bostonian ladies, could have been suggested every time Eliot read 'Complainte sur Certains

Ennuis'. Even *Crime and Punishment*, a French edition of which
he read in Paris, has left slight traces, in the thought of having
time to murder or turn back down the stair, the raising
of Lazarus, and the Hamlet disclaimer,[12] which echoes
Raskolnikoff's conclusion that he was no Napoleon. Jamesian
heroes who could not pluck up courage to address women, in
'The Beast in the Jungle', for example, had a general effect, a
more specific influence coming from the middle-aged hero of
'Crapy Cornelia', who, not having dared, feels he is old and
ready to retire from the stage of life.

The Prufrock who feels that he must make his visit but is
deterred by the thought of women conversing superficially
about Michelangelo, and of numerous evenings, mornings, and
afternoons he has spent among such culture-sipping groups,
remains at home, a prey to his reflections. His procrastinating
indecisiveness is reflected in the broken repetitiousness of his
musings, as he thinks of time in hand, or dwells with encroaching
scepticism on the worthwhileness of action, until the thought of
it fades out of mind. He knows, from philosophical speculation
as well as from habit, how subject he is to revisions, of decisions
or points of view, which will be reversed the next minute. Like
the poet of 'Preludes' he has found some satisfaction in observing
life in narrow streets, but the streets suggest to his obsessional
mind lines of thought leading to a question so overwhelming
that momentarily the postponed visit seems preferable. (The
image of squeezing the universe into a ball to roll it to some
overwhelming question seems to derive from Symons on
Laforgue: 'sentiment is squeezed out of the world before one
beings to play ball with it'.) He could wish he had seen beyond
this life like Lazarus, but concludes that he is no great prophet,
that, like John the Baptist's, his head has been brought in on a
platter, and that he has been seen out by the eternal Footman.
His bafflement makes him think of the yellow fog (Mrs Eliot
said it was remembered from St Louis, but it must be
appropriate to Boston; if it derives from any other source,
Baudelaire's 'Les Sept Vieillards' in *Tableaux Parisiens* cannot be
excluded). He lingers on the subject, delighted in the thought of
its feline movements, until he evolves an Imagist poem. The
final sleep of the fog expresses his love of excluding the world; it
reflects the coma or anaesthesia which afflicts Prufrock's intellect
with indecisiveness, though he pursues, at intervals, a course of

self-centred analysis to justify his inaction. His sense of failure makes him disclaim being another Hamlet; he is no more than his attendant, another Polonius (a tedious old fool to his lord), sententious (on this Eliot recalls Chaucer's Clerk of Oxenford), deferential, and obtuse.

Puritanical or valetudinarian fears ('Do I dare to eat a peach?') and a sensuous imagination (the evening sleeps peacefully as if stroked by long fingers) betray his inhibited nature. Nervously shy of bare braceleted arms, he is excited by their light brown down in lamplight. With his thin legs and balding hair, he feels he must dress in the latest fashion, and walk on the beach. He has heard mermaids singing; he has seen them seaward borne, combing their white hair in waves blown backward, but he has not indulged in imaginary frolics with them, like Tennyson in 'The Merman'. If he dares to dream of love, he has no hope of a response to his 'love song'. Awakened from his trance, he is lost or drowned. He feels alien, a misfit, like a crab scuttling across the sea-floor. Hamlet's remark to Polonius (ii.ii), 'for you yourself, sir, shall grow old as I am, if, like a crab, you could grow backward', might seem as appropriate an epigraph as Eliot's Dantean extract on the self-torment of Guido da Montefeltro (*Inferno*, xxvii.61–6), but it is in the latter that we see the full force of the poem: 'since nobody ever returned alive from this depth, if I hear truth . . .'. Prufrock is a tragi-comic figure.

8

Incidental Poetry

During his second period at Harvard University Eliot concentrated on his philosophical studies, and seems to have found little time for poetry, producing only one poem which he chose to include in his *Collected Poems*. This is the haunting lyric 'La Figlia che Piange', the title (suggesting grief, not tears) being that of a sculptured design which Eliot regretted having missed when he was in Italy. In the girl whom he poses for a parting with her lover, there may have been subsumed a recollection of Emily Hale with the sunlight in her hair. His poetic persona imagines how he would have the grieving lovers part, the girl with her hair over her arms, and her arms full of flowers, the lover leaving as the soul departs from the torn, bruised body. Aesthetically distanced and detached, he hopes to find some wonderfully deft, controlled way for the lover to leave, paradoxically 'Simple et sans foi comme un bonjour' like that imagined by Laforgue in 'Pétition' (*Derniers Vers*). The girl haunts his imagination for days, but he counts himself fortunate to have seen a subject to which he would like to give an artistic pose and gesture. This way of converting an experience which has stirred him troubles the poet, and one is left conjecturing what the complicated poem conceals. The epigraph from Virgil's *Aeneid* (i.327) recalls the meeting of Aeneas and Venus, and his asking how to address her, for neither her face nor voice is mortal.

Eliot inherited from his mother a keen interest in mysticism and lives of saints, and he spent much of his leisure time on these allied subjects during his final year at Harvard, writing a number of religious poems. After leaving for Europe, and being struck by pictures of religious suffering in Belgian and Italian galleries, he wrote 'The Love Song of Saint Sebastian', which suggests how terribly morbid and obsessional his imagination could be. The poem presents the conflict of flesh and spirit, the saint wounding himself with flagellation, and abasing himself before the lady, whom he then strangles. Here Eliot's disgust with sex anticipates the form voiced by Sweeney in 'Fragment of an Agon', when he remarks that any man, at some time or other, will want to 'do a girl in'. Another hagiopoetic subject, 'The Death of Saint Narcissus', completed at the end of 1914 or early in 1915, and included, with some textual changes, in Hayward's 1967 edition of Eliot's *Poems Written in Early Youth*, indicates the supervention of a more balanced, but controversially ascetic, outlook. It also shows in a strange way the emergence of the kind of symbolism which was to become important in *The Waste Land* and Eliot's later poetry.

As he knew from studying Evelyn Underhill's *Mysticism*, the indwelling creative power of the universe (Coleridge's 'one Life' or the fire of Heraclitus) was regarded by some philosophers as the dance of Nature. 'As the chorus about its choragus, says Plotinus . . . so do we all perpetually revolve about the Principle of Things.' When we behold Him, we 'form a truly divine dance about Him; in the which dance the soul beholds the Fountain of life'. The idea of dancing in rhythm with the whole creation is found in Yeats's *Words for Music Perhaps* (cf. xxi, 'The Dancer at Cruachan and Cro-Patrick'); it relates to Eliot's image of the still point at the centre of the turning world in 'Burnt Norton'; experience of it gives release from time, or communion with God; the dance is at the still point, without which there could be no dance (or ecstasy, in the old, mystical sense of the word). This concept is basic to 'The Death of Saint Narcissus'.

Narcissus is Eliot's creation, not the second-century Bishop of Jerusalem. Before he danced to God, he had delighted in the smooth movement of his limbs as he walked between the sea and the high cliffs (the unseen world and the margin of the sensory world); his rhythm had both soothed and stifled him as he traversed the meadows. He is like the Narcissus of classical mythology: by the river (leading to the sea) his eye is ever on himself. (In 1919 Eliot described the egoism of Donne as 'an Eye curiously, patiently, watching himself as a man'; at the end of *Ash-Wednesday* he calls on the spirit of the river and the spirit of the sea to ensure that he is not debarred from union with God.) In cities (one version of the poem, like *The Waste Land*, includes Carthage, St Augustine's city of unholy loves) Narcissus seemed, like Virgil and Dante in the *Inferno* (vi.34–6) to be treading on bodies. So, being too physically minded, he abandoned the world, but in the desert he is the victim of his imagination, which makes him feel he is a tree, then a slippery fish in his own grip, then a young girl caught in the woods by an old man. Such sensations had gratified him. As a dancer to God he was imperfect because his self-gratification continued to the end; when the arrows came he gloried in seeing his white skin invaded by red blood.

With a complete change of implication, the opening, invitatory lines were reduced and modified for incorporation in the first part of *The Waste Land*. The promise in the original text[13] was to show a shadow different from that of the person addressed, whose shadow is seen either sprawling across the sand at sunrise or as the reflection on red rock of a figure huddled by the fire – later, as a leaping shadow reflected by the flames. (As in *The Waste Land*, the red rock has its religious significance; the figure huddled by the fire may have been intended to recall Peter just before his denial of Christ.) The critical shadow is that on St Narcissus's mouth, where his body lies in the shadow of the grey rock; the shadow that stains his mouth and the greyness of the rock are related. Between the idea and the reality the shadow of 'The Hollow Men' has fallen. Unlike the white happy bones of *Ash-Wednesday* (II), Narcissus was unable to die unto the world of his natural self; his body therefore remains after martyrdom, spiritually dry and stained, having assumed the green of the natural world. To him may be applied an adaptation of Eliot's epigraph from St John of the Cross to 'Sweeney Agonistes': 'Hence the soul cannot be possessed of the divine union, until it has divested itself of the love of [the created self].'

Making literary friends in London, working on his thesis at Oxford, then marrying and having to find full-time employment as a teacher until the end of 1916, Eliot had little time for the writing of poetry. In October 1915 three of his poems appeared in *Poetry*; all are light and mildly ironical at the expense of Bostonian relatives he remembered. 'The "Boston Evening Transcript"' begins imagistically, and touches briefly on dull bourgeois routine with the evening paper, at a time when appetite for life is wakened in others. Most interesting is the simile adduced to indicate the degree of boredom with which Cousin Harriet's paper is delivered: wearily turning, as if to bid farewell to La Rochefoucauld, assuming the street were time and he were at the end of the street (a comparison based on a recollection from the *Purgatorio*, Eliot told Desmond MacCarthy, according to Virginia Woolf). The humour of 'Aunt Helen' would hardly amuse a reader of Dickens; the most telling point in this sketch is the silence in heaven as well as in the street when Miss Helen Slingsby died. The rhythm of 'Cousin Nancy' announces a livelier subject. Nancy Ellicott, who strode and rode across the barren, puritanical hills of New England, was a modern young woman who shocked her aunts, still bound by the tenets which they awesomely attributed to Ralph Waldo Emerson and Matthew Arnold (the second of whom Eliot's mother probably heard lecture in St Louis). For them the works of these two religious guardians represented the last word (George Meredith's 'army of unalterable law' in the sonnet 'Lucifer in Starlight' refers to the stars).

'Mr Apollinax' gives a memorable impression of Bertrand Russell; the epigraph is from Lucian's 'Zeuxis and Antiochus': 'What novelty! O Hercules, what paradoxes! How inventive man is!' When Russell was teaching at Harvard, he and his student Eliot were guests at a tea-party, where the pretentious hosts were reduced to little more than discreet etiquette by Russell's free-thinking talk and laughter. The party took place not at Circe's but at another 'palace', that of dowager 'Mrs Phlaccus' (described by Russell as an 'arrant snob') and Professor and Mrs 'Channing-Cheetah'. So absorbing was his companion's performance that the poet could remember his hosts by little more than a slice of lemon and an unfinished macaroon. His expression is lively, and his imagery original and effective. He could hear a centaur's hoofs beating over the turf as Mr Apollinax's talk 'devoured the afternoon'; rather misleadingly he was reminded of Fragilion and Priapus in Fragonard's painting *The Swing* as he noticed his laughter tinkling among the teacups. It seemed to come from deep down, as if from the old man of the sea, beneath coral islands where the bodies of the drowned, after falling from streaks of surf, descend through green silent waters ('worried' evokes a picture of corpses attacked and torn by devouring sea-creatures). As he laughed, Mr Apollinax's face resembled a foetus shaking uncontrollably; the reverberations of his laughter suggested that his head was rolling independently under a chair or grinning, tangled with seaweed, over a screen. The poet imagines comments after their departure, with a reference to Apollinax's satyrically pointed ears, and professional egoism insisting that something he said was open to challenge.

Eliot had come to scorn traditional poetic subjects, particularly those of nature and the countryside which were to become popular in Georgian anthologies doomed eventually to be branded as 'week-end' verse. While looking down from a window in Bedford Square, he noticed the foggy impressions of 'Morning at the Window', a short poem which appeared in September 1916. The fog seems to have entered his spirit; he thinks he is aware of damp souls of housemaids 'Sprouting despondently at area gates' along the pavement. The brown fog tosses twisted faces up to him, and tears from a passer-by with a muddied skirt a smile that seems to hover in the air before vanishing along the roofs. The last image has a pleasing mobility; it recalls the smile which fell heavily among the bric-à-brac of a Boston hostess, and is not uncharacteristic of an author who was apt to see human states or dispositions in parts of the body such as hands, feet, or eyes. Eliot is trying to express an inner reality through the observable, but the live, key imagery is, after all, subjective.

'Hysteria', published in Ezra Pound's *Catholic Anthology* (so named after its diversity) and substituted for 'Ode' in the first American edition of *Ara Vos Prec*, is remarkable mainly for being in prose. One can find varieties of prose poetry which appeal mainly, it may be, for rhythmic reasons or, as in Conrad's *Heart of Darkness*, for rhythm and imaginative intensity. But few would expect to find 'Hysteria' in a collection of prose poetry; to some readers it might appear unsuitable in subject. Some of its imagery is striking, especially in the description of teeth exposed in hysterical laughter as 'accidental stars with a talent for squad-drill'; and the 'if' anaphora of clauses imposes its rhythm. The passage is not free verse masquerading as prose; the whole piece is studied, and Eliot probably wrote it with the conviction he expressed in 'Reflections on *Vers Libre*' (*The New Statesman*, 3 March 1917) that unrhymed verse had much to do to equal the standards of good prose. One of his principal aims was to write poetry which avoids the artificial, and is syntactically as near as possible to prose or conversation. As 'Hysteria' has excellent denotative and imaginative qualities, both of which he regarded as essential to poetry, it may presumably be considered a poetic exercise. It raises some minor questions: when, if ever, did Eliot overcome his adolescent, puritanical obsession with sex; was his first wife the subject of this carefully subtle study; and, if so, how coldly could he, as artist, regard her? The critical detachment which characterizes the passage in general is confirmed by both the sense and the hard alliteration of the final statement, which recalls the conclusion of a very different subject in 'La Figlia che Piange'.

Eliot obviously wished to keep up a language he had learned and read assiduously in France, and further reading of French poetry and prose may have stimulated him to try his hand at French verse. Perhaps he preferred this method in order to draw less public attention to his subjects in England and America. 'Le Directeur', 'Mélange Adultère de Tout', and 'Lune de Miel' appeared in *The Little Review* of July 1917. The first is aimed at *The Spectator*, a Conservative journal; the 'directeur' who made the breeze stink could have been no particular person, and the ending carries no conviction. It seems strange that Eliot could have been sufficiently pleased with such a petty rhyming *tour de force* to preserve it among his collected poems; had something closely comparable appeared in English, few readers would have had much patience with it. 'Mélange Adultère de Tout' makes fun of the ubiquitous American professor who aims at being in the swing wherever he is, 'jemenfoutiste' in Paris or excitedly ascending philosophic heights in Germany. There may be some retrospective self-deflation in this *Emporheben*, in addition to Eliot's more obvious reference to himself as journalist in England and 'un peu banquier' in London. The ridicule reaches a peak with the thought that the American professor will one day be seen wearing a giraffe skin at an African oasis, and that his cenotaph (an empty tomb) will be found in the torrid clime of Mozambique.

More typical and worthy of Eliot is 'Lune de Miel', and one could wish he had made more of it in English poetry. It is the first of several memorable passages where the effect depends on ironical juxtapositions. No doubt the background detail was pieced together from his own hurried visit to northern Italy in the summer of 1914. A honeymoon couple, on an extensive sight-seeing tour, have reached Ravenna, where they lie perspiring, flea-bitten, and sleepless one hot summer night, knowing that they must be up early to catch the train for Milan, where they hope to see Leonardo da Vinci's mural of the Last Supper. As they lie supine, 'écartant les genoux De quatre jambes molles tout gonflées de morsures', the husband is thinking of costs and economies. Not far away, in Classe, outside the walls of the city, is the church of the early Christian martyr Saint Apollinaire, recommended to visitors by Baedeker, and now degraded to some kind of works, its Byzantine form still preserved despite its crumbling stones. The poetry is remarkable for its persistent dependence on the precise and factual, on an anti-romantic asceticism which eschews verbal overtones, to reinforce an impressive contrast of decline between divine self-sacrifice and art devoted to the greater glory of God, on the one hand, and hurrying, superficial, mercenary modernity, on the other.

If there is nothing humanly sordid in 'Lune de Miel', there is little else in 'Dans le Restaurant'. No recollection of happy childhood, with sunshine and garden imagery, enters this poem. A dirty dribbling waiter with itching head and fingers must relate his experience when he felt a sexual urge for the first time. He was only seven, and the girl smaller than he; the weather was wet and dirty, and a sudden shower drove them to the shelter of wet willows near budding brambles. Afterwards, when a big dog came to paw them, he ran off. The restaurant scene closes with the unwilling listener giving the waiter ten sous, so that he can go and cleanse himself in the *salle-de-bains*. The dog seems to be developing as a repulsive image in Eliot's poetry. Far more important is the cryptic conclusion, on the drowning of Phlebas the Phoenician off the coast of Cornwall, which once had strong ties with Phoenician traders (the echo of Baudelaire's title 'La Vie Antérieure' is interesting but not significant). In a modified form this was to be the only part of 'Death by Water' which was retained in *The Waste Land*, but no stretch or 'logic' of the imagination can bring to light any necessary link between physical cleansing and spiritual salvation in the final imagery of 'Dans le Restaurant'.

9

Quatrains

Though Eliot asserted that *vers libre* did not exist, and had good reason to be confident that his own poetry had not suffered from any freedoms he had employed in the length of lines or incidence of rhyme, he knew as well as Ezra Pound that 'free verse' could lead to degeneration in the style of writers who were not constantly alert to the necessity of keeping language alive. In *The Criterion* of July 1923 Pound inveighs against 'the general dilution of vers libre, Amygism,[14] Lee Masterism' and 'general floppiness' gone too far, and recommends Théophile Gautier's *Émaux et Camées* as a remedy. He probably had the example of Eliot in mind, for the latter began writing poems in Gautier quatrains in 1917. Eliot knew that every type of poetry imposed its own discipline, and that whatever its outward form there was only good poetry or bad. He did not wish to fall into any particular style, as Spenser or Milton had done, knowing as keenly as Gerard Manley Hopkins that self-imitation soon leads to dull 'Parnassian'. For him every poem was a new beginning, and imposed its own pattern; it was, in the words of 'East Coker', 'a raid on the inarticulate With shabby equipment always deteriorating'. At this time he was turning more and more to Elizabethan and Jacobean dramatists in his search for ways of revivifying his own poetic language. Like Wordsworth, who frequently, over a period of many years, turned the 'prison' of the sonnet form into glorious gain, he knew he could benefit from working strictly to a formal pattern.

Eliot's allegiance to Gautier was temporary; he was soon to find that he had accumulated poetry in many voices which was to prove unamenable to any one form. Though it produced a number of poems which excited the younger generation with their daring and wit, the Gautier period must be regarded as temporizing and preparatory. Eliot had realized from Gautier's example how much he could gain in shorter poems which were likely to shock, and he was not likely to disagree with the conclusion of his model:

> Oui, l'oeuvre sort plus belle
> D'une forme au travail
>   Rebelle,
> Vers, marbre, onyx, émail.

Everything passes, Gautier continues in 'L'Art', his concluding address to the 'Gardiens du contour pur': only a robust art is eternal; the sculptured bust survives the city, and an austere medal found by a workman reveals an emperor.

'The Hippopotamus', which has the common hymnal metric, appeared in the July 1917 number of *The Little Review*; and its satire, as the epigraph confirms, is directed against the lifelessness of the Church of England. The broad-backed hippopotamus prone in the mud represents the torpor of the spiritually dead in *The Waste Land*; he is merely flesh and blood. The wit depends on a series of collocations, the weakness of the hippopotamus being contrasted with the self-assurance of a Church founded on a rock. The hippo may make business losses, but the Church does not need to strive for spiritual gain. At mating time the hippo's voice is hoarse, but every week the Church can be heard rejoicing in being at one with God. The impudent truth of the satire continues: the hippopotamus sleeps by day but hunts at night, whereas (God working mysteriously 'His wonders to perform') the complacent Church can sleep and feed simultaneously. The verse rises in accord when Eliot describes the flight to heaven, and the redemption, of the hippo in the familiar imagery of a comfortable faith. Rarely has the Church received such an aggressive indictment, and there is no let-up. The poem concludes with a devastating swipe: while the purified hippopotamus is kissed by all the martyred virgins in heaven, the Church remains below, 'Wrapt in the old miasmal mist'. It would be a mistake to think this poem just a youthful sally; the miasmal mist is old, and Eliot's criticism was to continue. The ironical emphasis on 'True' is recurrent; it implies a Church too self-satisfied to face the truth. When Eliot renounced his Unitarianism, he joined a Church which stressed human sin and the need for purgatorial redemption; only such attitudes, he believed, could improve the state of the world.

The next three poems in this quatrain pattern of four-stressed lines appeared with 'Dans le Restaurant' in September 1918. One of them, 'Mr Eliot's Sunday Morning Service', continues the attack on the Church from another angle. Those who feed the Lord's flock are sapient; their polyphiloprogenitiveness lies in their propensity to propound new theological theory. So it was in the early days of Christianity, when a 'superfetation' of the One produced the Neoplatonic interpretations of Origen. (Eliot's use of 'mensual' for 'monthly', from one of the plural genitives of 'mensis', is unorthodox; 'enervate' alludes to the tradition that Origen suffered sexual mutilation.) Here, in conjunction with the epigraph from Marlowe's *The Jew of Malta* (a remark made in Act IV, when two friars appear), Eliot implies that learned exegesis can destroy the vitality of the religion on which it depends for its nourishment. His thoughts return to the polyphiloprogenitive expositors of the 'subtle schools', who perform an epicene function like the bees passing between stamens and pistils. Their changing viewpoints make him think of Sweeney shifting from ham to ham in his bath. Perhaps this is the most metaphysical of Eliot's poems. Through the collocation of images and ideas it has a coherence of subject rather than artistic unity. Yet, as is typical of Eliot, beauty of poetic tone indicates the religious centre around which the poem turns. Only when the words 'Still shine the unoffending feet' are read in the context of the Baptism painting can their full effect be felt. They form part of a recognition scene of lasting truth, the Word made flesh, a light in the darkness of this world. Eliot's seriousness is reinforced in the penitential contrast of pustular young men with their 'piaculative pence' and the souls of the devout who burn 'invisible and dim'. Henry Vaughan's poem 'The Night', from which this phrase is taken, expresses the soul's yearning to leave the world of sin for heaven, and its conclusion suggests the Cloud of Unknowing:

> There is in God (some say)
> A deep, but dazzling darkness; As men here
> Say it is late and dusky, because they

See not all clear
O for that night! where I in him
Might live invisible and dim.

Although Eliot owed the title 'Sweeney among the
Nightingales' to Elizabeth Barrett Browning's 'Bianca among
the Nightingales', his poem has nothing in common with hers
except the nightingale's significance. As in *The Waste Land* the
inviolable Philomela voice is a protest against the defilement of
love. A discarded epigraph, that the nightingale sings adulterous
wrong, seems to allude to Cassandra's wish, after her prophetic
vision of the hero's death in the *Agamemnon*, to be released like
Philomela; and it probably accounts for Eliot's daring transfer
of Agamemnon's murder to a nightingale-haunted wood. In
changing but integrated imagery, the expression of which
admirably suits sense and intention, the last stanza voices a call
for true life and a protest against its denial; the positive call is
sustained in the full-throated life and spirit of the nightingales'
song, while the direction of their faecal discharge provides apt
comment for a sordid crime. Agamemnon's cry is Eliot's
epigraph for a poem devoted to Sweeney and his entourage at
some South American dive. Sweeney is no Agamemnon, but,
though his facial features give him a status no higher than that
of the animal kingdom, he seems an innocent compared with
the sinister figures which animate the scene. Eliot once said
that all he set out consciously to achieve in this poem was a
sense of foreboding, which is evident at the outset in the stormy
moon, the veiled constellations, and the drifting of Death and
the Raven. The cinematic charade, however, creates mystery
and suspense rather than fear; few readers are likely to worry
about Sweeney's fate, though he soon falls asleep, and the
significance of the horned gate could be drawn less from
classical sources than from the *revenge* theme of Thomas Kyd's
The Spanish Tragedy: 'the gates of horn, Where dreams have
passage in the silent night'. The poem is redolent of animality
and death: a silent man who has been sprawling and watching
by the window suddenly contracts with concentration, then
withdraws, no more than a vertebrate. Rachel *née* Rabinovitch
tears murderously at grapes from fruit just served by the waiter.
She and the 'person' in the Spanish cape (prostitute nightingales)
are thought to be in league; knowing which, a heavy-eyed man

declines their gambit, walks out, and leans in at the window, where a wistaria surrounds the grin of his gold teeth. The image is vivid and vaguely portentous. Meanwhile the host talks with someone indistinct by the door, and the nightingale sings in the Convent of the Sacred Heart. True love springs from true religion.

'Whispers of Immortality' bears an ironical title; it does not seriously fit the poem at any point, even at the end. The mystical term 'whispers', which is recurrent in Eliot's later poetry, expresses hints or intimations of the 'still small voice'. It is not heard in Webster or Donne; such were their desires and terrors, they could never really forget flesh and bone; so obsessed did they become with life's ephemerality they could never escape a sense of the skeleton beneath the skin. Donne's love-poetry shows that no fleshly contact could subdue the ague of this skeleton; Webster's death-ridden imagining of life anticipates the buried skeleton with its lipless grin or, it may be, with daffodil bulbs growing in its eye-sockets. Yet their vision beyond death affords a powerful contrast to current philosophies of love, which see the highest spiritual ('pneumatic') bliss in Grishkin's uncorseted bust, and associate even the 'Abstract Entities' (such as Platonic Beauty) with her charms. (The first lines on Grishkin are modulated on Gautier's 'Carmen'.) Eliot's counter-arguments are on two levels. The first is anti-feminist and ineffectual, reflecting his own physical disgust rather than a neat cynicism: even the jaguar in a dark Brazilian forest, he says, does not emit so strong a female stench as Grishkin. The second indicates that there can be no spiritual progress except 'between dry ribs', beyond the flesh, a subject to which he returns more explicitly in *Ash-Wednesday*.

The early critical history of 'A Cooking Egg', which was first published in May 1919, in a new illustrated quarterly, demonstrates the difficulty presented by the kind of poetry Eliot was developing, in which images, thoughts, and scenes are assembled without the linkage normally provided by authors to ensure communication of the whole as a coherent unit. By omitting superfluous elements of explanation and relationship, he could concentrate on essentials, give his poetry greater intensity of appeal, and leave integrating processes to the 'logic of the imagination'. In a preliminary explanation of this phrase (which is particularly applicable to a longer and more complex poem such as *The Waste Land*), Eliot writes in the preface to his translation of St-John Perse's *Anabase*,

> any obscurity of the poem, on first readings, is due to the suppression of 'links in the chain', of explanatory and connecting matter, and not to incoherence, or to the love of cryptogram ... the sequence of images coincides and concentrates into one intense impression. .... The reader has to allow the images to fall into his memory successively without questioning the reasonableness of each at the moment; so that, at the end, a total effect is produced.

The interpretative problem with reference to 'A Cooking Egg' is well known, and came to a flourish in 1953. Starting with the contradictory views of two eminent critics that the Pipit who sat upright was (1) the hero's retired nurse, (2) a young girl, it was argued that she was (3) a Bloomsbury *demi-vierge*, and (4) the hero's fiancée. A round of academic attack and counter-attack revealed commonsense, critical ingenuity, and persistent error or oversight; it was rounded off with the argument that the 'penny world' connotes the 'shabby, second-rate lives that Pipit and the narrator had been living'.[15] After such knowledge, what forgiveness can be expected for further error?

The poem is a soliloquy or meditation, a series of reflections in three stages, the first recalling a past scene, the other two turning to the present. It is not strictly an interior monologue, since the hero does not address himself, as Prufrock patently does; and this rules out the use of terms such as 'narrator' or 'speaker'. The hero's recollection of Pipit does not tell us where she lives; it indicates traditional values in her family, respectability above all. Whether the appearance of *Views of the Oxford Colleges* on the table suggests that her friend the hero or one of the family was an Oxford student or about to become one is neither deducible nor specifically significant. Like the *Invitation to the Dance* on the mantelpiece, the detail points to a kind of socio-economic and moral English ambience similar to that which the poet himself knew at home and with some of his Boston relatives. The elegant invitation card is not physically supported by family photographs and silhouettes; they are visible counters which lend their weight to the dignity of the dance which links higher society with Pipit's family. Possibly the hero and Pipit were present on that splendid occasion; they had been friends from childhood.

Now, disillusioned after the 1914–18 war, and having rejected his former bourgeois standards in no half-measure (as the epigraph from Villon makes very plain), he has adopted a flippant attitude towards the honour, capital, and society which he once held in high esteem. He amuses himself with the thought that he will have as much of these as he wishes in the next world, and the cynicism is not limited to himself; post-war disillusionment has killed respect for heroes as well as financiers. Instead of the respectable upright Pipit, he can have Lucrezia Borgia as his bride in heaven;[16] she will tell him amusing stories beyond the reach of Pipit's experience. And, instead of Pipit to give him religious guidance, Madame Blavatsky will instruct him in the Seven Sacred Trances. Eliot could empathize as readily with this kind of frivolous scepticism as he could with scorn expressed for the dealings of financial potentates in debt-ridden western Europe. He probably regarded it as the height of cynicism for his hero to assume Piccarda's readiness to be his heavenly bride, for she was the lady whose spirit spoke to Dante, as he entered the first sphere of Heaven (*Paradiso*, iii), on the acceptance of God's will, whatever the station of the blessed: 'His will is our peace; it is that sea to which everything created by it and nature moves.'

Having pursued that line of thought far enough, the hero reflects gloomily on the world in which he finds himself. He is not sentimental, but his feelings get the better of him. He recalls boyhood happiness when he enjoyed some cheap confection behind the screen (another token of period respectability) with Pipit, and looked forward to an era of greatness (the eagles and trumpets of imperial glory). Now he broods on post-war debts and depression, and contrasts the prospects of his youth with those of multitudes in cheap ABC restaurants. The final image is not apocalyptic, but, in expressing the depression of the masses, it has the prophetic voice and vision of Blake. The egg set aside for cooking has lost its freshness.

'Burbank with a Baedeker: Bleistein with a Cigar' and 'Sweeney Erect' were published in the summer number of *Art and Letters*, 1919. The first confronts us with the problem of poetry which depends on the recognition of quotations and literary allusions for the full realization of its imaginative effects and of its thought. The Venetian background which is flashed in quick succession by a cento of quotations in the epigraph is a bonus, almost a poem in itself, though the poem exists independently of them. First, we are reminded of Gautier's 'Variations sur le Carnival de Venice'; then, most critically of all, of the text of one of Andrea Mantegna's paintings of Saint Sebastian, 'nothing but the divine is stable; the rest is smoke'. Then follow a snatch of narrative from the first chapter of *The Aspern Papers* by Henry James, a cry from the maddened Othello, Browning's thoughts of the dear dead women, 'with such hair, too', in 'A Toccata of Galuppi's', and lastly, its origin and non-Venetian context quite lost on almost every reader, the final stage direction in a work by John Marston,[17] intended presumably to contrast a virtuous lady with the princess of Eliot's poem.

Eliot's strictures on the spiritual decline of western civilization (at the 'smoky candle end of time') are marred by intensive anti-Semitism. He thinks of Shylock on the Rialto, of the rats beneath the piles, and, beneath them all, the wealthy Jew, making money from furs. His antipathy against rootless, free-thinking, money-lending, materialist Semitic representatives was fuelled by Ezra Pound, never to more vitriolic effect than in Bleistein, 'Chicago Semite Viennese', with 'lustreless protrusive eye' staring from 'protozoic slime'. Even the dawn has a touch of death, the horses of the sun-chariot (an image descended from Seneca and Chapman[18]) introducing with 'even feet' the 'pallida mors' of Horace's ode (i.iv). There is a notable stress on 'little' and 'small' in the opening lines. The descent to the 'small' for a Ruskinian aesthete intent on studying ancient splendours has its irony; a slight change of direction, and he falls a prey to Princess Volupine, whose name ('voluptuous', 'vulpine') was undoubtedly a collateral offspring of such clever Laforguian neologisms as 'ces voluptés à vif', 'sous la céleste éternullité'. 'They were together, and he fell' echoes a line from Tennyson's 'The Sisters'. The 'defunctive music' of Shakespeare's 'The Phoenix and the Turtle' which announces that 'love and constancy' are dead merges with the music which signifies that Antony's god Hercules has left him. Like Cleopatra's, Volupine's barge burns on the water; in the evening, with blue-nailed phthisic hand, she climbs the water-stair to entertain Sir Ferdinand Klein, whose name signifies a worthless grandee. Burbank, the deflated romantic, is left reflecting on how the power of the winged lion, once the religious symbol of Venice, has been curtailed. He thinks of Ruskin's seven laws (*The Seven Lamps of Architecture*) which indicate how moral greatness is reflected in buildings, and of their application in *The Stones of Venice* to the period of Gothic growth and Renaissance decline. The loss of divine grace which this implied with the advent of wealth and worldly pleasure lends weight to the one positive section in the epigraph, the text of Mantegna's painting. Wealth and corruption are the key notes of the poem.[19]

The sudden transition in 'Sweeney Erect' from romantic pictures of the deserted Ariadne to the sight of Sweeney getting out of bed provides a contrast which is intended to shock. The title refers to the broad-bottomed hero as he stands upright and prepares to shave, lathering his face in the confidence that he knows all there is to know about the female temperament. He waits for the shriek from the recumbent epileptic to subside as he tests the razor on his leg. Ladies appear in the corridor, protesting against the disgrace, and Mrs Turner ventures to say that it does the house no good; but Doris comes towelled from the bath, with sal volatile and a glass of brandy. Unlike Ariadne, the epileptic is not deserted, though Sweeney's indifference seems to cast him in the role of Theseus.

The romanticism of the first two verses is dramatically forced in accordance with the context of the epigraph from Beaumont and Fletcher's *The Maid's Tragedy* (ii.ii), where the heroine Aspatia, after being deserted by her lover, is critical of an embroidery by one of her ladies-in-waiting which depicts Ariadne abandoned on an island after Theseus has sailed away. Aspatia poses dramatically as Sorrow's monument ('Mine arms thus, and mine hair blown with the wind, Wild as that desart') for an improved picture, insisting that the embroidered rocks be made to groan with continual surges, and that the island behind her be nothing but desolation. She concludes by asking her ladies to look at her, the miserable life of the poor picture; even the picture as she imagines it falls short of her suffering. Such a parade of feeling invites comment, and it is implied in Eliot's opening lines, where Aspatia's egoism and dramatized indulgence in the luxury of grief are eloquently captured, and the poet gives more than is asked, with a picture of Aeolus above reviewing the work of his gales, which produce the desired effect in Ariadne's hair and (not without a sly irony) speed Theseus's departure. The transition to Sweeney is swiftly graduated by reference to risings of female beauty and male ugliness, Nausicaa and Polyphemus, in the *Odyssey*.

Without other implications, the poem would be an anticlimax. A clear reference to Emerson is given, but how many readers could be expected to see any link with Rousseau in the poem? The two are associated in Eliot's mind, but what was familiar is not communicated. Though some of its overtones may be lost, 'Burbank with a Baedeker: Bleistein with a Cigar' retains a coherence which 'Sweeney Erect' fails to give. The chances are that it remains chiefly a caricature. The hero is hardly human; he is like an orang-outang when his sweaty, steaming self emerges from the sheets; after jack-knifing upwards and straightening his legs, he pushes against the framework of the bed, and claws at the pillow, to get up. His face, slitted and gashed with eyes, might be the hurried work of a crude cartoonist; he is described as an old root with knotted hair. Such features are part of a passage quoted by Eliot, in his Harvard lectures of 1932–3, from Shelley's *The Triumph of Life*, where one of a 'deluded crew' appears as an old, strangely distorted root; the grass is his thin discoloured hair, and the holes he vainly seeks to hide are, or have been, his eyes. This 'grim Feature' (Sweeney is grimmer) is Rousseau, who confesses that, had his genius been 'with purer nutriment supplied', he would not have been as corrupted as he is now. In his essay 'Self-Reliance' Emerson, who had not seen the silhouette of Sweeney 'straddled in the sun', states that 'An institution is the lengthened shadow of one man: as the Reformation, of Luther; Quakerism, of Fox . . .'. The tenor of Emerson's thought, like Rousseau's, is that the individual should be free, that he should not conform to institutions. We should not be ashamed of the 'divine idea which each of us represents'. 'Trust thyself', he wrote; 'No law can be sacred to me but that of my own nature.' 'I ought to go upright and vital.' That is the attitude guyed by Eliot: Sweeney is erect and vital. He is Eliot's symbol of degenerate man. 'What kind of shadow does he cast on our civilization?' he seems to ask. Twentieth-century history did not support the view that human nature is divine, and Eliot's opposition to the Emersonian principle that the individual should trust himself placed him on the side of Jeremiah (xvii.5): 'Thus saith the Lord; Cursed by the man that trusteth in man, and maketh flesh his arm, and whose heart departeth from the Lord.' The thought imaged in the penultimate lines of 'Preludes' finds one of its worldly manifestations, an 'objective correlative', in 'Sweeney Erect'.

10

Preliminaries to *The Waste Land*

About the time that 'Sweeney Erect' made its first appearance, in the summer of 1919, Eliot completed 'Gerontion', an interior monologue like 'The Love Song of J. Alfred Prufrock' but in far more concentrated dramatic verse, without rhyme. With special reference to the Treaty of Versailles which brought the First World War to its official conclusion, the poem turns analytically to the persistence of human fallibility in history, and the failure of man to learn from history until it is too late (aspects of both being strikingly illustrated in *The History of Henry Adams*, which Eliot had just reviewed). War and heroism produce crime and political follies; history deceives; what can be done to be saved? Until dissuaded by Ezra Pound, Eliot had intended the poem as an introduction to *The Waste Land*.

'Gerontion' signifies an old man, shrunken in body and soul, quite different in spirit from Henry Newman's Gerontius, who, at the point of death, trusts in God and wakes spiritually refreshed. As if remembering Newman's 'What can this world offer comparable with that insight into spiritual things . . . ? Let us beg and pray Him day by day to reveal Himself to our souls more fully, to quicken our senses, to give us sight and hearing, taste and touch of the world to come',[20] Gerontion asks how he can use his failing senses for closer contact with God. He is addressing his conscience deliberately, not from terror of death, but from experience of the terror which has assaulted him from time to time after the loss of holiness. Like Mary in *The Family Reunion* he knows the agony of the spiritual compulsion to be reborn, the ache that ensues after Christ has

96

sprung like a devouring tiger in the new year. He wishes he could see a sign of new birth, the Word made flesh, but the 'word within a word' is 'unable to speak a word', and lies wrapped in darkness. Eliot's preliminary words to this quotation from Lancelot Andrewes imply that the age is corrupt: 'An evil and adulterous generation seeketh after a sign' (Matthew, xii.38–9). A discarded epigraph (*Inferno*, xxxiii.122–3) shows that Gerontion had reminded Eliot of Alberigo, still alive though soulless:[21] the poem, however, does not present such a state, though it indicates that Gerontion's intensively activated conscience is soon quiescent.

Eliot uses 'house' in more than one sense. The first recalls Tennyson's in 'The Deserted House' and 'By an Evolutionist', where it represents the body occupied by the soul. Gerontion's is rented, and he will soon have to leave it; his thoughts are its tenants, and they are dry, the thoughts of one without faith, in an age which produces no sign of hope for the rain of spiritual rebirth. The symbolism obviously anticipates *The Waste Land*. But Gerontion is no mere individual; he is the voice of a decaying western civilization financed by Jews. The anti-Semitism is undisguised: 'squats on the window-sill', 'Spawned in some estaminet'. The decayed house has no sign of vitality or health; its environmental features are rocks, stagnant moss, stonecrop, iron, and excrement. Even the goat on the windy hillside coughs. The woman who keeps the kitchen sneezes as she tries to clear the drain. Gerontion has no ghost, no spiritual life; he lives in a draughty house under a windy hill. 'Vacant shuttles Weave the wind.' Here Eliot combines key phrases from the book of Job (vii.6) and the first chapter of Joyce's *Ulysses*: 'My days are swifter than a weaver's shuttle, and are spent without hope'; 'The void awaits surely all them that weave the wind'. Joyce's emphasis is more in accord with Eliot's meaning, and his words are immediately followed by Haines's wish not to see Britain fall into the hands of German 'jews'.

Gerontion's hopelessness comes from contemplating western religion. Instead of springing like a tiger, and shocking people into a sense of the error of their ways, it is unreal and evasive; it may be no more than ritual, and it is sometimes spurious. Those who profess it are cosmopolites of no abiding city, unctuous (Mr Silvero with fondling hands), penumbral, furtive, lacking in candour (Madame de Tornquist, who shifts the candles in a dark room), or unconvinced (Fräulein von Kulp turning, one hand on the door). There is concern for art treasures but not for treasures in heaven; there is little assurance or little light. The Churches are guilty of betrayal, the poet suggests; the spring of the year is associated with the bloom of the judas-tree and the depravity of May. What forgiveness can there be, after awareness of these things (without action), Gerontion asks, turning the maxim 'Tout connaître, c'est tout pardonner' inside out.

Attention is drawn to the effect of religious insincerity and shallowness in political affairs. With dramatic iteration, Gerontion asks us really to *think* about the mistakes of history, alluding to the Treaty of Versailles (the Polish Corridor in 'contrived corridors') and to the Hall of Mirrors in which the treaty was signed by politicians astray in a wilderness. History illustrates how people are deceived by ambition and vanity; it gives opportunities which are lost through distraction, which increase expectations and demands out of all due proportion, or which come too late, when no longer believed in or believed in only on reconsideration. The tree of knowledge of good and evil, whence all our woe has proceeded, has become the tree of wrath; error or sin is part of the human inheritance. Such are the thoughts of one who did not fight on any of the war-fronts. The allusion is not confined to the 1914–18 conflict; the hot gates signify Thermopylae, and have a universal overtone. The warm friendly rain and the salty swamp, as *The Waste Land* and the origin of some of its symbolism reveal, connote spiritual renewal or stagnation.

Finally Gerontion thinks of his own end. Eliot's imagery may have sprung from the scene in *Measure for Measure* (III.i) which provided his epigraph: 'Ay, but to die . . . To be . . . blown with restless violence round about The pendent world . . .', as Claudio anticipates with dread. Gerontion (and here Eliot alludes to Rutherford's latest atomic discovery) wonders whether he and others, including the Fresca who appears in the original script of *The Waste Land*, will be scattered in split atoms beyond the circuit of the Bear; Eliot, it will be seen, returns to the Senecan image employed by Chapman in *Bussy D'Ambois*. The dull head in windy spaces, on the verge of sleep, imagines himself a gull helplessly driven by strong winds, in the straits of

Belle Isle or in snow near Cape Horn, or blown by drying Trade Winds to death by water in the Gulf of Mexico. His dream-vision is as American as the image of flowering dogwood and judas in the depravity of May, which originates from *The Education of Henry Adams*. Recalling the spring at Washington, Adams mentions these trees and others in his description of the beauty squandered by the Potomac and its tributaries. More significantly for 'Gerontion', he describes the 'brooding heat of the profligate vegetation' as 'sensual, animal, elemental'. No European spring had shown him the 'intermixture of delicate grace and passionate depravity that marked the Maryland May'.[22]

Old and comatose, Gerontion has ignored the boy who is reading to him. The opening of Eliot's poem was suggested by A. C. Benson's description of Edward FitzGerald: 'Here he sits, in a dry month, old and blind, being read to by a country boy, longing for rain.'[23] The epigraph comes from the speech in which the Duke bids Claudio prepare for death; the lines that follow seem even more relevant:

> for all thy blessed youth
> Becomes as aged, and doth beg the alms
> Of palsied eld; and when thou art old and rich,
> Thou hast neither heat, affection, limb, nor beauty
> To make thy riches pleasant. What's yet in this
> That bears the name of life?

The varied, predominantly dramatic style of 'Gerontion' reflects the influence of Jacobean dramatists, one line echoing the opening of a passage from Thomas Middleton's *The Changeling*, in which Eliot found the virtues of 'a great poet, a great master of versification'.[24] One can observe how he manipulates it to reflect the disturbed conscience of an old man. Often the thoughts are disjointed; almost as often they rely on repetition for emphasis, as if Gerontion (Eliot thereby achieving his purpose with the reader) makes a special effort to sustain a clear sequence of ideas. Sometimes the syntax suggests a tiredness and impatience with complete thought-clarification, notably at the opening, with the thought of fighting for life in the marsh, and at the end, in the image of the gull finally claimed by the Gulf.

Although Eliot was anxious to proceed with his 'long poem' at the end of 1919, he chose to add to the critical essays and reviews on which he had concentrated during the year, until he had a selection suitable for a volume; this appeared as *The Sacred Wood* in November 1920. The following year he regretted his inability to find a period long enough for concentration on poetry, and it was not until he had left his wife, and was under treatment at Lausanne, that he was able to complete the bulk of the scripts from which *The Waste Land* emerged. With them were poems or fragmentary sketches which had been written earlier, from some of which passages in the original five-part poem were drawn. One was 'The Death of Saint Narcissus', the opening of which was adapted for the first section, just as the ending of 'Dans le Restaurant' was changed to form the climax of 'Death by Water'.

Whether contributive or not to *The Waste Land*, some of the satellite poems submitted for Pound's consideration in January 1922 have their own independent interest.[25] 'What the Thunder said' owes much to the earliest of these, 'So through the evening', which was written before Eliot left America in 1914. Tortured with fruitless meditation on the sacramental words 'Do this in remembrance of me', which should give release and freedom, but seem addressed to unresponsive desert houses, the narrator has strange visions as he continues along the twisting road of conjecture, accompanied by another person. A woman fiddles whisper-like music on the strings of her black hair, and a man creeps down a wall, seeing inverted towers which are tolling reminiscently; the spiritual drought of Christian churches is confirmed by voices chanting from cisterns and wells which are by implication empty. As the two men leave the town their confusion persists; the narrator feels like a deaf mute in the sea who knows neither up nor down, and continues swimming down in water where there is neither life nor movement. The imagery is different from that which concludes *The Waste Land*, but the quest is the same. In 1919 Eliot was significantly impressed by the following passage from Donne's 'Mundus Mare' sermon: 'All these wayes the world is a Sea, but especially it is a Sea in this respect, that the Sea is no place of habitation, but a passage to our habitations.'[26]

Conscious of an irony in the two forces which gave him no

rest, the urge for literary success and the inner demand for spiritual salvation, Eliot ridiculed the desire for earthly fame in 'Exequy'. Mockery is conveyed through egotistical emphasis, the light elation of deliberately artificial verse, and the vainglory of visionary posthumous hero-worship in antique pagan style. Eliot's narcissistic persona thinks with rapturous absurdity of the lovers who will visit his suburban tomb when he is worshipped as a local god in some Italian grove, with celebrations concluding festivals in his honour. He will be one of the shades, like the spirits of whom we are reminded in 'The Burial of the Dead', having done little harm and no good (cf. *Inferno*, iii.36). The putative arrival of the second, self-sacrificial self is conveyed in verse which reflects a deeper, more troubled spirit. This critical conjunction is not managed felicitously, however. If, the poem continues, the imagined outsider comes to the Mound, his beauty diminished by shadow and stains of dead autumnal colour (rather like the dead Saint Narcissus), he will hear a ghostly subterranean chuckle and the words of Arnaut Daniel: 'Ara vos prec . . . sovegna vos a temps de ma dolor' (*Purgatorio*, xxvi.140ff: 'Now I beseech you . . . remember my suffering in good time'). It is as if the Mound of past celebrations is becoming strangely merged with Dante's Mount of Purgatory.

In 'Song' the awakened, or the dreamer, catches a glimpse of the golden foot he may not touch (a deleted ending to the effect that he awaits that touch after thirty years seems autobiographical); the reference must be to the risen Christ of Revelation (i.15). This image within the shadow of his bed is the ghost that makes him feel he bleeds between one life and another (the second powerless to be born, like Arnold's new world of faith). The sound of bells is cut off by a sudden wind; the blackened river recalls a face sweating with tears (Jesus in the garden of Gethsemane), and across it he sees the waving, minatory (spearlike) flames of camp-fires. Besides hinting at a biblical scene, the poet's vision is Dantean: the ante-Hell episode with a crowd of the spiritually lifeless by the river ends with a wind which rises from the tearful earth and flashes a crimson light (*Inferno*, iii.55–7, 70–87, 106ff.) A transition from 'Song' to the Crucifixion imagery in the opening lines of 'What the Thunder said' may be found in an early fragment, 'After the turning', where the shaking of spears that accompanies the flickering of lights signifies the menace of spiritual senescence or Gerontionism in the western world.

'The Death of the Duchess' brings us to the 'Unreal City', particularly to the silk-hatted inhabitants of Hampstead. Their weekly habits (a foretaste of the citizens in choruses of *The Rock*) and their thoughts are routine; they are never free from the turning wheel. They suggest non-human images, including dogs' eyes over the edge of a table, or wordless bird-beaks. The poet would like to join a host of such beaks; it is distressing for him to be alone with another person. So, with reference to Webster's plays, he turns to the marital problem that is central to 'A Game of Chess'. While his surrealistically tailed but wingless thoughts hang on the chandelier, or fall one after another to the floor, his wife brushes her hair and make it glow with words spoken by the Duchess when she thinks she addresses her husband as she regards her hair in the mirror: 'You have cause to love me; I enter'd you into my heart, Before you would vouchsafe to call for the keys' (*The Duchess of Malfi*, III.ii). All the poet can think of is escaping; it would make no difference whether he told his wife he loved her or did not love her. This deadness of love contrasts with the passion of Webster's duchess and her husband, but, except at one point, the circumstantial references in the remainder of the poem are to the bedchamber scene in Webster, which Eliot found fraught with 'breathless tension'. The exception is familiar; it consists of five lines, which were reduced to the three on the closed car and the game of chess in *The Waste Land*. Perhaps Vivienne realized the autobiographical truth of a line which indicated that the only companionship shared by the neurotic woman and her husband came from the chess pieces; it was withdrawn at her request. She wrote a story about a caged woman, and 'In the Cage' was the title at one time for both 'The Death of the Duchess' and 'A Game of Chess'.

The creative idea of 'Elegy' seems to be rooted in this marital impasse. The poem, which reads rather like one of Emily Brontë's, concerns the death of a wife who had been wronged like the heroine of *The Maid's Tragedy*. As if in a story by Edgar Allan Poe, she returns from her charnal vault to plague the poet despite his remorse. If only she had come like a heavenly visitant (the cyclamen image is elucidated in 'Difficulties of a

Statesman'), he would have mourned her death. Now, for his sins, he is pursued by God in a rolling fiery sphere; and flames of anger and of desire, like that of 'The Hound of Heaven' by Francis Thompson, threaten to consume him.

'Dirge' introduces Bleistein as a possible alternative to Phlebas the Phoenician in 'Death by Water'. The sea-change he suffers below the level of the wharf rats is gruesomely detailed, and echoes of 'Full fathom five' (*The Tempest*, i.ii) recur, to end with ('Hark! now I hear them') a scratching assault by lobsters' claws.

Much of the material Eliot accumulated for Pound's consideration was still in the rough, showing no attempt at integration. A projected title, 'He Do the Police in Different Voices' (from Dickens, *Our Mutual Friend*, xvi), suggests that he had ultimate hopes of a greater degree of collocution than Pound could recommend. Instead Pound discouraged additions, and discarded large portions of the main work; he was particularly vigorous in resisting the inclusion of 'Song', 'Exequy', and the Bleistein dirge. He examined closely 'The Death of the Duchess', and it is noteworthy that he recommended relatively few changes in the section which includes its essence, part II ('A Game of Chess'). Part V ('What the Thunder said'), for which the most poetical ideas and imagery came from 'So through the evening', received hardly any criticism. Eliot had this last section in mind when he stated that composition may, after being contemplated for a long period, suddenly take shape and words which require little revision. He thought it was the best part of the poem, the only part that gave it justification.

Eliot did not accept all Pound's minor criticisms, but was quick to profit where weaknesses were made apparent. Pound's deletion of the parenthesis, that it was John who saw and heard these things (cf. Revelation i.1–2), with reference either to the crowds of people circumambulating in Madame Sosostris's prognosis or to the whole of it, makes it seem strange that he did not question the role of Tiresias in the poem. The longest passages he rejected, generally with good reason, were in parts I, III, and IV. The original opening is a dramatic narrative of night-life in down-town Boston, increasingly dreary and pointless the more it is prolonged. No doubt it was suggested by *Ulysses*, but Joyce could do this sort of thing more poetically and significantly, and with greater instantaneous effect. An introduction of this kind would no doubt have been popular, but it adds nothing, and is quite out of key with its immediate sequel, the opening as we now have it, with its profound poetic implications and arresting dramatic tones. The Boston background may have been intended to emphasize the universality of the poem, but its retention would have weakened a unity of effect which was not at first apparent. Pound's lack of discernment is seen in the cancellation of the sea-change reference which accompanied the drawing of the drowned Phoenician card from the Tarot pack; his failure to see Eliot's meaning in the dead sound of St Mary Woolnoth's at nine o'clock in the morning is also evident.

More than half of part III ('The Fire Sermon') was withdrawn, including the whole of the initial section on Fresca, and many stanzas from the encounter scene between the typist and her carbuncular client. The Fresca passage is imitative of Pope, the first two lines ending in the rhymes with which Belinda is introduced in *The Rape of the Lock*; in Eliot's white-armed heroine there is a Homeric overtone reminiscent of Pope's translations. Eliot thought highly of his couplets, but Pound did not hesitate to tell him that, if he couldn't write better than Pope, it would be foolish to burlesque him. Eliot could not equal Pope; he surprises less by his wit than by the itch to shock, which leads to more original effects than in the Boston scene. Fresca's first act on rising from pleasant dreams of love and rape is to slip quietly to the w.c., where her labour is eased by reading Samuel Richardson's pathetic story of Clarissa Harlowe. After writing a letter, she takes a bath; the second action provides Eliot with an opportunity to indulge the kind of anti-feminist distaste which marked his description of Grishkin; the first, to satirize society. Elsewhere in another age Fresca might have been a weeping Mary Magdalene, for it is the same strong besetting urge which makes a bitch or a martyr (a similar idea is developed with Celia Coplestone in *The Cocktail Party*). Then follows an indirect onslaught on the mish-mash of European literature which was popular among culture-seekers; it is particularly antipathetic towards Pateresque aestheticism: Fresca was born from the soapy waves of John Addington Symonds, Walter Pater, and Vernon Lee; she is bemused by Scandinavian, and thrilled to hysteria by Russian, authors. Misbred by fate, and deceived by flattery, she is ranked by the nine Muses as a vulgar can-can frequenter of pretentious cultural circles. A Venus Anadyomene, under the patronage of Lady Katzegg, she becomes acquainted with the wealthy and the fashionable. Aeneas recognises his mother in her, just as the rabble recognise a goddess on the cinema screen. It seems unfortunate that Eliot did not have the time to polish and continue his satirical couplets in self-contained scenes or portraits.

The Fresca sketch, more discreetly handled and dextrously finished in its Augustan voice or mode, could have presented a light, engaging facet of a 'waste land' which would have given greater variety in the sex-motivated scenes of the poem as a whole. Had he succeeded in it, he would still have had to solve the problem of its collocation, how to place it so that what followed did not break the imaginative sequence. It is regrettable that he was unable to develop the possibilities of the brief passage on London which precedes the numerous quatrains on the typist. As in the Hampstead lines, and like Hardy,[27] he looks upon the people of London as victims of the wheel of worldly forces. Philosophers may think they can trace the clue to life in their perceptions of the noise, movement, and lights of this metropolis. The answer, the poet adds, addressing Glaucon in an allusion to the ideal city of Plato (*The Republic*, ix.592), is not here but in heaven. Known as the City of God to Stoics and early Christians, this ideal was in Arnold's mind when he wrote bitterly in *Culture and Anarchy*:

> And the work which we collective children of God do, our grand centre of life, our *city* which we have builded for us to dwell in, is London! London, with its unutterable external hideousness, and with its internal canker of *public egestes, privatim opulentia*, – to use the words which Sallust puts into Cato's mouth about Rome, – unequalled in the world!

Eliot's different voices assume a variety of forms. From couplets of the 'heroic' kind practised by Pope he turns to quatrains in the style of Dryden for the typist scene. His admiration for Dryden's mastery and variety of technique, especially for his genius in lifting the prosaic and ordinary to the imaginative heights of poetry, is manifest in an essay he wrote on Dryden in 1921, when he was anxious to complete *The*

Waste Land. Much of the detail in the original version of this section is realistically trivial and commonplace, and so coarse with superfluous intent at one point that Pound assumed it would be offensive. Eliot's reduction and improvement of this passage, with no real loss and much gain in movement and impression, points first to tired, rather laborious writing, then to a period of alerted critical judgment, which is particularly telling with a change of verb in the second line of the final quatrain. The sordid associations of the river before and after this scene suggest that Eliot may, by adopting the *Annus Mirabilis* stanza, have hoped to remind the reader of the city's punishment for its sins, and ironically, as with his reference to Spenser's 'sweet Thames', to recall the silver Thames of Dryden's concluding vision, with its new prospects of prosperity and glory for his '*London*, Empress of the Northern Clime'.

Pound's one written comment on the manuscript of part IV ('Death by Water') was an unqualified condemnation, but he couldn't launch his attack until he received a typescript copy. This he criticized to such effect that all of it was withdrawn except the Phlebas passage, which had been anticipated in the Tarot-pack introduction, and was probably recommended for no other reason. Pound's insight seems to have failed, and Eliot knew that the isolated Phlebas lines would prove baffling to the reader. It might be better to omit them, he wrote, only to receive the categorical answer that the passage must remain because it had been introduced in the card-pack. Eliot's compliance was at fault, for helpful pointers to the significance of his marine symbolism were lost.

The narration of 'Death by Water', which is dramatic at times, describes with intimate detail the voyage of a fishing-schooner, its crew disaffected by the food and the inadequacy of the ship in a storm, as it makes its way from Gloucester past the Dry Salvages, the eastern banks (where they make a good catch), and the most northerly islands, until the ship sinks among ice-floes. The account contains some of Eliot's finest blank verse, in plain language that moves from the factual to the poetical with fluent economy. When the catch is good, the fishermen are happy, and think of home, dollars, girls, drink, and pleasing violin music at Marm Brown's, an important link with the bar in Lower Thames Street, where lounging fishmen enjoy the playing of a mandoline at noon. Fishing is symbolical,

and Eliot hints at its meaning through repeated allusions to
Tennyson's 'Ulysses': an apparent quotation (combining 'Much
have I seen' and 'have suffered greatly'), the moaning of the sea
with 'many voices' (repeated in 'The Dry Salvages'), and the
reference to the Hyades. The Ulysses of Tennyson's poem is not
merely a geographical explorer:

> Yet all experience is an arch wherethrough
> Gleams that untravelled world, whose margin fades
> For ever and for ever when I move.
>   . . . Life piled on life
> Were all too little, and of one to me
> Little remains: but every hour is saved
> From that eternal silence, something more,
> A bringer of new things; and vile it were
> For some three suns to store and hoard myself,
> And this gray spirit yearning in desire
> To follow knowledge like a sinking star,
> Beyond the utmost bound of human thought.

Ulysses, like Eliot, wishes his knowledge to extend beyond what
seems knowable, beyond the normal confines of this world, this
life.

In the height of the storm which follows the harvest of
fishing, nobody dares to look in his neighbour's face, or to
speak in the horror of a world that screams all round them;
('The horror! the horror!', from Conrad's *Heart of Darkness*, was
Eliot's first epigraph for *The Waste Land*). All is quiet as the ship
sinks and the last entry is made in the log-book. The recorder
wonders whether a higher Being is aware of what is happening.
His term for the Unknown is uniquely Dantean, a clear
reference to the ending of the Ulysses story in the *Inferno*
(xxvi.85–142), with the sinking of the ship 'as pleased Another'.
Ulysses and his men had just caught sight of a mountain,
undoubtedly the Mount of Purgatory, dimly in the distance;
and it is of this, and of Arnaut Daniel gladly accepting the
flames of purgation, that we are reminded by the recorder's
request that he be remembered ('sovegna vos'), written amid
the ice-floes, a purgatorial symbol which recurs, together with
the detail of the leaking garboard, in 'Marina', where the
timber and paint of an age-worn vessel have suffered badly

from ice and heat. It might have been better had Pound encouraged Eliot to revise 'Death by Water' for publication as a separate poem; as it is, no more than the final Phlebas adjunct, without any of the preliminary indicators to its spiritual connotation, it remains *inherently* incomprehensible.

11

Influences

Some scholarly writers have depended considerably for their imaginative sustenance on literature; none, probably, more than T. S. Eliot. Thomas Hardy, who admitted that bookishness was the most consistent feature of his life, created the main phases of his plot, the principal character, and some episodes, in *The Mayor of Casterbridge*, largely as a result of conceiving a Wessex story in terms of Sophocles' *Oedipus Rex*, the love–jealousy–hatred relationship of Saul and David, an important situation in *King Lear*, and much more in Hugo's *Les Misérables*. The full impact of *Tess of the d'Urbervilles* cannot be felt until it is seen as a comment on Richardson's *Clarissa*. Hardy's incidental allusiveness and love of quotation is marked, but it is usually less concentrated, as one would expect in novels, than it often is in Eliot's poetry.

A minor example of a possible literary influence in Eliot's earlier poetry is worth considering. Charles-Louis Philippe's *Bubu de Montparnasse* may supply a clue, not to the third section of 'Preludes', but to crucial lines in the fourth. Eliot read this novel at an impressionable age, and it remained for him a 'symbol' of the Paris he knew in 1910. In it Pierre communes with God, as he thinks of the evil in the world, and of the heavy crosses women have to bear. He and Berthe are joined by Louis Buisson, who tells them how, while Jesus (God's love on earth) prayed in the garden on the Mount of Olives, his disciples slept. Jesus felt that 'the night of the earth' covered him, and said, 'For years I have been spreading my soul over the world to bring it to life. Forgive me, my Father, but I see that all has failed.' The symbolism of this description must have appealed deeply to Eliot's religious imagination; he may not consciously

109

have remembered it when, in 'Preludes', he wrote of one straining after the realization of an immanent Spirit, but it undoubtedly seems inherent in his notion of a Being whose capacity for suffering is as infinite as its compassion.

Reference has been made to the influence of shorter stories by Henry James on the creation of Prufrock's character, on his Bostonian ambience, and that of the conscience-troubled hero of 'Portrait of a Lady'. The title of another story by James, 'In the Cage', must have been in Eliot's mind when he wrote 'The Death of the Duchess' and 'A Game of Chess'. It reminded him of the passage in Petronius's *Satyricon* where Trimalchio boasts of seeing the aged and shrunken Sibyl hanging in a bottle; when the boys asked her what she wanted, she would say, 'I wish to die.' The effect of Eliot's concentration on Elizabethan and Jacobean plays at various times from 1918 to the publication of *The Sacred Wood* in 1920 has already been noticed; their impingement on *The Waste Land*, and the relatedness of Wagner's operas at important points, will be referred to later. Here the primary concern is with influences which played an important part in the genesis of the poem.

Of all the French poets of the nineteenth century, it was Baudelaire whose thought and imagery made the deepest impression on Eliot's poetry. How could Eliot fail to admire one who maintained that true civilization depended not on material progress or on 'les tables tournantes' but on 'la diminution des traces du péché original'? Taking his words from the last chapter of Pater's *Marius the Epicurean*, he characterized Baudelaire as 'a soul *naturaliter* Christian', whose certainty of human damnation expressed some hope for salvation from 'the ennui of modern life'. The 'hypocritique lecteur! – mon semblable, – mon frère!' which ends 'The Burial of the Dead' concludes the 'Au Lecteur' introduction to *Les Fleurs du Mal*, where Baudelaire finds in the infamous menagerie of our vices nothing more ugly, wicked, and vile then Ennui; it is capable of swallowing the whole world, and the hypocritical reader, the poet's 'semblable', is familiar with it. Eliot did not believe that Baudelaire's images of sordid metropolitan life would have as lasting a poetic appeal as those of Cavalcanti or Dante, but he knew that his elevation of such imagery of the contemporary world 'to the *first intensity*', his presentation of the actual and of something beyond it, provided an example which he could follow.[28]

In 'Le Cygne' Baudelaire presents thoughts and impressions in Paris, and recalls seeing one morning an escaped swan scrabbling over the dry pavement, and dragging its white plumage over the rough earth, its wings twitching nervously in the dust as it reaches a dry stream-bed. 'When will it rain? When will it thunder?' it seemed to ask as it looked up to an ironical, cruel blue sky. The same question, with similar overtones, is raised at the end of *The Waste Land*. The sense of life proceeding incessantly from hell to the unknown which came to Baudelaire as he witnessed a phantasmagoric succession of bent, ragged old men shuffling in the snow and mud of a foggy street is the subject of 'Les Sept Vieillards'. Its imagery and symbolic significance lived in Eliot's mind, as he indicated by his association of its opening lines, 'Fourmillante cité, cité pleine de rêves, Où le spectre en plein jour raccroche le passant!' with his 'Unreal City' and the crowd flowing over London Bridge in a brown wintry fog. At the end of 'Mademoiselle Bistouri' Baudelaire beseeches God to have pity on the 'monstres innocents', the 'fous' and the 'folles', of the swarming town; God, he says, may have given him his sense of horror to convert his heart, healing at the point of a knife. This is the subject of 'L'Heautontimoroumenos' (a title repeating that of Terence's play *One's Own Executioner*), where, thinking of the tears shed in his Sahara, he writes,

> Je suis la plaie et le couteau!
> Je suis le soufflet et la joue!
> Je suis les membres et la roue,
> Et la victime et le bourreau!

'I am the Resurrection and the Life', a brief ancillary poem among the scripts considered for *The Waste Land*, has the same purgatorial thoughts, with the idea of the butter for the sacrifice coming from similar paradoxical expression in the *Bhagavad-Gita*.[29] Baudelaire's 'L'Irrémédiable' contains three images, of the soul seeking light or a key in 'un Styx bourbeux et plombé', which bear some resemblance at least to images in Eliot's poetry, the last of them in *Ash-Wednesday* (III): a swimmer struggling in adverse waters; a ship trapped in polar ice; one of the damned descending lampless on the edge of an abyss, or of endless stairs without a hand-hold, where slimy monsters with large phosphorescent eyes make darkness darker. The symbolical ending of the voyage in the original 'Death by Water' most probably originated from the second image. 'Moesta et Errabunda', with childhood happiness presented as a green paradisal garden of flowers, music, and song, seems to anticipate in most respects a dominant image in *Four Quartets*.

The sixth book of Virgil's *Aeneid*, in which the Sibyl of Cumae escorts Aeneas to the Underworld, had a special significance for Eliot. Their route lay through the 'sacred wood', the forests concealing the golden bough which had to be plucked and carried to Proserpine by anyone wishing to enter her domains. The dismal waters of Acheron, where the unburied dead stretch imploring hands toward the shore beyond (they were translated to Dante's Ante-Hell, and to 'The Hollow Men'), delay the passage to Hell. Arrived there, Aeneas speaks to his father Anchises, and learns that the multitude by a stream in a pleasant valley are those who are destined for reincarnation, and who drink oblivion from the Lethe river. Anchises then tells them how the immanent Mind makes the whole universe work. The Life force in all creatures is fire (a Heraclitean idea which the *poet* in Eliot accepted); and they originate from Heaven. Unfortunately they are deadened by their sinful bodies, and cannot see Heaven from their dark prison. Evil does not relinquish souls when death comes; in purgatory some hang empty (the 'hollow' men) in the winds; some are purged in a vast whirlpool ('death by water'); some, by fire. There are two gates of Sleep, one of horn through which genuine visions pass, another of ivory through which delusive dreams are sent; and it is through the latter that Anchises directs Aeneas and the Sybil back to earth.

Echoes of the Bible are more common in Eliot than is generally suspected; a simple expression such as 'set . . . in order' at the end of *The Waste Land* is biblical. At this stage it suffices to stress the importance of the book of Ezekiel, in which the expression 'Son of man' occurs frequently. It is, in fact, peculiar to it, and its use by Eliot is bold, indicative of a voice that speaks for God, in the old Hebraic sense of 'prophetic'. For allusions in *Ash-Wednesday*, it should be noted that the book of Ezekiel originated during the Israelites' exile in Babylon; in the last chapters the prophet's concern is with the rebuilding of the Temple, and with the inheritance, the division of the land, on their return. The vision of the holy waters (xlvii.6–12) is particularly relevant to *The Waste Land*:

> And he [the Lord God] said unto me, Son of man, hast thou seen this? Then he brought me, and caused me to return to the brink of the river. Now when I had returned, behold, at the bank of the river were very many trees on the one side and on the other. Then said he unto me, These waters issue out toward the east country, and go down into the desert, and go into the sea: which being brought forth into the sea, the waters shall be healed. And it shall come to pass, that every thing that liveth, which moveth, whithersoever the rivers shall come, shall live: and there shall be a very great multitude of fish, because these waters shall come thither: for they shall be healed; and every thing shall live whither the river cometh. And it shall come to pass, that the fishers shall stand upon it . . . their fish shall be according to their kinds, as the fish of the great sea, exceeding many. But the miry places thereof and the marishes thereof shall not be healed; they shall be given to salt. And by the river upon the bank thereof, on this side and on that side, shall grow all trees for meat, whose leaf shall not fade, neither shall the fruit therof be consumed; it shall bring forth new fruit according to his months, because their waters they issued out of the sanctuary: and the fruit thereof shall be for meat, and the leaf thereof for medicine.

The river in *The Waste Land* is squalid, but the most surprising juxtaposition, at the very centre of the poem, introduces 'fishmen' and a flashing hint of salvation; by the contrast of its implication the river of Life stresses the meaning.

In his notes to *The Waste Land* Eliot acknowledges his indebtedness to vegetation ceremonies in two volumes (*Adonis, Attis, Osiris*) of Frazer's *The Golden Bough*. In 'The Myth of Adonis', at the opening of the first of these volumes, there is a lament for Tammuz, or Adonis, which, being of Babylonian origin, may relate to Ezekiel's vision, as the following lines show:

Her lament is for a great river, where no willows grow,
  Her lament is for a field, where corn and herbs grow not.
Her lament is for a pool, where fishes grow not.
  Her lament is for a thicket of reeds, where no reeds grow.
Her lament is for woods, where tamarisks grow not.
  Her lament is for a wilderness where no cypresses (?) grow.
Her lament is for the depth of a garden of trees, where honey
    and wine grow not.
Her lament is for meadows, where no plants grow.

A brief passage in 'The Ritual of Adonis' chapter may be related to Eliot's hyacinth image. People were reminded of the annual death of Adonis, which was associated with the cutting of the corn, by the red leaves of autumn; and human beings were slain on the harvest-field to propitiate the corn-spirit. As the dead, it was assumed, revived in the sprouting corn, so it might be thought that they returned in the spring flowers. 'What more natural than to imagine that the violets and hyacinths . . . sprang from their dust, were empurpled or incarnadined by their blood, and contained some portion of their spirit?', Frazer asks, quoting from the *Rubáiyát*:

> I sometimes think that never blows so red
> The Rose as where some buried Caesar bled;
>   That every Hyacinth the Garden wears
> Dropt in her Lap from some once lovely Head.

Initially the title of Eliot's poem may have occurred to him when he read in Malory's *Morte d'Arthur* (xvii.3): 'and so befel there great pestilence and great harm . . . for there increased neither corn nor grass, nor wellnigh any fruit, nor were fish to be found in the water. Therefore it is called . . . the Waste Land.' He was familiar with Tennyson's use of the expression in the last book of *Idylls of the King*, where, with the ruined chapel on 'a dark strait of barren land' over which blew a cold, shrill wind (foreshadowing the derelict chapel, visited by nothing but the wind, of 'What the Thunder said'), it connotes the defeat of religious hope and idealism. Eliot's title, however, was determined more by its recurrence in Jessie Weston's *From Ritual to Romance*, a study of the Grail legend which owed its initial inspiration to *The Golden Bough*. It gave him, as he admitted, 'a good deal of the incidental symbolism' in *The Waste Land*, and, more than any other book, helped to mould its thematic development.[30]

Jessie Weston's work may have drawn Eliot's interest to the Tarot pack of cards, which seems to have been used in Egypt 'to predict the rise and fall of the waters which brought fertility to the land'. Without observing its hieroglyphics exactly, Eliot uses this divining-pack as an arresting but rather cryptic introduction to his themes. In the old myth both vegetable and human fertility were lost when Tammuz died; he is the spring god or Life force. Eliot makes much of sexual infertility, and elevates the Life force from the physical to the spiritual in 'The Burial of the Dead'; his spring god (the tiger in 'Gerontion') is not welcome to the modern world. More important in *From Ritual to Romance* is the Fisher King, whose death, sickness, wounding, or old age is responsible for the infertility and desolation of his land. Its recovery depends on the King's restoration, and the role of the healer or quester in effecting this desired end varies considerably. The Fisher King being dead in one legend, and the King's brother in another, Eliot turns this uncertainty to advantage in 'The Fire Sermon'. Miss Weston gives prominence to the fish as 'a Divine Life symbol, of immemorial antiquity', and to its adoption by the early Christians. Whereas Lawrence in *Etruscan Places* asserts that Jesus was represented as a fish because it was 'the *anima*, the animate life' of the sea, she suggests that its Life significance arose from the belief that all life came from water. She quotes Dr R. Eisler to the effect that 'the Fish was sacred to those deities who were supposed to lead men back from the shadow of death to life'. Her reference to the many hymns in the Hindu *Rig-Veda* which were addressed to Indra for rain may have reminded Eliot of the meanings ascribed to thunder in one of the *Upanishads*. Her rapid survey of the Healer's transformation, in fertility ritual drama, into a Redeemer may have given him a hint for the Crucifixion and road-to-Emmaus overtones in 'What the Thunder said'; and her description of this mysterious evolution as something 'rich and strange' may have awakened, or re-awakened, him imaginatively to the key role of Ferdinand ('Those are pearls that were his eyes').

In some of Conrad's stories of western commercialism Eliot found much to admire, in both the outlook and the imagery of

that powerfully creative writer. Two stories in *Tales of Unrest*
show affinities with the opening of *The Waste Land*. 'The Return'
creates an intensively externalized impression of the time-
ridden, vacant-eyed City business man who reaches home to
discover that he and his wife have been skating on the surface
of things; for them the profound river of life has become frozen.
This is related to the river in 'The Dry Salvages', but comes
more closely in its imagery to 'The Burial of the Dead'. The
story of 'An Outpost of Progress' emphasizes the irony of its
title, and the hypocrisy of colonial commercial representatives
who claim to bring the progress and virtue of civilization to
western Africa. The outpost is aptly sited in a void surrounded
by immense forests. Extreme privation suddenly brings out the
worst in one of the two white men left behind, and fright makes
one kill the other. The next morning, in a deadly white mist,
like a man who wakes up from a dream to find himself
'immured for ever in a tomb', he calls on God for help. Rather
than be taken for judgment to the 'rubbish heap' of civilization,
he hangs himself; the 'stony rubbish' of 'The Burial of the
Dead' is allied in thought and imagery to both these stories.

Eliot's interest in Conrad's *Heart of Darkness* is indicated in
the original epigraph of *The Waste Land* and the closely related
one he used for 'The Hollow Men'. His 'heart of light' seems to
admit the connection, which is borne out when we find in 'The
Fire Sermon' details from Conrad's opening scene ('barges
drifting', 'red clusters of canvas') followed by recollections of
Elizabethan glory. Conrad's narration begins with an ominously
glooming sky at sunset; at the end, the river flows 'sombre
under an overcast sky' and seems to lead into 'the heart of an
immense darkness'. The commercial centre which profits from
business in dark African forests lies across the Channel. To gain
his appointment Marlow crosses over to a city like a whited
sepulchre, and makes his way to an office up a staircase 'arid as
a desert'; two knitters of black wool sit before the door of
Darkness with downcast eyes; after signing a document, he feels
he is in a house in 'a city of the dead'; when he returns to it at
the end, he resents 'the sight of people hurrying through the
streets to filch a little money from each other'. In Africa he
meets emissaries of light, and, after glimpsing brutality and
horror for which they are responsible, he is certain that he has
never seen anything as 'unreal' as the 'imbecile rapacity'

that bewitches these ivory-collectors. The silent wilderness surrounding a mere speck of an outpost appears 'something great and invincible, like evil or truth, waiting patiently for the passing away of this fantastic invasion'. Jealousy of his enormous success, especially in oratory, is the reason Kurtz is left to die. Such was his brilliance that one who knew him said he could have been a splendid leader of any extreme party. *Corruptio optimi pessima*: a man proclaiming high ideals, his success as a dealer had depraved him; rumour had it that 'he had collected, bartered, swindled, or stolen more ivory than all the other agents together'. He was 'hollow at the core', madly haunted with 'images of wealth and fame'; the powers of darkness had 'claimed him for their own'. Only on the brink of death, when he cried out, 'The horror! the horror!', did he recognise the truth, and pass judgment on his soul. In the eyes of Marlow it was a moral victory over the pride, ruthlessness, and abominable terrors and satisfactions, of which he had been guilty in the extreme.

Of all the influences on Eliot's poetry, none is greater or more pervasive than that of Dante; it is especially significant at the opening and conclusion of *The Waste Land*. The unreal city with its business-geared pedestrians may recall Conrad, but deeper import is conveyed with the crowd passing over London Bridge to resume their commercial routine: so numerous was the procession, 'I had not thought death had undone so many'. This repetition of the *Inferno* (iii.55–7) is a reminder of the spirits of the pusillanimous who congregate with sighs and lamentations in Ante-Hell, on the desert shore of the great Acheron river. They are the unfortunate who were never alive and will never be remembered, who missed 'the benefit of the intellect' (the awareness of God), lived without infamy or praise, have no hope of death, and are envious of every other lot. Eliot's impression of his contemporary world is similar to Arnold's in 'The Scholar Gipsy':

> Vague half-believers of our casual creeds,
>   Who never deeply felt, nor clearly will'd,
> Whose insight never has borne fruit in deeds,
>   Whose weak resolves never have been fulfill'd.

In both 'Death by Water' and 'What the Thunder said' the

use of 'you', 'we', and 'I' suggests that Eliot is thinking more in terms of the reader and himself. The question whether he should set his lands in order points toward some of the Ariel poems and *Ash-Wednesday*, though the imagery it introduces is that of the Fisher King. Fishing on the shore corresponds to the bone's prayer on the beach in 'The Dry Salvages'. The arid plain behind the fisher is foreshadowed in Dante's Ante-Purgatory, and has the same spiritual connotations. (Purgatory, the mountain dimly perceived by Ulysses, rises from the ocean.) After returning to earth with Virgil, Dante finds himself on a lonely plain, where his guide removes the stains of Hell from his face with dew. On the desert shore, by the sea that never saw its waters navigated by any person who returned, Virgil then girds him with the rush of humility, in preparation for a meeting with the first of God's ministers. The seashore and the first preparations for healing hint at a relatedness between Eliot's Dantean overtones, the healing of the river waters in the sea of Ezekiel, and the sea-change of the drowned Phoenician sailor.

12

The Waste Land

Eliot's allusiveness through imagery and quotation in *The Waste Land* is exceptional in degree; it can call up literary scenes and overtones of thought and feeling, all in all equivalent to an epic, as I. A. Richards said, of far greater import to the modern world than *Paradise Lost*, and comparable rather to Joyce's *Ulysses*. This kind of imaginative concentration is not original; it will be found in novels and poems by other writers, but never in all probability at the same sustained intensity. What is peculiar to *The Waste Land* is the collocation of images and scenes in a manner calculated to evoke feelings and accordant ideas, without overt statements of meaning. There is no contextual narrative or thought, as in a poem by Baudelaire, to give more explicit significance to the imagery. Coherence depends on imaginative interlinking and unification, Eliot's 'logic of the imagination'. Scenes from life, presented sufficiently in symbolical terms to communicate their deeper meaning, are interwoven with passages informed allusively or abstractly with symbolism, to form a whole which creates not a reasoning-process or a completed pattern of illustrated thought but, to use Richards' terms, a response in feeling and attitude which might metaphorically be described as a 'music of ideas'.[31]

Original creative symbolism is elaborated by Lawrence in *Sons and Lovers*, *The Rainbow*, and *Women in Love*, notably in moonlit scenes, but the description of the blighted garden through which Hardy's Tess is drawn by Angel's music is much closer in quality to Eliot's symbolism by virtue of its literary overtones, its kinship with Swinburne's 'Ilicet' and a well-known passage in *Hamlet*. More interesting, though it has an explanatory conclusion, is the key passage in the ulterior theme of George Eliot's *The Lifted Veil,* since it anticipates *The Waste Land* in some respects; the imagery which it shares with T. S. Eliot is biblical in origin. Nothing indicates or suggests that the latter knew the vision of Prague; it expresses George Eliot's apprehension that with the decay of the Christian faith no religion would succeed it, and humanity would become spiritually dead:

a city under the broad sunshine, that seemed to me as if it were the summer sunshine of a long-past century arrested in its course – unrefreshed for ages by the dews of night, or the rushing rain-cloud; scorching the dusty, weary, time-eaten grandeur of a people doomed to live on in the stale repetition of memories, like deposed and superannuated kings in their regal gold-inwoven tatters. The city looked so thirsty that the broad river seemed to me a sheet of metal; and the blackened statues, as I passed under their blank gaze, along the unending bridge, with their ancient garments and their saintly crowns, seemed to me the real inhabitants and owners of this place, while the busy, trivial men and women, hurrying to and fro, were a swarm of ephemeral visitants infesting it for a day. It is such grim, stony beings as these, I thought, who are the fathers of ancient faded children, in those tanned time-fretted dwellings that crowd the steep before me; who pay their court in the worn and crumbling pomp of the palace which stretches its monotonous length on the height; who worship wearily in the stifling air of the churches, urged by no fear or hope, but compelled by their doom to be for ever old and undying, to live on in the rigidity of habit, as they live on in perpetual mid-day, without the repose of night or the new birth of morning.

There are six movements in the first part of *The Waste Land.* Lines vary through the whole range from the two-stressed to the six-stressed, from lyrical to narrative and descriptive, from orthodox dramatic narrative to the arrestingly dramatic which implicates the reader. The first two movements are combined, and their subject extends from spring to winter. Keeping to the vegetation myths, Eliot's year begins with spring; it is the season of rebirth, the time for a renewal of spiritual life. Such is the higher implication of Lancelot Andrewes' comment on 'better travelling to Christ' in the spring, which the poet quoted in one of his 1919 reviews. It is because Christ comes tiger-like when genuine spiritual rebirth occurs that the metaphorical April is so cruel; for the same reason Mary in *The Family Reunion* (i.ii) associates the terror of the soul tormented into new life with the vernal sacrifice of tree and beast and the fish that thrashes itself upstream. Most people prefer the spiritual quiescence or indifference of winter; wealthy pleasure-seekers partake in the worldly pastimes of rootless cosmopolitanism in western Europe. Whether Eliot met the Countess Marie Larisch in 1911 or 1914 is uncertain; he probably read her memoirs, a not very exciting record of European court scandals, mingled with sexual intrigue and corruption, which was published in 1916. Marie had several archduke cousins, and was related to Ludwig II, the Bavarian king who was drowned in the Starnberger-See. The sense of freedom associated with the mountains is ironical, referring to a patriotic poem ('Auf den Bergen wohnt die Freiheit') about Ludwig, who became a prisoner in his own castle, and may have been drowned while trying to escape. The sledding descent probably alludes to the catastrophic 1914–18 war,[32] and the moral slump which confronted young people in its wake. The irony of the freedom claimed by those who could afford amoral lives is stressed in 'We think of the key, each in his prison' near the end of the poem.

The poet asks almost with exasperation what spiritual growth can be expected from 'stony rubbish'. In the heat of the desert it is impossible to answer this question, for one knows only a mass of 'broken images'. The question is one of knowledge, not of praying to broken stone as in 'The Hollow Men'; the metaphor may originate from the broken glass which, in 'Caprices in North Cambridge',[33] Eliot had associated with other species of squalor and decay to produce a vacant-lot or waste-land image; the broken images, though destitute of religious connotation, resemble the 'broken lights' in Tennyson's prologue to *In Memoriam*. The truth about the age and its possibilities of religious awakening are unascertainable, for knowledge is restricted to an accumulation of impressions, subjective, limited, disparate, and of small account. Combined with this philosophical implication there are overtones of Ezekiel's waste-land prophecy (vi.1–7) in which altars are laid waste and images broken as a sign of God's anger in a post-war world. The red rock which offers the only relief in the parching desert is the Christian faith. The Church's interpretation of 'the shadow of a great rock in a weary land' (Isaiah, xxxii.2) as the 'blessings of Christ's kingdom' is undoubtedly implied; the rock symbolizes the Christian Church (Matthew, xvi.18), and 'red' hints at the Crucifixion ('The dripping blood our only drink', Eliot writes in 'East Coker'). The business man striding to and from his work is but a shadow of a man, reminiscent of the hero of Conrad's 'The Return'.

The fourth movement introduces the most important aspect of Eliot's theme. In principle at least he is at one with D. H. Lawrence: religious dearth or superficiality is reflected in despiritualized love. For Eliot there was a divine spark in true human love; it is ultimately the love of God, he said in his later years. The hyacinth girl (after 'flos hyacinthinus' in Catullus's poem (no. 61) which begins 'Collis o Heliconii') finds that her passion is not reciprocated. Though he knows that he is looking into the true light, the young man's eyes fail; he is neither alive nor dead, and knows nothing. The truth of living, 'the heart of light', is a spiritual perception, to be found in childhood happiness (the garden vision of 'Burnt Norton'), and in devoted love. Eliot's image of spiritual death in love merges with the openings of the first and third acts of *Tristan und Isolde*: a young sailor at the masthead sings a farewell to his Irish girl as Tristan (whose love glance does not fail) and Isolde begin their voyage to Cornwall; '*Oed' und leer das Meer*' is the announcement of the shepherd that there is no sign at sea of the ship which is to bring Isolde to her dying lover. The sea from which love (Venus) was born is bare and desolate. The innermost meaning of this allusive imagery is summed up in *Ash-Wednesday*, 'No place of grace for those who avoid the face'.

Madame Sosostris (whose name, after Aldous Huxley's 'Sesostris, the Sorceress of Ecbatana' in *Chrome Yellow*, 1921, suggests that her cold was catarrhal) draws cards from the Tarot pack which are positive or negative pointers to other features in the poem. The most important is that of the drowned Phoenician sailor, which she links with the resumed song heard by Ferdinand when he laments 'the King my father's wreck' in *The Tempest* (i.ii.387ff.):

> Full fathom five thy father lies;
>   Of his bones are coral made;
> Those are pearls that were his eyes;
>   Nothing of him that doth fade
> But doth suffer a sea-change
>   Into something rich and strange.

The one-eyed merchant merges with the Phoenician sailor, and the two-in-one are not altogether distinguishable from Ferdinand, we are told in Eliot's notes. As the drowned sailor and the song heard by Ferdinand relate to a sea-change from evil to good, there is reason to think that the one-eyed merchant is related to the one-eyed Riley of the song in *The Cocktail Party*; taking its meaning from Matthew, vi.22–3 and xviii.9, 'one-eyed' could indicate the will to change from darkness to light. Belladonna (possibly with a hint of poison in her name) plays a varied role in the poem. Eliot identifies the Man with Three Staves as his Fisher King; the Wheel is the wheel of Fortune, and, as it plays no specific part in the poem, it would be superfluous to look for another meaning. Thought to be the most perceptive woman in Europe (and the intentional irony of this need not be stressed), the clairvoyante Madame Sosostris warns against submarine death. She is unable to find the Hanged Man (which Eliot identifies as much with Jesus as with Frazer's hanged god), and sees masses of people walking in a circle, a foretaste of the conclusion to 'The Hollow Men'.

This brings us to the spiritually dead, the crowds walking to work in the commercial and financial centre of London, each preoccupied, not looking far ahead, as Eliot knew from daily experience; the deadness with which Saint Mary Woolnoth strikes nine is not so much fact as a reverberator of the somnolence which affected even the Church. The desert in the city (close beside you in the tube-train), Eliot wrote in *The Rock*) is imaged in the dense fog of a winter morning. The recognition of Stetson, with mingled exclamation, questioning, and concern in rapid remarks, brings animation to verse which has come to a slow plod in conformity to its subject. With the fade-out of Stetson, and the merging of speech into a frontal attack on the reader, part I ends at the height of climax. Though it probably hints at the 1914–18 war (like the Thermopylae of 'Gerontion'), the Mylae reference imparts a

universal reference; its association with Carthage, a city of
unholy loves, gives it a special aptness in *The Waste Land*. The
buried-corpse image which follows, thought startling in its time,
is now rather a damp squib. It has obvious overtones of ancient
vegetation ritual, but the question raised seems to be whether
the late war sacrifice has not been in vain. The sudden alarm
about the Dog is inseparable from the accusation levelled at the
reader; the unwanted Dog is friendly to men, the majority of
whom are dead to the need for religious revival. The reference
is to the Dog Star or Sirius, which, according to J. G. Frazer in
'Osiris', appeared above the horizon when the Nile valley was
inundated. With one significant change, of 'foe' to 'friend', Eliot
echoes the ending of Cornelia's song in Webster's *The White
Devil* (v.iv): 'But keep the wolf far thence, that's foe to men,
For with his nails he'll dig them up again.' His attention to the
possibilities of these lines in connection with the sea-change
which is as much desired as it is inevident may have arisen
from a footnote in the Mermaid edition, a quotation from
Charles Lamb's *Specimens of English Dramatic Poets*:

> I never saw anything like this dirge, except the ditty which
> reminds Ferdinand of his drowned father in the Tempest. As
> that is of the water, watery; so this is of the earth, earthy.
> Both have that intensiveness of feeling, which seems to resolve
> itself into the elements which it contemplates.

*   *   *

'A Game of Chess' takes its title from Thomas Middleton's
Jacobean play *Women Beware Women*, an absurd entanglement of
love, lust, incest, and revenge, in which affluence takes
precedence almost unquestioningly over virtue, and plans to
ensure that Leantio's wife Bianca becomes the Duke's mistress
are discussed allusively in terms of chess (ii.ii). Perhaps Eliot
could empathize with the disillusioned husband:

> What a peace
> Has he that never marries! if he knew
> The benefit he enjoyed, or had the fortune
> To come and speak with me, he should know then
> The infinite wealth he had, and discern rightly
> The greatness of his treasure by my loss.

He uses the phrase 'a game of chess' as a euphemism for contrived or loveless sexual gratification.

The opening is heavily elaborate with sensuous imagery; it may aim at a fleeting recall of Pope's exquisite effects in the description of Belinda's toiletry at the end of the first canto of *The Rape of the Lock*, but it deliberately stultifies any such parallelism. The allusions to Cleopatra ('The Chair she sat in, like a burnished throne') and to Dido ('laquearia') are to love and passion, and to genuine, royal splendours, quite inconsistent with the loveless sexuality of 'A Game of Chess' and its sequel. They have an ironical or pejorative purpose, emphasizing the pretentiousness of a setting indicative of self-admiration and indulgence, with mirror effects, profusion of jewels, and satiety of perfumes. The stress on glass and glitter suggests artificiality; the burning 'sevenbranched candelabra' have an ambience which sets them far apart from the seven lamps of Revelation (iv.5) or the seven 'candelabri' which represent the sevenfold gifts of the Spirit in the *Purgatorio* (xxix). Virtue does not reside in perfumes which 'lurk', are 'strange' and 'synthetic', and 'fatten' the candle-flames; the elongation of the latter (Eliot introduces a deliberate ambivalence by *prolonging* them), and the artificially induced colours of the burning logs, introduce a theme which ends only with denunciations of fleshy appetites by Saint Augustine and Buddha at the end of 'The Fire Sermon'. From its conglomerate opening scene, with its sad firelight and overtones extending to the classical world, to garrulous contraceptive gossip in a cockney public-house at closing time just after the First World War, 'A Game of Chess' has a range in time and social class which confirms the universality of Eliot's theme.

The change from the solidity of this setting to the dramatic presentation and extension of the situation first portrayed in 'The Death of the Duchess' is cinematic and vaguely surrealistic. Attention is called first to the picture above the fireplace of Philomel's metamorphosis after being raped by her brother-in-law Tereus, King of Thrace; the 'sylvan scene' recalls Satan's irruption into the garden of Eden (*Paradise Lost*, iv.130ff.); and Eliot's lyrical intensity asserts the persistence of virtue even in the desert of a 'dirty' world:

> yet there the nightingale
> Filled all the desert with inviolable voice
> And still she cried, and still the world pursues
> 'Jug Jug' to dirty ears.

The scene fades with glimpses significant of decay and lifelessness ('withered stumps of time') on the walls, and vague staring forms which hush the room as strange shuffling steps are heard on the staircase. Then the fire lights up points of a woman's brushed-out hair, and voices, almost impersonalized, are heard, expressing the void in the lives of two married people, the woman edgy and fractious, the husband resigned.

He cannot communicate with her, and is on the point of leaving. She appeals to him, her words expressing a high-strung impatience mounting repeatedly almost to hysteria, with final interrogative interation (as in 'What are you thinking of? What thinking? What?'). She threatens to rush out with her hair down, asks desperately what will they do tomorrow and tomorrow and tomorrow. Only the same routine, ending in a game of chess, the answer comes; the closed car in the rain reflects the unhappiness of caged lives. The man thinks they are in an alley of rats (which introduces one of the motifs in 'The Fire Sermon'), where the buried dead or spiritually inanimate (kept warm by winter) lost the bones which might bring them life (Ezekiel, xxxvii.3: 'Son of man, can these bones live? And I answered, O Lord God, thou knowest'). The wind under the door voices the nothingness of their lives; and the remembrance of 'Those are pearls that were his eyes', followed by a snatch of American ragtime, renews the sea-change theme which links all five sections of the poem. This interlinking would have gained had Eliot not deleted at this point a reference to his hyacinth-garden, which stood in significant conjunction with Shakespeare's metamorphic line.

Like the knocking in 'Sweeney Agonistes', the knock on the door for which the couple wait as they press lidless eyes is death; it is renewed in the ambivalence of the recurrent public-house closing-time call, which combines the poet's handful-of-dust motif with the popular 'Eat, drink, and be merry, for tomorrow we die' philosophy. Poor Albert, who has been in the army during the war, expects to have an enjoyable time, and, if his wife doesn't oblige, others will, she is told. These low-class disclosures follow those made on abortive practices by the Eliots' charwoman when they lived in Crawford Street, and are highly mimetic, especially when Lil is told what a fool she is, and asked why she married if she didn't want to have children. The good-night farewells at closing-time merge into the 'Good night, ladies, good night, sweet ladies, good night, good night' of the mad Ophelia (*Hamlet*, IV.v), whose love is dead. The death to which Eliot looks forward, and which is implied in the epigraph of *The Waste Land*, is not like Ophelia's; it is like that for which the narrator of 'Journey of the Magi' yearns, a dying unto one kind of life for spiritual rebirth.

*   *   *

So, at the opening of a many-voiced section, with rueful recurrence to the sweet Thames of Spenser's 'Prothalamion' (a poem redolent of summer flowers and love and beauty), we come to the same metropolitan river in the waste land of the twentieth century. It is winter; the last decaying leaves are drawn into the wet muddy bank, and the wind blows over a brown land. The litter and other nocturnal evidence of the summer have disappeared, with the 'nymphs' (an ironic echo of Spenser) and their friends, 'the loitering heirs of City directors'. The echo of the psalm 'By the waters of Babylon we sat down and wept' (hinting at Eliot's convalescence at Lausanne on Lake Leman – the Lake of Geneva – and anticipating the 'exile' of *Ash-Wednesday*) suggests the yearning for a new Jerusalem or renewal of spiritual life in the western world. Such a thought is implicit in the presentation of a Ferdinand figure fishing on a winter's evening in a dismal canal behind a gasometer, a conjunction of images which originated, with the rats and bones, from Eliot's recollections of the funeral in Joyce's *Ulysses*. The fisherman's melancholy reflections on the loss of the king, first his brother, then his father, combine two Fisher King legends, thereby giving greater contemporary definition to the subject of the lament: it is for his fellow-men, 'brother' reinforcing the early address to 'mon frère' the reader. The unburied dead, fated like those by the waters of Acheron on the margin of Virgil's Hell, may be seen in these rat-infested surroundings, bodies and bones lying low, the one on the damp soil, the other in a garret which keeps them dry.

Here there is no answer to the question whether the dry bones of Ezekiel's vision can live; nor is there any indication of revival, for, but for the rattling of the bones by rats, the dead lie undisturbed from year to year. This, not the deserts of eternity, is the desert Eliot associates with Marvell's winged chariot of Time, which brings a chilling reminder of Death with his broad chuckle, and, more wittily, in a parody of lines on Actaeon and the chaste huntress Diana, of the one certain renewal of spring, when Sweeney comes with sound of 'horns and motors' to Mrs Porter. Sweeney, a representative sex-seeker, is governed not so much by nature as by the exercise of appetite; the horns, as in the 'hornèd gate' of 'Sweeney among the Nightingales' are not innocent of sexual connotation, and the motor image anticipates the 'human engine' which waits like a throbbing taxi at the onset of the encounter between the carbuncular clerk and the typist.

The collocation of a bawdy song on Mrs Porter and her daughter (which was popular with Australian troops during the 1914–18 war) with '*Et O ces voix d'enfants, chantant dans la coupole!*' creates a startling antithesis which is magniloquent with shame. Verlaine alludes to the conclusion of Wagner's *Parsifal*, where the hero, who has been anointed after *his* feet-washing ritual, restores the wounded Amfortas to health by touching him with the sacred spear, and announces that he is to succeed him as keeper of the Grail. The restoration of the kingdom is shown in the glow of the Grail, the downpouring of a halo over the whole scene, and the hovering of a white dove over the head of Parsifal as a sign that he is God's chosen (cf. Matthew, iii.16–17). All, including the boys high up in the dome, join in sacramental song, and with it the work closes in spiritual triumph. In juxtaposition to this, the echoing allusion to Lyly's *Campaspe*, with its '*Jug, jug, jug, tereu!*' reference to the barbarous king Tereus and the ravished Philomel, underlines Eliot's irony, for Lyly's birdsong lyric is a welcome to spring.

The dead are recalled when, in thick wintry fog, the Smyrna merchant Mr Eugenides (the one-eyed merchant of Eliot's Tarot pack who merges into the Phoenician sailor), speaking common French, invites the narrator to have lunch with him at the Cannon Street Hotel, the resort of commercial travellers from the Continent, and then spend the weekend with him at the Metropole on the sea-front at Brighton. That the implications are far from respectable is attested by the placing of this invitation cheek-by-jowl with the Sweeney-Mrs Porter evocation and the prostitute-typist scene. The poetic tones in the expression of these two sexual encounters are entirely different, the first being lyrical in accordance with the irony of background allusion which includes two kinds of singing, the second being unusually precise in conformity with the assurance of the young man and the indifference of the typist; matter-of-factness and prosaic exactness reflect what Eliot in his essay on Baudelaire describes as the 'cheery' sexual 'automatism' of the contemporary world.

Whether Tiresias, who perceives the latter scene, and has 'foresuffered' everything enacted on the divan bed, is as necessary to the poem as Eliot and some of his critics claim seems dubious: he soon fades out. Repeatedly we are reminded that the poem is a succession of scenes with different voices; sometimes the emphasis is such that there can be little doubt that Eliot is heard addressing the reader; at other times (very clearly in the Eugenides invitation) the identity of the individual indicated by the use of the first person remains obscure. The introduction of 'me' in such a passage illustrates Eliot's problem. No person – and he may have considered Gerontion in this role – could have witnessed all the scenes, especially as they developed in the original scripts; but they could all have been cogently described, narrated, dramatized, or imagined, as if by the poet himself. As he was the only begetter of them, it seems an unconvincing ingenuity (an idea possibly which occurred late as the solution of an artistic dilemma) to claim that Tiresias, an aged man with withered dugs, fated to live as man and woman, to become endowed with prophetic vision, and to live to a great age, is the 'most important personage' in the poem, because what he *sees* is its 'substance', the men all merging into one, the women being all one woman, and both sexes meeting in him. *The Waste Land* has a considerable degree of universality, but it contains much that is restricted in significance to the post-war period of 1919–21; in relation to this the Theban prophet, who could have been made redundant by appropriate artistic measures, is a fantastic incongruity.

The synecdochic use of eyes and back for 'office workers', which sharply undercuts the romance of the 'violet hour' (in a Sapphic glimpse of a civilization close to nature), creates a generalized depersonalization, almost a reflex action, which is not finally eliminated until the bored typist, relieved like the workers that business is over, smoothes her hair mechanically, and resorts to mechanically played music. The antithetical recall of Goldsmith's 'When lovely woman stoops to folly' stresses her shamelessness. Here follows one of those rapid metamorphoses which prove the inadequacy of describing Eliot's technique in terms of collage, or even kaleidoscopic, effects. In *The Tempest* Ferdinand's recollection of the music which crept by him upon the waters, as he mused upon 'the King my father's wreck', is followed by a resumption of Ariel's song, with its sea-change into 'something rich and strange'. It is precisely what happens at this point of *The Waste Land*. We have a sudden ebb and flow, a sea-change from the gramophone music to the 'fishmen' significance of a mandoline pleasingly played outside a public house in Lower Thames Street. From the sordid we are translated into magnificence, the bar melting into the church of St Magnus Martyr, with its 'Inexplicable splendour of Ionian white and gold'. This turning-point at the centre of the poem releases hope, but the element of uncertainty – the mandoline is heard occasionally – is solemnized in an appeal to the city which is a reminder of the lament of Jesus over Jerusalem, with its reference to the desolation which follows the rejection of prophets or the word of God (Matthew, xxiii.37–9 or Luke, xiii.34–5).

A contraction in the verse announces a change of scene, the unpleasant face of the Thames sweating with oil and tar. Images evocative of the soulless commercialism of Conrad's *Heart of Darkness* are part of a drift motif which, by its inclusion of the Isle of Dogs, almost certainly connotes the first sense of the canine symbolism in 'Marina'. The 'Weialala leia Wallala leialala' refrain is the motif of Wagner's Rhine-daughters, who lament the loss of the river's beauty when the Rhine-gold is stolen. The deterioration of the Thames is given additional emphasis by the contrast drawn between historic Greenwich with its royal palace and Elizabethan splendour, and the Thames-daughters with their unpleasant associations. The beating oars of the former scene combine with a brisk swell (as opposed to twentieth-century drift), pealing bells, and white towers, all indicative of purposeful religious life. (Eliot's note on the Elizabeth–Leicester source introduces some nonsense on the subject of Spanish intrigue, which unfortunately is often misconstrued with reference to the poem at this point.) In a surprising graduation from the factually sordid to the disconsolately prophetic, the lament of the Thames-daughters takes us downstream from Richmond to Moorgate and on to Margate, north of which the sullied waters mix with the sea. The trams and dusty trees associated with the first daughter indicate the mechanical and soiled, with implications like those for the typist, sexual willingness being expressed merely in the raising of knees; she is indifferent, passive, and supine. 'Highbury bore me. Richmond and Kew undid me' echoes Dante (*Purgatorio*, v.134). The second of the trio is almost neutral between self-centred contrition and acceptance. The third seems to assume the voice of Eliot, as if on Margate sands *he* could connect 'Nothing with nothing', which is almost a repetition of the vacuity expressed by the wind in 'A Game of Chess'. The 'broken fingernails of dirty hands' resurrects an image which he included in his early poem 'Interlude: in a Bar', where it symbolizes soiled and damaged lives.[34] Finally the voice recalls that of an Old Testament prophet, speaking for God, as in Micah, vi.3: 'O my people, what have I done unto thee?'

'The Fire Sermon' concludes with references to Saint Augustine and Buddha. In his *Confessions*, at the opening of book III, Augustine recalls his youthful lust in Carthage; in book x he examines the snares of the senses, and writes on the lust of the eyes: 'Thou pluckest me out, O Lord, Thou pluckest me out; *because Thy loving-kindness is before my eyes*. For I am taken miserably, and Thou pluckest me out mercifully.' This section on the spiritual dangers of sensuous allurements is closely connected with the Fire Sermon in which Buddha urges his disciples to pursue the ascetic life, eschewing the pleasures of all the senses, which burn with appetite. Hatred of life 'is an important phase – even, if you like, a mystical experience – in life itself', Eliot wrote in his essay on Tourneur.

*   *   *

Eliot's note on the Phoenician sailor is not entirely helpful, though the non-inviduation of the latter, coupled with the address to the reader, lends something to the universality of the

poem; it is difficult to see how he can be associated with
Ferdinand of Naples, since the source reference to the recurrent
sea-change motif which is heard in *The Waste Land* is to
Ferdinand's father. The submarine current which whisperingly
denudes his bones of their sinful flesh connotes an early process
of spiritual rebirth, 'whispers' being a metaphor for mystical
communion with God or intimations of the Divine. The
imagery of the stages indicates a return to the state of childhood,
and seems to imply, in conjunction with the ending of 'Dans le
Restaurant', that the seed which flowered at the opening of
'Burnt Norton' had long been sown: to enter the kingdom of
heaven one must be as a little child (Luke, xviii.17); a man
cannot see that kingdom unless he is born again, and 'born of
water and of the Spirit' (John, iii.3,5).

Eliot may have been influenced in making a Phoenician
sailor the subject of drowning at sea by the knowledge (to
which Jessie Weston refers in *From Ritual to Romance*, xii) that
the spreading of the idea of the resurrection or spiritual rebirth
which was common to Mithraism and Christianity was due to
Syrian merchants, who were 'as ardently religious as practically
business-like', and travelled widely through the Roman Empire;
if so, the commercialism of dried grapes c.i.f., as opposed to the
true vine of Christ, accentuates the wordliness of the one-eyed
merchant before the process of redemption. The name 'Phlebas'
was suggested by *Philebus*, Plato's dialogue on pleasure, Eliot
supplying a clue in his allusion to Socrates' comment on one
type of the self-ignorant (48e): people 'who think themselves
taller and more handsome and physically finer' than they really
are.

The whirlpool may have come from a conflation of images:
the whirling round of Ulysses' ship, before it sank in a perilous
passage, with Mount Purgatory dimly visible in the distance
(*Inferno*, xxvi), and Baudelaire's wish at the end of 'Le Voyage'
to leave the oasis of ennui, embark on the sea of darkness, and
plunge 'au fond du gouffre' in order to find a *new* life. Our will
is tranquillized by the strength of love, and blessedness depends
on submission to God's will: 'His will is our peace; it is that sea
to which all things move', Dante writes (*Paradiso*, iii.70–87). We
are reminded too of the sea 'to which all things move' in the
Ezekiel passage on the river of life which is healed when its
waters enter the sea. 'The true mystic – the person with a

genius for God – steers a compass course across the "vast and strong sea of the divine"', Evelyn Underhill observes in *Mysticism*, a book on which Eliot made copious notes. Submitting to God's will is implied in sailing to windward, which the sailors of the original 'Death by Water' could not do in their faulty ship. In this, as in *The Waste Land*, the attached Phlebas passage concludes with a patent appeal to readers. It does not say that we can all control our courses; the address is to those who take charge of the wheel and look windward. (The wind brings life to picked or dry bones, as in Ezekiel and *Ash-Wednesday*.) They are asked to consider Phlebas, who was once like them. If Mr Kurtz can at the very last see the horror of his ways, and hope can be entertained for Sweeney ('Fragment of an Agon'), even one who is identified with the Smyrna merchant of the Metropole weekend can repent. Eliot believed that a sense of damnation offers a better hope of salvation than Dante thought possible for the spiritless who achieved nothing, good or evil (*Inferno*, iii.34–51).

*   *   *

'What the Thunder said' gives a more Christian emphasis to Eliot's subject, both in the opening lines, which image scenes leading up to the Crucifixion, and in the fourth paragraph, which hints at the sudden appearance of Jesus, after his resurrection, to two of his disciples on the road to Emmaus. The setting is desert, as in 'So through the evening'; as the Christian faith declines, so does the spiritual life of the individual and the community: 'He who was living is now dead We who were living are now dying.' Eliot reveals further overtones in the vision on the road, these lines being prompted by an account in Sir Ernest Shackleton's *South* (1919) of an Antarctic expedition in which 'the party of explorers, at the extremity of their strength, had the constant delusion that there was *one more member* than could actually be counted'. Christ may be thought a delusion in the modern world, but man is sometimes made conscious of something beyond the world of the senses and science.

Drought, rock, and sand characterize the scenery the road follows, with memorable images of a dead mouth among the mountains, showing 'carious teeth that cannot spit', of 'dry sterile thunder', and of 'red sullen faces' sneering and snarling at the doors of cracked mud houses. This rising strain of surrealist impressions drops gently into the limpid, slow lyricism of yearning, which quickens in lengthening lines at the thought of the sound of nothing but flowing water, with no cicada (a flashback to the cricket that gives no relief, almost at the start of the poem) or wind in dry grass, only the sound of water dripping over a rock and accompanied by the song of the hermit-thrush in the pine trees. This birdsong recalls Walt Whitman's 'When Lilacs Last in the Dooryard Bloom'd'; the poet shows an admirable command of mimetic effects, as delicate as they are simple, in creating a sense of a trickle which reaches sustained increase. The vision of the third person on the road is followed by a surrealistic intensification: first, of maternal lamentation high in the air, as hooded hordes are discerned swarming over extensive plains, or observed, on closer view, stumbling in cracks in a vast expanse ringed by the flat horizon. Eliot's note draws attention to the effect of the Communist revolution in Russia, with half of eastern Europe on the way to chaos, driven drunkenly in spiritual delusion to the edge of the abyss. The image of a city disintegrating over the mountains is a reminder of the fall of great metropolitan civilizations, and the list extends to the unreal city London. Then follows the colourful vision of 'So through the evening', except that baby-faced bats (darkness-loving creatures) crawl down a blackened wall to present the vision of inverted towers from which 'reminiscent' bells are heard. The voices from empty wells and cisterns take their meaning from Jeremiah (ii.13): 'For my people have committed two evils; they have forsaken me the fountain of living waters, and hewed them out cisterns, broken cisterns, that can hold no water.' This impression of dead or overthrown religion is confirmed when the Chapel Perilous is reached in a 'decayed hole' among the mountains, an empty windowless ruin with a swinging door; it houses only the wind, which can be heard singing in the dry grass over the 'tumbled graves'. There is hope for dry bones, as *Ash-Wednesday* will show; hope too is announced by the crowing cock, as lightning flashes and a gust brings a scud of rain. The bird's role is ambivalent, however: he proclaims the dawn, which traditionally dispelled evil spirits (*Hamlet*, I. i. 147–64);

equally important, at least, in this context is the cock-crowing which connotes the denial of Christ (Matthew, xxvi.69–75).

Though the critical significance of the poem applies to western civilization, the change of scene at this point to the Ganges and Himalayas, and the adoption of the thunder-message from one of the *Upanishads*, contribute, like the pairing of Buddha with Saint Augustine at the end of 'The Fire Sermon', to the enhancement of the poem's universality, in the sense that the radical problems of living the good life are basically the same wherever we are, and the wisdom of experience is vital for all of us, whatever its source. The Da-Da-Da of the thunder (and here Eliot had the benefit of his Sanskrit tutor at Harvard) is interpreted 'Damyata, Datta, Dayadhvam': 'Control yourselves; give; be compassionate.' Changing the order, to end with the most important of these three commands, Eliot begins with 'Give', in the sense of 'self-surrender' or the scriptural 'he that loses his life shall find it'. In a society governed by money and self-interest, self-surrender or living for the sake of others becomes rarer in the life of the individual; yet only by giving ourselves do we live, Eliot asserts, adding sardonically that such charity is not measurable in terms that will be found when last wills and testaments are opened in the rooms of the dead; he is less convincing when he speaks of obituaries. In translating 'Dayadhvam' as 'sympathise', he does not shift his hortatory viewpoint a great deal, but the basis of his thought has changed. It is philosophical; our self-centredness ('each in his prison') is confirmed by F. H. Bradley: experience is limited to each one's circle, 'a circle closed on the outside'; 'the whole world for each is peculiar and private to that soul'. The sound of the key in the lock recalls the cruel imprisonment and death of Ugolino and his children in 'the horrible tower' (*Inferno*, xxxiii). Loss of individuality through the accelerating process of organizing society in larger entities may or may not have been in the poet's mind, but the isolation of the individual diminishes his powers; any belief he holds in the greater possibilities of life is short-lived. Here Eliot's Coriolanian image derives from Arnold's 'Isolation': 'in the sea of life enisl'd . . . We mortal millions live *alone*'; in spring, on moonlit nights, when nightingales are heard, a longing like despair reaches the innermost caverns of these islands, which feel they were once 'Parts of a single continent';

> Who order'd, that their longing's fire
> Should be, as soon as kindled, cool'd?
> Who renders vain their deep desire? –
> A God, a God their severance rul'd;
> And bade betwixt their shores to be
> The unplumb'd, salt, estranging sea.

Eliot could not accept such inevitability; the key to right living is self-control, and he presents it in nautical terms, emphasizing the joy that self-control brings, true happiness or serenity depending on submission to God's will; the calmness of the sea is inseparable from the Dantean thought 'His will is our peace'. It is comparable to Wordsworth's in 'Ode to Duty':

> Flowers laugh before thee on their beds
> And fragrance in thy footing treads;
> Thou dost preserve the stars from wrong;
> And the most ancient heavens, through Thee,
>   are fresh and strong.

Whether the fifth part is the best of *The Waste Land*, as Eliot thought, is arguable; some will not be able to give poetical assent to its didacticism; some may wonder whether its didacticism is adequate. Some may justifiably object against the obscurity of its conclusion. The concentration of quotations, given or echoed, equals that of the more homogeneous collection which forms the epigraph of 'Burbank with a Baedeker: Bleistein with a Cigar'. The question whether he should put his lands in order is addressed almost as much to the reader as to the Fisher-King poet himself. The nursery rhyme on London Bridge suggests for the second time the decline of western civilization. It is followed by a reminder of the purgatorial fire which cleanses but does not consume, and is gladly accepted by the repentant Arnaut Daniel. 'Quando fiam uti chelidon' ('When shall I be like the swallow?') occurs at the end of the 'Pervigilium Veneris', which has for its Latin refrain 'Tomorrow shall love be for the loveless', and concludes with a reference to the barbarious king Tereus; the words which introduce Eliot's quotation, 'quando ver venit meum?' raise the general question of spiritual rebirth. 'O swallow swallow' is related, for Procne, wife of Tereus, was changed, like her wronged sister Philomela, into a bird, Philomela into a nightingale, Procne into a swallow; though an echo of the opening of Tennyson's lyric (*The Princess*, iv.75ff), it has no literary overtones, and simply reiterates the yearning for a new life. Like the Prince of Aquitaine in Gérard de Nerval's sonnet 'El Desdichado' ('The Disinherited'), the poet feels sadly deprived of the light of heaven:

> Ma seule étoile est morte, – et mon luth constellé
> Porte le Soleil noir de la Mélancolie.

The Waste Land is no more than fragments shored up against his ruined tower (there may be a reference to the tower struck by lightning in the Tarot pack, but, if so, it is strange that Eliot gives no hint of it). The quotation from *The Spanish Tragedy* by the Elizabethan dramatist Thomas Kyd expresses Hieronymo's agreement ('Why then Ile fit you') to present the entertainment which he uses to wreak revenge for the murder of his son; in this each actor is to play his part in a different tongue, in Latin, Greek, Italian, or French, for example. 'Why then Ile fit you' is Eliot's apology for his fragmentary poem: Hieronymo continues,

> When I was young, I gave my mind
> And plied myself to fruitless poetry:
> Which though it profit the professor naught,
> Yet it is passing pleasing to the world.

'Hieronymo's mad againe' (the sub-title of Kyd's play) is an apology for over-allusiveness in different tongues. The 'Shantih shantih shantih' ending from the *Upanishads* serves as a blessing; Eliot's note implies no less than the traditional Church benediction, 'The peace of God, which passeth all understanding, keep your hearts and minds in the knowledge and love of God . . .'.

*   *   *

Impatient readers who enjoy the shock of realism in Eliot, as he enjoyed it in Joyce's *Ulysses*, may be resentful of the steady Christian undercurrent by which his evaluations are made; it is seen emerging more frequently as he progresses. His early verse is often the product of a tortured Christian conscience; increasing religious assurance acts like a light which accentuates the darkness of the objects behind which, for the most part, it is concealed. The more clearly one follows his poetry, the more consistent it will be found from beginning to end, from 'Preludes' to *Four Quartets*. The subject of the earlier poetry is primarily the world; in the later poetry, from Ariel poems and *Ash-Wednesday* onwards, the religious search, almost a complete turning away from the world, the flesh, and the devil, is his continuing subject. The certainty of faith by which the western world is measured and found wanting in *The Waste Land* is conveyed in pervasive symbolism, such as fog, wind, light and darkness, infertility, rock and water, emptiness or vacancy; above all, in striking collocations, as when a change of music brings 'fishmen' and the splendour of the church of St Magnus Martyr into sudden apposition with the automatic typist. Nowhere is this technique more gloriously or devastatingly successful than in the conjunction via Verlaine of the ending of Wagner's *Parsifal* with the world of Sweeney, Mrs Porter, and her daughter. To know Eliot's background implications is not the supreme task for the reader, but, the more they are known, the more astonishingly abundant his art will be revealed. The creativity of its imagery, allusions, and references, opens up a world which, for all its wide-ranging multiplicity, is closely integrated.

To describe *The Waste Land* as insignificant and splenetic, a rhythmical grouse against life, as Eliot did,[35] is a euphemistic understatement in the extreme, an evasive rather than a modest dismissal. He is much nearer the mark in 'Virgil and the Christian World' (1951) in stating that a poet may believe he speaks only for himself when he in fact expresses the secret feelings of his readers and of a whole generation. A prophet, he adds, does not need to know how much his utterances signify.

His notes on *The Waste Land* belong to two categories, the first of which supplies references for his quotations. In his essay 'The Frontiers of Criticism' he says that this is all he intended in the first place, 'with a view to spiking the guns of critics of my earlier poems who had accused me of plagiarism'. The poem first appeared without reference, in *The Dial* and *The Criterion*. Then, when it was to be issued as a slim book, and was found to be 'inconveniently short', the notes were expanded to fill more pages with printed matter at the publisher's request.

Eliot told Arnold Bennett in September 1924[36] that the notes were to be taken seriously; in 1956 he stated that the extension had resulted in a 'remarkable exposition of bogus scholarship'. Padding takes the form of redundant internal references and of irrelevant expansion. Eliot refers the reader from one 'Jug jug' passage to another, and from the rats and bones of part II to the rats and bones of part III. He obviously had difficulty in filling the vacant pages, and did not hesitate to quote Ovid (*Metamorphoses*, iii) at length on Tiresias. (When Jupiter and Juno disagree on which sex derives greater pleasure from love, the question is referred to Tiresias, who has been made to experience love as both man and woman, after striking two snakes when·they were copulating. He agrees with Jupiter that women get more pleasure from love than men do, and Juno indignantly makes him blind; Jupiter then compensates him with the gift of prophetic vision.) 'The whole passage . . . is of great anthropological interest', Eliot writes tongue-in-cheek. A pedantic and somewhat pretentious note on the hermit-thrush must have been composed in a similar mood, one feels; it begins, 'This is *Turdus aonalaschkae pallasii*, the hermit-thrush which I have heard in Quebec Province. Chapman says. . . .'; it ends, 'Its "water-dripping song" is justly celebrated.' The lack of explicit reference, especially in the second note on Saint Augustine's *Confessions*, suggests that Eliot was not over-conscientious, and took just what came to hand. The conclusion of the same note exemplifies either a fit of padding pomposity or, as one likes to think, a superb piece of poker-faced mischief. Years later, in 'The Frontiers of Criticism', he concluded that his example had done no harm to other poets; he could think of no good contemporary poet who had 'abused this same practice'. Unfortunately he had 'stimulated the wrong kind of interest among the seekers of sources'. He was justified in acknowledging his indebtedness to Jessie Weston, but regretted sending 'so many enquirers off on a wild goose chase after Tarot cards and the Holy Grail'.

13

Critical Essays

i CHIEFLY *THE SACRED WOOD*

Eliot's criticism was stimulated by some of the course-work he did for evening classes in London, even more by studious application in the continual reviewing of books from 1916 to 1919. The first of his collected essays, 'Reflections on *Vers Libre*', appeared in *The New Statesman* of 3 March 1917. In it he states categorically that *vers libre* does not exist, and ridicules the notion that there is such a school of poetry. This kind of claim arises when society is 'sluggish', when tradition lapses, novelty is in demand, and theorizers attempt to make much of little art. After identifying *vers libre* with Imagism, he considers its form with reference to pattern, rhyme, and metre, devoting most attention to the latter. He does not consider rhythm, but remains at a rather elementary prosodic level,[37] and reaches the obvious conclusion that vitality in verse is incompatible with metrical monotony. He is all for making the most of rhymeless verse, because rhyme-addiction has 'thickened the modern ear'. His views on the use of rhyme illuminate his own practice: verse without rhyme imposes greater demands than rhymed verse; used only when necessary, 'for a sudden tightening-up, for a cumulative insistence, or for an abrupt change of mood', rhyme will be much more effective than when it supports weak verse. The life of verse depends on metrical liberties, which are not found in Swinburne; as soon as one is accustomed to his metres, there is nothing surprising in his movement, none of the inexplicable wonder of music beyond the reach of alternative words. Eliot's interest in early seventeenth-century drama is prominent: Tourneur and Shirley wrote a more regular verse than either Middleton or Webster, who was more technically adept in some respects than Shakespeare. Some semblance of metre is necessary in poetry, and Edgar Lee Masters, whose *Songs and Satires* Eliot had reviewed five months earlier, would have done better had he given his prose material a more regular verse form, as Crabbe had done with his. One striking feature in the essay is the assertion that the advantage of rhymeless verse lies in the poet's being required to reach the standards of prose. The conclusion is memorably absolute: there is no division between traditional verse and *vers libre*; 'there is only good verse, bad verse, and chaos'.

'Ezra Pound: His Metric and Poetry' was published anonymously as a pamphlet in New York late in 1917, after being corrected and revised by Pound; Eliot preferred anonymity because at the time he was relatively unknown. A compilation rather than an essay, it traces Pound's first ten years as a poet, with copious quotations from the poems and the reviews. Pound's mastery of *vers libre* arose from expertise in handling regular forms and a variety of metres; he never chooses words for the sake of the 'tinkle'. Eliot's prejudice against Swinburne extends to Shelley: such is the importance Pound attaches to every word in contributing effectively to rhythm and sense that he could not write like Shelley, 'leaving blanks for the adjectives', or like Swinburne, 'whose adjectives are practically blanks'. Pound's music is very different from that of these two poets, for music in verse (on which Pound quotes Pater's dictum with approval) does not require that poetry should be meaningless. Eliot's admiration of the definition and concreteness of Pound, as opposed to the 'resonant abstractions' of Swinburne or the 'mossiness' of Mallarmé, reflects his own poetic predilections. He refers to Tennyson with deliberate scorn: people who know Malory will perhaps realize that the *Idylls of the King* are 'hardly more important than a parody, or a "Chaucer retold for Children"'. Many years were to pass before Eliot recognised seriously that his youthful posturings resulted as much from ignorance as from the heady uplift of one of those inevitably recurrent waves of anti-Establishment modernity.

The tenor of Eliot's 1920 introduction to *The Sacred Wood* suggests that he saw himself, at a time when criticism lacked direction, as Arnold's heir to the guardianship of the golden bough in the sacred wood of tradition, particularly with respect to poetry. Were Arnold alive, he would have to do all his work again; the critic's duty is to preserve tradition, and judge how far the creativity of writers is animated by critical intelligence alert to the best that is known and thought. Unfortunately Arnold allowed his critical interest to be turned to extra-literary affairs, in the attempt to raise his country's standards. It would have been astonishing if he had turned to the novel, compared Thackeray with Flaubert, shown why George Eliot was more serious than Dickens, and Stendhal more serious than either. Criticism can be performed by minds of a second, not second-rate, order, but they are hard to find; they need to stimulate ideas, their business being to see the best work of their age and that of the past in true perspective. Creative writers (those of the first order) will, like the poet of the age of Pindar or of Shakespeare, benefit from working in 'a current of ideas', as Arnold urged. To emphasize his point, Eliot refers to Johnson's commendation of those metaphysical poets who succeeded because they realized the supreme necessity of reading and originality of thought over spontaneity, imitation, and volubility.

The critical work of Rémy de Gourmont, recommended by Pound, was especially formative when Eliot wrote the 1919–20 essays which comprise *The Sacred Wood*; he is the exemplar of 'The Perfect Critic'. Creative critics, impressionists such as Symons who are contented with their own emotional responses, can never satisfy, Eliot maintains; we may find that we disagree with their impressions. Swinburne, who could express his feelings in his poetry, is much more reliable; his reaction as a reader is more detached, more subject to critical analysis. The wholeness of critical response, emotional and intellectual, depends upon perception, which it is the critic's task to elucidate, in order that his reader can form his own judgment; the essays of Eliot's later years show that his respect for the reader's final judgment never changed. Technical critics such as Campion have limited aims; Dryden is more disinterested but still hampered by legislative tradition; Coleridge, who had more ability than any other modern critic, allows his critical intelligence to become subordinate to his metaphysical interests. The enjoyment of poetry is not complete until a state of pure contemplation which transcends all personal emotion or interests is reached; and the true critic is one who has the Aristotelian ability not only to see the object as it really is (Arnold's desideratum) but to analyse perception 'to the point of principle and definition'. For this one needs Rémy de Gourmont's assets: high sensibility, a historical sense, and the power to generalize or organize responses. Criticism is a statement of this kind of structure; it is also 'a development of sensibility', and, as sensibility is rare, the critic and creative writer are frequently one.

At the opening of 'Imperfect Critics' Eliot turns to critics of the 'Tudor–Stuart' dramatists he had examined as poet–critic. Among them he finds Swinburne unequalled, despite the tumultuousness of his style, his enthusiasm being matched by his undiverted attention to the literature. Unfortunately he does not go far enough; he is an appreciator rather than a critic. Had Swinburne been able to concentrate further and distinguish the finer differences and resemblances between poets, he would have seen Chapman's likeness to Donne, in sharing a gift for sensuous thought which was characteristic of so much drama of their period but hardly apparent in nineteenth-century poetry. Eliot uses Swinburne's critical relevance to snipe at Pater, A. C. Bradley, and Swinburne's editor.

In choosing to include George Wyndham and Charles Whibley as types of imperfect critics, Eliot seems to be paying respect to Whibley, Wyndham's editor. Wyndham's essays show the same zestful romanticism which characterized his political and country life. His scholarship, chivalrous outlook, and imperialist sympathies may qualify him to write well on North's Plutarch, but he lacked critical depth and proportion. Nor did he understand Elizabethan rhetoric, the appreciation of which in Elizabethan drama was just as essential as the appreciation of sentiment in Victorian literature and Wyndham. In his assertion that there is no place for romanticism in literature, and that the arts demand that a man shall concentrate exclusively on art, Eliot is not thinking of art for art's sake but of the need for objectivity in criticism.

Charles Whibley lacks critical insight but conveys the taste for the best literature of a period, and this is no mean achievement in 'a country destitute of living criticism', where few talk intelligently about Stendhal, Flaubert, or Henry James. He does not exercise either of the critic's tools, comparison and analysis; otherwise he would see that Surrey anticipates some of Tennyson's best qualities. The important critic will wish to bring 'the forces of the past' to bear on the problems of the contemporary artist. Eliot's memoir on his friend Whibley (1931) appears in *Selected Essays*, and in it he follows the method which is often typical of himself but not of Whibley: 'he did not, as I and most people do, have to think up half a dozen subjects to talk about and then shuffle them into the most suitable order'; the transitions suggested themselves. The subjects suggested by Whibley's works include Eliot's ideas of 'journalism' in literature, 'conversational' style in writing, invective, the need for writers to converse a great deal, and the importance for critics of choosing only those subjects which interest them. Eliot is drawn to Whibley by the latter's love of authors, such as Rabelais and Petronius, who have a touch of the gentleman and the ragamuffin in them. He has interesting comments on Wyndham Lewis, Henry James's later style (the way he dictated to his secretary), free speech (which includes talking freely on sex, its irregularities and perversions, but rarely risks *plain speaking*), and 'dusty noble statues' in the hall of literary fame. Whibley did not worship 'mummified reputations'; he could distinguish the living from the dead, even in authors to whom he was not partial.

Eliot continues 'Imperfect Critics' with thoughts on two American critics and one French. Paul Elmer More and Irving Babbitt, though closer to the European tradition than English critics since Arnold, are excluded from it by transatlantic shortcomings. More is a moralist rather than a critic, but Babbitt's weaknesses are left obscure, Eliot being ready to challenge and take up the cudgels later. His critical judgment is at stake when he writes of the conspicuous absence of seriousness in *In Memoriam* or the seriousness which directs 'Amos Barton' but not *The Mill on the Floss* (how wrong he could be may be seen in *The Egoist* of April 1918: 'George Eliot who could write *Amos Barton* and steadily degenerate'). Julien Benda is selected to represent French intelligence. He is not his generation's 'critical consciousness', like Rémy de Gourmont, rather the 'ideal scavenger' of contemporary rubbish. His analysis of decadence in artistic taste could apply to London; the only person who has performed such a role in England, Eliot states, is Arnold (though Wordsworth protested loudly in his preface to *Lyrical Ballads*). The difference is that Benda writes in a society alive with ideas, and therefore his analysis of the second-rate facilitates the task of the creative writer. There is no one in England to kill the reputation of the Charles-Louis Philippes; George Meredith is still considered a master of prose, 'or even a profound philosopher'. Eliot saw himself as a slayer of reputations; no doubt the time had come for radical reassessments, but he was over-reaching himself, and he had yet to learn the wisdom of confining his criticism to authors he had mastered.

Readers who turned to *The Sacred Wood* for enlightening practical criticism were generally disappointed; the stir it created in the older generation arose from its challenge to traditional insular literary values; students were preoccupied with its critical theory, particularly in 'Tradition and the Invididual Talent', which reflects a Babbitt-inspired disapproval of individualistic writers who express their own limited feelings, or romantically assume that they have the imaginative or philosophical key to the universe. The question is examined with reference first to tradition, then to the process of poetic creation. For Eliot the tradition is European, as it was for Matthew Arnold in his campaign against British provincialism. The tendency in criticism is to look for the peculiar characteristics of an author, though it often happens that the best of his work, where in fact he is most individual, derives from tradition; there 'the dead poets, his ancestors, assert their immortality most vigorously'. Eliot speaks for his own poetry, and asserts that this historical sense is indispensable to anyone who wishes to remain a poet after the age of twenty-five (the writer's resources being otherwise too small). He states his case in absolute terms: the historical sense 'compels a man to write not merely with his own generation in his bones, but with a feeling that the whole of the literature of Europe from Homer and within it the whole of the literature of his own country has a simultaneous existence and composes a simultaneous order'. This assumes the impossible, for writers are continually forgotten or resurrected, and any author's knowledge of the past is limited; few poets can be expected to be as familiar with the European tradition as Pound in the years covered by Eliot's introductory pamphlet. Eliot's exaggeration proceeds from abstract or ideal euphoria: 'what happens when a work of new art is created is something that happens simultaneously to all the works of art which preceded it'; the mind of Europe or of the poet's own country is a mind which changes without ever abandoning anything *en route*.

He describes the artistic process as an act of depersonalization which is almost scientific, illustrating it by reference to a catalytic experiment. The progress of an artist is 'a continual extinction of personality', and a poet's maturity depends on the degree to which his mind is perfected as a medium for the fusion of varied feelings into new wholes. It is the intensity of the process that counts; 'the more perfect the artist, the more completely separate in him will be the man who suffers and the mind which creates'. Wordsworth had such a distinction in mind when he wrote on 'emotion recollected in tranquillity', though his general formula is inexact, as Eliot notes, even though poetry can be based on the recollection of an emotional experience. For the impersonal theory of poetry Eliot's chief model was undoubtedly Dante, from whom he draws illustrations, differentiating between the *emotion* of a situation and the *feelings* of the poet in communicating it.[38] How the latter are inherent in words and images is illustrated with reference first to a dramatic passage, where the 'floating feelings' which are awakened in the poet by his subject combine with the 'structural emotion' of the latter in generating a new emotion which is aesthetic; secondly, to the Brunetto Latini episode (*Inferno*, xv), which indicates that great poetry can be written without any originating emotion. In concluding that poetry is an escape from emotion, Eliot opposes the 'turning loose of emotion'; he rightly insists that the artist can create poetry from emotions he has never experienced as successfully as from those with which he is familiar (reflection on Wordsworth's sonnet 'Why art thou silent!' and its origin will confirm that Eliot is not overstating his claim). So we are brought to the world of the imagination. Much in this essay needed to be said, and has never been better said. For effect, it sometimes carries the argument to the extreme. The imaginative selection of a poet, in accordance with his 'feelings', depends very considerably on his personality, inherited and developed. A great poet, however cool and deliberate his poetic processes, transmits a unique personality.

The essay on Blake illustrates what happens to genius when it turns inward, away from tradition. In enunciating the sheer honesty of Blake's vision, the kind of honesty which is always accompanied by technical skill, Eliot seems unable to disengage himself from the task of the poet *vis-à-vis* his own sick epoch. Blake's early expression of genius reflects his innocence, his escape from the amassing of knowledge, usually regarded as education, which is apt to impose conformity or 'parasitic opinion' (as it did on Tennyson, Eliot hastens to add, without having given the question full consideration). Blake assimilated much from Elizabethan poetry and from eighteenth-century verse which had been subject to 'the discipline of prose'. Had he remained a traditional poet, we should have been spared the cranky individualism of thought which often affects a writer outside the Latin traditions, and led to the formlessness of his prophetic books. Unlike Dante, a classic with the 'gift of form which knows how to borrow', Blake remains 'only a poet of genius'.

Eliot's indebtedness to Rémy de Gourmont on the subject of self-education, and his extremism in expressing the theory of impersonality in art, are clear from passages he quotes approvingly in 'Philip Massinger'. Man's aim, Rémy wrote, is 'de nettoyer sa personnalité, de la laver de toutes les souillures qu'y déposa l'éducation'; Flaubert 'incorporait toute sa sensibilité à ses oeuvres. . . . Hors ses livres, où il se transvasait goutte à goutte, jusqu'à la lie, Flaubert est fort peu intéressant.' In a later essay (1932), on the dramatist John Ford, Eliot states that one could write many fine poetic passages or poems and yet not be a great poet, unless they were felt to be unified by 'one significant, consistent, and developing personality'. He returns to the subject in his 1940 lecture on Yeats, his most important statement being that on impersonality which is derived from intensely personal experience, but transcends it to create general (not universal) truth or symbol (recognisable, that is, to those of the same traditions).

If Eliot used the term 'objective correlative'[39] with some ambiguity in 'Hamlet' ('Hamlet and His Problems'), its use by critics and students has made it more obscure or nugatory. There is no reason why it should be applied to an image which comprehends or symbolizes an idea or 'feeling' integral, but incidental, to the resolution of a poem as a whole. Eliot applies it to 'a set of objects, a situation, a chain of events', the question being whether such circumstances validate Hamlet's emotions. Shakespeare, recasting an old play, failed to find an 'objective correlative' because something in his experience, or something he had read in Montaigne,[40] occasioned a disgust which makes Hamlet's emotions disproportionate to his circumstances. It is unfortunate that Eliot fails to dissociate 'the mind which creates' from 'the man who suffers' in imaginative fiction: Shakespeare may fail to find his objective correlative, but what has Hamlet to do with any absence of objective equivalent? Such is his state of mind that he thinks he has reason enough for more than he can ever decide to do. The most damaging criticism of the play, Eliot begins, comes from creative critics such as Goethe, who made Hamlet a Werther, and Coleridge, who made him Coleridge; it was fortunate, he adds, that Pater did not turn his attention to the play.

Like a number of essays in *The Sacred Wood*, Eliot's study of Marlowe's blank verse (written during the period when he was working on 'Gerontion') suggests a poet–critic who reads with an eye to the writing of successful verse plays. His greatest weakness is a tendency to make comparisons by brief quotations regardless of whether or not they were written for drama. He ignores Wordsworth's 'Michael' when he claims that after 'the Chinese Wall of Milton' (where he follows Ezra Pound's prejudice) blank verse suffered retrogression; and his inclination is for Kyd rather than for Tennyson, the quotation from whose 'Dora' is by no means representative. His condemnation of Shakespeare's 'tortured perverse ingenuity of images' shows a classical approach which aligns him with traditional French critics, with Dryden also and Arnold. He makes much of Marlowe's evident borrowings from Spenser, and stresses the obvious when he states that the 'torrential imagination' of this poet resulted in his working within sentence continuities rather than in customary end-stopped lines. He is most interesting when he illustrates a trend in Marlowe's verse towards a serious Jonsonian style which borders on caricature.

An exercise in sustained criticism, the essay on Ben Jonson opens with the conclusion that his reputation has been deadened probably because of his neglect by poets, for appreciation has a kinship with creation, and we have to go back as far as Dryden to find a live criticism of his work. Jonson's poetry is 'of the surface'; lacking the evocativeness found in Shakespeare and Marlowe, it does not stir the feelings, and is qualified to reflect 'the lazy reader's fatuity'. In approaching the question of

T. S. Eliot, aged about seven, with his Irish nursemaid Annie Dunne

(left) T. S. Eliot with his father Henry Ware Eliot in 1898
(right) Eliot aged ten, from a portrait by his sister Charlotte

2

(*left*) Eliot's brother Henry Ware Eliot at Harvard, 1902
(*right*) Eliot at the age of twelve

(*above*) View of Gloucester Harbour, towards Boston, from the Eliots' summer-house on Eastern Point, Cape Ann

(*below*) the Dry Salvages, as they appeared in Eliot's day

4

Photographs by Henry Ware Eliot, junior, in 1921:
(*above*) London Bridge, with Christopher Wren's church of St Magnus Martyr in the background
(*below*) Mrs Eliot with Tom and his sister Marian

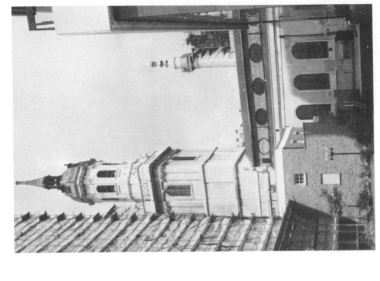

City churches in 1984: (*left*) St Mary Woolnoth   (*right*) St Magnus Martyr

(right) Vivienne Eliot at Garsington Manor, 1921

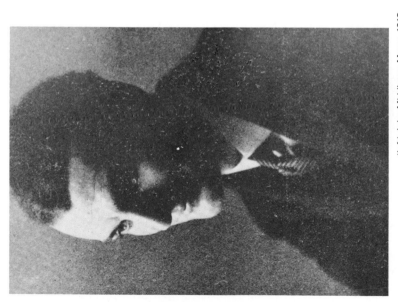

(left) John Middleton Murry, 1918

7

(left) Bertrand Russell by Roger Fry, c. 1923   (right) Wyndham Lewis

(*left*) Ezra Pound in the garden of his Paris studio, 1923
(*right*) T. S. Eliot outside Faber and Gwyer's, 1926

9

(*left*) Vivienne in one of the London flats she shared with Tom

(*right*) 'Uncle Tom's Cabin', where Eliot lived and worked in 1933, after leaving Vivienne

Crowhurst Church, where Eliot worshipped in 1933; its ancient yew illustrates the rebirth-death significance the tree had come to symbolize for Eliot

(*left*) St James's Church, Chipping Campden   (*right*) sunshine and the dry pools, one upper and two lower, at Burnt Norton

12

(*above*) The rose-garden at Burnt Norton   (*below*) the church at Little Gidding

(*above*) Jacob Epstein's bust of T. S. Eliot, 1951   (*below*) Eliot at a rehearsal of *Murder in the Cathedral* in 1951

(*above*) At the University of Sheffield, in May 1959, where Eliot opened the new University Library and received an honorary degree   (*below*) with his wife Valerie on this occasion

(*above*) The church of St Michael at East Coker   (*below*) the memorial plaque to T. S. Eliot in its north-west corner

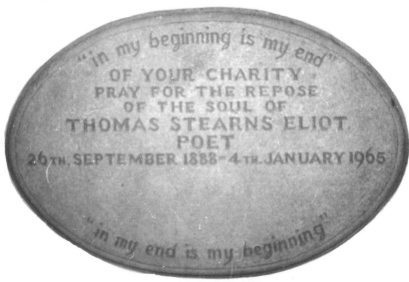

"in my beginning is my end"
OF YOUR CHARITY
PRAY FOR THE REPOSE
OF THE SOUL OF
THOMAS STEARNS ELIOT.
POET
26TH. SEPTEMBER 1888 - 4TH. JANUARY 1965
"in my end is my beginning"

16

'humours', after referring to the indissociability of character and environment in Flaubert's *L'Éducation Sentimentale,* Eliot writes dangerously of characters in drama as outlines to be filled in, and, again, in maintaining that Shakespeare's characters could be transposed to different settings. Not so with Jonson, where the life of the central character is the life of the plot, from which the emotional tone of the drama derives; his 'unity of inspiration . . . radiates into plot and personages alike'. In the works of Shakespeare, Donne, Webster, and Tourneur, words often have 'a network of tentacular roots reaching down to the deepest terrors and desires' (as in 'Gerontion'), whereas the verse of Beaumont and Fletcher is superficial like cut, slightly withered flowers stuck in sand and drawing no sustenance from below (an image suggested by Swinburne, as quoted in 'Swinburne the Critic'). The surface of Jonson is solid, however; he creates his own world, with its own illuminating logic or point of view, simplification of character giving relief to an emotional impulse which for the purpose of satire works like caricature; so the personality of Jonson infuses his work. Eliot claims that his brutal lack of sentiment, his surface polish, bold designs, and continual regard for theatre would have a modern appeal, at the same time blaming the 'flaccid culture' of the twentieth century for preferring 'faded literature to faded shows', and pointing out that *Comus,* which spelt death to the masque, is read for its poetry by hundreds for every ten who read *The Masque of Blacknesse.*

Massinger, not a model to follow, has been lucky with his critics. In his two complementary reviews of A. H. Cruickshank's *Philip Massinger* (1920) Eliot's aim seems to be 'finally and irrefutably' to put him into place. On the subject of literary borrowings he sheds light on his own practice: 'Immature poets imitate; mature poets steal', turning what they take into something better or different. Good poets usually borrow from remote authors; Massinger's borrowings from Shakespeare and other contemporaries show a lack of sensuous thought or imaginativeness, a feeling for words rather than for things. Like Fletcher, he is one of Milton's precursors; had he inherited a nervous system like that of Middleton, Tourneur, Webster, or Ford, his style would have been a triumph; as it is, it suffers from 'cerebral anaemia'. He deals not so much with emotions as with emotional abstractions; when his ladies resist temptation they appear as 'lubricious prudes', unable to support conventional moral standards with genuine feeling. Though inferior to Marlowe and Jonson, he is most successful in comedy. Brilliant technically, he could not create great art out of a defective personality. He is one of those writers who can judge of manners but, just at the time when a new view of life is needed, look at it through their predecessors' eyes.

'"Rhetoric" and Poetic Drama', one of the two more general essays on drama in *The Sacred Wood*, was occasioned by the death of Rostand, author of *Cyrano de Bergerac*, and a practice among critics of labelling bad verse 'rhetoric'. Eliot discusses the imprecisions of the term with reference to Elizabethan drama, finding time circuitously to comment on the 'conversational' in American *vers libre* and inferior types of English 'Wordsworthianism'. Returning to *Cyrano* as an extended illustration of the dramatic awareness which characters have of themselves, he argues that the word 'rhetoric' be used specifically for the kind of speech, good or bad, in which a character regards himself as a dramatic figure. Otherwise the term should apply to any kind of speech inflation which results from the desire to be impressive.

A creative urge inheres in 'The Possibility of a Poetic Drama'. The claim that Elizabethan blank verse was more accomplished than it has been ever since is made more precisely than in the essay on Marlowe. The subsequent loss of the poetic tradition in drama was reinforced by Charles Lamb's 'autopsy' of it, for 'a form is not wholly dead until it is known to be'. In his comments on later blank verse, Eliot is particularly antagonistic to Tennyson, who turned out 'large patterns on a machine'. The non-emergence of contemporary poetic drama is due to the age and its expectations; it is not divorced from the egoism of actors. Unfortunately, too, instead of keeping to the presentation of events (a characteristic of permanent literature, including *L'Éducation Sentimentale*), drama has shown a partiality for philosophy, from Goethe to *Peer Gynt* – vision has precedence in *The Dynasts* – and hybrids such as the Shavian and Maeterlinckian types. The idea of a play should be inherent in its presentation of life, which should be simplified to give greater universality than will be found in Ibsen or Tchehov. Eliot is drawn to the possibility of converting a form of popular entertainment, music-hall in particular, to dramatic art.

He held out more hope for dramatic art from the music-hall than for the rehabilitation of Greek literature from Gilbert Murray's translations. We need capable expository scholars, he maintains, if the classics are to remain an important part of western culture or 'the foundation for the literature we hope to create'; or if it has to be decided whether Aristotle is no longer a moral leader in Europe. Similarly, if Greek poetry is to retain its vitality, educated poets will be required to prevent its 'masquerading as a vulgar debasement of the eminently personal idiom of Swinburne'. After this, one hardly needs to follow Eliot's attempts to justify his pronouncement against 'the most popular Hellenist of his time'. With Arnoldian irony he insinuates many changes for the worse with the advancement of learning; there is, for example, 'a curious Freudian-social-mystical-rationalistic-higher-critical interpretation of the Classics and what used to be called the Scriptures'. Greek is no longer 'the awe-inspiring Belvedere' it was to Winckelmann, Goethe, and Schopenhauer; Pater and Oscar Wilde have produced a rather inferior version. Eliot admits outdated claims for the classics, but puts in a good word for Petronius. Greater exertion is required to assimilate expanding knowledge: we need to digest both Homer and Flaubert; we need a close study of Renaissance humanists and translators such as Pound has begun; and we need the 'creative eye' to ensure that the past lives in the present.

In 'Swinburne as Poet' Eliot endeavours to do general justice to an author for whom he had little sympathy; he is often right, but his analysis is just as often too sweeping. Assuming that human feelings have no place in Swinburne's poetry, and that his language fails because he does not present the object, as Conrad and Joyce do, he concludes that only a genius such as Swinburne could dwell 'so exclusively' in words. With reference to a poet whose Hellenic protest voiced the suppressed feelings of honest Victorians, this critical extremism is quite untenable. There *is* a case for the general epithet in 'the tideless dolorous midland sea', and it is absurd to suggest that the object does not exist, only words, in 'Snowdrops that plead for pardon And pine for fright'. Eliot tells us that the object that was not there disappears, while that of the daffodil in Shakespeare's 'daffodils' that 'take the winds of March with beauty' remains. Shakespeare's daffodils remain because they have been deservedly quoted for ages; Swinburne's snowdrops are relatively unknown. They belong to the same category of poetical genesis but, in accord with the subject, which is sensitively conceived, lack the Shakespearian resonance. The swallow disappears from 'Itylus', Eliot adds; perhaps the image was not there in the first place. If the poem is read with the horrible Procne–Philomela–Itylus legend in mind, it may be seen that Eliot has ignored Swinburne's purpose. Like a conjuror, he waves the wand of quotation, and, hey presto, the case is proved. He does little to evaluate either Swinburne's strength or his weaknesses, and remains superbly vague. Selecting three poems, which any volume of Swinburne should contain (why 'The Leper'?), he states that it ought to contain many more, though there is perhaps none which it would be a mistake to omit.

Eliot's early criticism was the product of enormous literary resources of observation and thought. If he did not make the most of them in 1920, it was because he was too anxious to secure his reputation. In *The Sacred Wood* he is, as he was to remain for several years, most revealing, most exciting, trenchant, and original (mainly on the drama and poetry of the sixteenth and seventeenth centuries) when examining works with a creative eye. He had launched a general strategic offensive with clearsightedness adulterated by prejudice and sometimes by hauteur, placing himself in a number of positions which were hardly tenable; in later years, after establishing himself as the major critic of his age, he began prudent stage-by-stage withdrawals from some of these positions. His refusal to budge from others, and from further entrenchments, arose from an inability to cultivate critical detachment when religious and moral issues were raised. The first explicit warning of this new uncompromising attitude appears in the preface to his 1928 edition of *The Sacred Wood*. He does not believe with Arnold that poetry is a criticism of life, or a substitute for religion, but he is convinced that criticism cannot end with technical or artistic analysis, and that it must include judgment of the moral, spiritual, and perhaps even the political, issues which literature raises. When he wrote this, a third book of his essays, largely religious, philosophical, and political, was near publication.

'The Function of Criticism' (1923) provides a kind of footnote to some of the essays in *The Sacred Wood*. Comparison with

Arnold's 'The Function of Criticism at the Present Time' soon shows how unprepared Eliot was for his subject; his essay is largely a piece of inspirational journalism, portentous in the sense that it 'offers – to deny'. Years later, in 'The Frontiers of Criticism', he admitted having re-read it and wondering what all the fuss was about. The issue round which it turns is whether, as Middleton Murry believed, the critic relies on the 'inner voice' or whether, like the creative writer with his 'ideal order' of tradition, he has external standards. To Eliot as a disciple of Babbitt, the inner voice suggests indiscipline, Arnold's 'doing as one likes'. The only common guidance for critics he can arrive at in the end is the pursuit of truth. He believes that any fact established in *Notes and Queries* is worth more than 'nine-tenths of the most pretentious critical journalism'. He acknowledges Rémy de Gourmont as the source for his critical recipe of comparison and analysis, but no longer assumes that creative writers are the *only* critics who are worth reading. Experience has taught him, however, that the critical work involved in creative writing is the most valuable kind of criticism.

ii SEVENTEENTH-CENTURY POETRY

The three essays in *Homage to John Dryden* (1924) appeared in *The Times Literary Supplement* as early as 1921, that on Andrew Marvell for the tercentenary of his birth, the other two, on Dryden and the metaphysical poets, as reviews. To Eliot the quality of Marvell's poetry, a 'precious liquor' to be squeezed from two or three poems, is not personal but that of a civilization; his best verse is a product of European or Latin culture. The kind of puritanism he represented was not like that we associate with Arnold's 'Dissidence of Dissent'. Cultured and receptive to French influences, he was more the voice of literary England than Milton, whose poetry suffered in the conflict between puritanism and the wider, more Gallic, outlook. Out of the 'high style' which developed from Marlowe to Jonson, the seventeenth century consciously cultivated wit and magniloquence. This wit is peculiar to the Caroline age; it is not the wit of Shakespeare or of Dryden. Eliot finds it in the songs of *Comus*, in Cowley's 'Anacreontiques', and in Marvell's

'Horatian' ode; he sees it as 'tough reasonableness beneath the slight lyric grace'. Discussing the image of Time in 'To His Coy Mistress' with reference to 'Latin' civilization, he quotes the passage in Horace which is echoed with a different application in 'Burbank with a Baedeker: Bleistein with a Cigar'. Marvell's wit is integral to his imagination; it is structural, not a fanciful offshoot, and for that reason Eliot argues (not comparing like with like) its superiority to the fancy of 'L'Allegro' and 'Il Penseroso'. The alliance of levity and seriousness which he finds in Marvell, Latin, Elizabethan and Jacobean poets, Gautier, and the *dandysme* of Baudelaire and Laforgue, reflects the kind of wisdom which precedes genuine synoptic religious awareness. Illustrations from Marvell's poems of the difference between fanciful and imaginative imagery follow, with a slighting remark on 'modern practitioners' of poetry; (Mr Hardy has already been dismissed as a 'modern Englishman' and therefore incapable of tough reasonableness in lyrical form). Whether Eliot focuses correctly or not in comparing a passage from William Morris with six lines from 'The Nymph and the Faun', the 'bright, hard precision' he finds in Marvell is unquestionable. The dream world of nineteenth-century poetry is contrasted with the 'visionary realities' of Dante and his contemporaries.

In the end Eliot returns to his principal concern, the problem of defining wit; it is not a form of erudition or cynicism, but 'involves, probably, a recognition, implicit in the expression of every experience, of other kinds of experience which are possible'. The major qualification with which this scrutiny opens, and the questionableness of 'implicit in the expression of every experience', make this explanation more obscure than helpful, but Eliot leaves it to attack poets of the Romantic period, and their successors, for their want of wit. The essay shows Eliot's strength and his weaknesses; he can draw effectively from wide resources to reinforce his views. On the other hand, certain impressions are becoming fixities or prejudgments, making his reactions rather automatic and predictable; he is too prompt, for example, in the use of comparison for denigratory ends. It would have been more to the purpose had he allowed himself room to discuss the 'magniloquence' of Marvell; his direct comments on the subject are negatively reserved for Milton, who 'used and abused' its possibilities, and eventually, by dispensing with wit, perhaps damaged the language (as Keats believed, for another reason).

Dryden is 'one of the tests of a catholic appreciation of poetry'. Few contemporaries could appreciate him in 1921, Eliot writes, because the twentieth century was still the nineteenth, which had no room for him. He is linked with Marlowe and Jonson as the transmitter of almost all the best qualities in the poetry of the eighteenth century. To enjoy him, one must obviously divest onself of nineteenth-century assumptions (at this point Eliot begins a comparison of Dryden and Shelley which betrays Johnsonian obstinacy in refusing to see the propriety of an image presenting a snake's renewal of her outworn 'winter weeds'). Eliot's analysis of the method by which Dryden ensures the union of satire and wit in *MacFlecknoe* is excellent, despite some introductory inexplicitness and the unconvincing and superfluous degradation of Cowley which he employs to hoist Dryden; many of Dryden's readers would have recognised the adaptation of Cowley as part of the wit, adding the delight of surprise and contrast to the pleasure of familiar rhythms. The well-known view which Arnold shared with Pater that the substance of Dryden's verse is prosaic is rejected, and the sentence in which Hazlitt places Dryden in the school of artificial poets, and Milton in the natural, receives the barrage it deserves for its obvious lack of discrimination. Eliot suspected that Hazlitt was the least intellectually interesting of all our well-known critics, and few would wish to disagree with his assertion that Milton is 'our greatest master of the *artificial* style', whereas Dryden's is natural to a high degree.

His analysis is based on the principle that poetical standards vary from poet to poet, a principle he sometimes overlooks in making comparisons. All he can hope to do, in an effort to bring some order into his preferences, is to enunciate clearly his reasons for enjoying the poetry he likes. He does this in the Dryden essay, it is worth noting, at the time when he had the composition of most of *The Waste Land* in prospect. His anti-romanticism is implicit everywhere. He finds much of Dryden's peculiar genius in 'his ability to make the small into the great, the prosaic into the poetic, the trivial into the magnificent'. Eliot admires his 'capacity for assimilation' and the splendid diction which gives life to his plays, especially when he can pursue the art of 'making the small great'. The main part of the contrast he draws between Swinburne and Dryden is cogent as a generalization: both are masters of words, but, whereas Swinburne's are suggestive and not denotative, Dryden's are precise; they 'state immensely, but their suggestiveness is often nothing'. Eliot has found that the attempt to reduce the essence of poetry, the common non-formal element among poets, leads to little of significance, but he has no doubt that the 'next revolution of taste' (which he was strenuously undertaking) could lead to interest in Dryden's verse; he is one of those who has set standards which it is dangerous to ignore.

'The Metaphysical Poets' is one of the best of Eliot's essays; it suffers very little from divarication, and it examines its subject closely and at long range. He distinguishes between the poetry of Donne (close to that of Chapman), courtly poetry derived from Jonson, and devotional verse, with Crashaw's Italianate style setting him almost in a class apart. The problem is to find what is common to all these poets in their use of figurative language. We have the ingeniously sustained parallelism of Donne's lovers and a pair of compasses, or of Cowley's world and a chess-board; elsewhere, rapid comparative changes; or startling effects briefly and suddenly introduced, a 'telescoping of images and multiplied associations' similar to those which give linguistic vitality in Webster, Tourneur, Middleton, and Shakespeare. Johnson's criticism of what he chose to call 'metaphysical' poetry, that 'the most heterogeneous ideas are yoked by violence together', may be justified by the worst of Cleveland and Cowley, but the unification to some extent of heterogeneity is characteristic of poetry in general, including that of the metaphysicals. Eliot illustrates this, comments on their pure simplicity of language, and observes that their occasional remoteness from simplicity in sentence-structure reflects changes of thought and feeling.

The question arises whether the metaphysicals had a poetic quality the disappearance of which must be counted a loss. Later Elizabethan and early Jacobean poets display lively 'sensuous apprehension of thought', and an ability to turn thought into feeling. By the nineteenth century this intellectual vitality was lost; Tennyson and Browning do not 'feel their thought as immediately as the odour of the rose'; they are reflective poets. 'A thought to Donne was an experience; it modified his sensibility.' Seventeenth-century poets, like the dramatists they followed, 'possessed a mechanism of sensibility which could devour any kind of experience'. To explain the change that followed, Eliot introduces the concept (which came to him from Rémy de Gourmont) of a 'dissociation of sensibility'. It was increased by the influence of Milton and Dryden (one great in magniloquence, the other in wit, Eliot writes in 'Andrew Marvell'), each of whom 'performed certain poetic functions so magnificently well' that the absence of others passed unnoticed. Language became more refined, while feeling became more common or general (Eliot writes 'crude', but Johnson contended that 'Great thoughts are always general'). Sentimentality began, Eliot assures us, in the early part of the eighteenth century, and continued; then Keats and Shelley died early, and Tennyson and Browning 'ruminated'. Eliot's bias or selective misrepresentation ends in manifest oversimplification; one carefully chosen word cannot comprehend two major poets.

The wit of the metaphysicals produces surprising collocations and ingenious parallels of thought; its intellectualizing may be trivial or wide-ranging, eccentric or philosophical, but at least it makes the reader think, and exercises more of his perceptions than most of the poetry of the eighteenth or nineteenth century. Had the dissociation of sensibility not taken place, Eliot continues, the term 'metaphysical' would not have been ascribed to seventeenth-century poets. Looking forward, he thinks it probable, as I. A. Richards did after him, that modern poetry must be difficult. The effect of a complicated civilization on a 'refined sensibility' will make the poet 'more comprehensive, more allusive, more indirect, in order to force, to dislocate if necessary, language into his meaning'. Eliot seems to be thinking of the problems he had experienced in writing 'Gerontion'; history has not proved the general truth of his assertion, however. He quotes Laforgue in support, and ends his case with the bizarre statement (mainly from de Gourmont, and anticipated in his essay on Massinger) that the poet must look not only into the heart but also into 'the cerebral cortex, the nervous system, and the digestive tracts'. Resisting the parodic temptation to vary the regions for a particular poet or poem, one can conclude that Eliot's consistent ideal in poetry is intensity of sensuous thought, with intellect and feelings working imaginatively in one clear, coherent process.

Although it has nothing startling to offer, a later tercentenary essay, 'Sir John Davies' (1926), has the virtue of a more mature integration; with no axes to grind, Eliot concentrates his scholarly power of critical analysis almost entirely on *Nosce Teipsum*, a long poem on the immortality of the soul. Its merit does not lie in its philosophy, which is oddly individual, but in the high poetic level it sustains, with felicity of expression and (though Eliot does not emphasize it) of imagery, in both of which it is clear and choice. The 'personal cadence' is never absent, and no stanza is rhythmically identical with another. No poet, including Gray, has employed the quatrain more successfully; and no poem in similar verse, Eliot adds, shows metrical superiority to *Orchestra*. There seems to be a hint of Spenser's influence in this poem, but the thought and expression of Davies belong to no school; his tone and language are those of a meditative solitary. He does not play with ideas in the manner of Donne, but follows his main line of thought unwaveringly, and has the ability, which is as remarkable as it is rare, of presenting it with feeling. The progression of *Nosce Teipsum* intensifies the feeling; variation comes from the metrics. Eliot finds only one parallel, and that is in passages on the soul by Dante, a much greater poet, with a more comprehensive and subtle philosophy; from these he quotes a brief sample (*Purgatorio*, xvi.85–93), which he recalls at the opening of 'Animula'.

'A Note on Richard Crashaw', written as a review a year or so later, and included in *For Lancelot Andrewes* (1928) is less creditable. In it Eliot reverts to the nonsensical extremism of his distaste for Swinburne's poetry, finding the same emptiness in Shelley's 'To a Skylark', which shows no brain-work, and is only sound without sense. Most of his comment was occasioned by an editorial remark that Crashaw's work foreshadows that of Keats and Shelley, two other poets of unfulfilled renown who found a retreat, and died, in Italy. Eliot sees nothing in common between Keats and Crashaw, or, after much cry, between Shelley's imagery and Crashaw's. Bias creates a stubborn literalness in his response to Shelleyan imagery, making him almost arrogantly explosive for a prosaic explanation; it is not the end of his derogation. Crashaw's pillow in 'The Tear' is preposterous, but it gives intellectual pleasure; Eliot describes it as a 'deliberate conscious perversity of language', and likens it to 'the amazing and amazingly impressive interior' of St Peter's.

It would be more correct to say that the perversity is not in the language, but in the use to which it is put. The pillow image must be judged in its continuity; it is an example of imagery fused with devotional thought, a salient example of the fantastic efflorescence of Crashaw's fecund and hyperbolical imagination. His verse is much more mature than that of Keats or Shelley, 'as one would expect', Eliot writes, adding for good measure that Keats and Shelley were 'apprentices' and 'not nearly as great' as they are thought to be, though *Hyperion* and *The Triumph of Life* suggest they would probably have surpassed Crashaw. He regards the latter as a devotional poet, since the word 'religious' is abused; even Shelley has been described as religious, and he is, in the sense in which the word is used when applied to Dean Inge or the Bishop of Birmingham. On this rather Arnoldian polemical level, Eliot prefers to remain provocatively inexplicit. On Crashaw he has little original to say. He finds an erotic element which renders his 'passion for heavenly objects' imperfect, stresses his saturation in Latin and Italian poetry, and gives Mario Praz as his authority for placing Crashaw above Marino, Góngora, 'and everybody else, merely as the *representative* of the baroque spirit in literature'.

Eliot's more temperate 1932 essay on George Herbert appears to disclose the difficulty he himself had experienced as a poet in distinguishing between genuine feelings and the seemingly appropriate, especially in devotional verse. He finds a kinship with a man of the world who agonized towards the spiritual life, sees *The Temple* as a structured whole, a work of spiritual stamina, and Herbert as a man who went 'much farther on the road of humility' than Donne. Modified and extended biographically and critically in 1962 as a general introduction for the 'Writers and their Work' series, *George Herbert* ends aggregatively with illustrations of Donne's influence on *The Temple* (and of its varied stylistic features), after emphasizing fusion of thought and feeling in both poets, with dominance of sensibility in Herbert, and of thought in Donne. The indebtedness of Vaughan to Herbert is noted.

iii   MORE ON ELIZABETHAN AND JACOBEAN DRAMA

'Four Elizabethan Dramatists' (1924) was intended as the opening of a study of Webster, Tourneur, Middleton, and Chapman, not so much as a supplement to the criticism of Lamb, Coleridge, and Swinburne as in the belief that such re-examination of the one 'distinct form' of English drama could exert a revolutionary influence. Eliot reached this conclusion after reading William Archer's *The Old Drama and the New* (1923). Archer's view that 'the difference between modern drama and Elizabethan drama is represented by a gain of dramatic technique and the loss of poetry' is implicit in Swinburne; and Lamb's *Specimens* had given the impression that plays can be read as literature without reference to the stage, thus setting in motion the idea that poetry and drama are distinct. These preliminaries tend to show that Eliot's real subject was the future of poetic drama. The main weakness of English drama, the demand for realism, began with the Elizabethans; it ends in 'the desert of exact likeness to the reality' which is seen by commonplace minds. Perhaps only in one play, *Everyman*, has English drama kept within the bounds of art. The Elizabethans had their stage conventions, but they had no convention to arrest the movement towards realism. The artist should 'consciously or unconsciously draw a circle beyond which he does not trespass'; he will draw from life, but 'an abstraction from actual life' is necessary for the creation of art.

This abstraction demands that the actor should become impersonal; his personality should become absorbed in the action of drama as in ballet. Convention has the same advantages for the actor as for the author: an artist cannot produce great art if he uses it to exploit his personality. The actor's interpretation of his part should not interpose between the play and the audience, yet (Eliot argues unconvincingly) greater dependence falls on the actor in realistic Drama. (It seems that the stress on the imperfect actor who wishes to impress his personality on the play or audience distracts Eliot from his real subject, which is the revival of drama as an art-form, through the use of conventions. What he has in mind by this can be judged best from *Murder in the Cathedral*.) Of the four writers he has chosen to study in the furtherance of his views, Eliot thinks Chapman the most classically minded, and the most independent in his pursuit of dramatic form. He illustrates very briefly the impurity of Elizabethan drama by reference to the combination of convention and realism in *Macbeth*, proposing to demonstrate that the weaknesses to which Archer objected are due to this kind of hybridization. The way in which genius proceeds towards chaos in *The Duchess of Malfi* exemplifies the 'artistic greediness ' of the Elizabethans, 'their desire for every sort of effect together' which was ultimately responsible for Sir Arthur Pinero and 'the present regiment of Europe'. Eliot ends with a slight crescendo of critical irony: by analysis of Elizabethan philosophy, dramatic form, and blank verse, it is possible to understand why Mr Archer is both the opponent and, unconsciously, the supporter of the Elizabethans, as well as 'a believer in progress, in the growth of humanitarian feeling, and in the superiority of the present age'.

Eliot's interest in the Senecan influence on Elizabethan drama came to a head in 1927 in two essays, the first of which, 'Seneca in Elizabethan Translation', introduces a reprint of Thomas Newton's edition of *Seneca: His Tenne Tragedies* (1581). Eliot's long, scholarly essay falls into three parts: the qualities of Seneca's plays, their influence on Elizabethan dramatists, and the history and merit of the translations. If the plays, as is generally agreed, were written for non-theatrical declamation, we can understand why the characters seem to speak with one voice, 'and at the top of it'. This theory lessens the problems raised by Senecan peculiarities, including horrors, many of which could not be staged without becoming ridiculous. The plays are admirably suited to 'an imperial highbrow audience of crude sensibility but considerable sophistication in the ingenuities of language'. Their Stoicism reflects a sceptical age which found compensation for its moral failings in ethical posturing. Death provided an opportunity for sententious aphorisms which the Elizabethans were quick to follow; half their commonplaces, 'the more commonplace half', are of Senecan descent. Seneca often obtains telling effects, and the lines of Hercules which impressed not only Chapman but Eliot himself (as can be seen in 'Gerontion') are instanced. His dramatic form is practical, and could be tried again; at one point Eliot suggests its suitability for broadcasting.

The question of Seneca's influence on Elizabethan drama

leads Eliot to note that he was regularly taught in schools, that translations of his plays appeared in quick succession from 1559, and that plays by Seneca, and imitations of Seneca, were produced in Latin at the universities about this time. By the time of *The Spanish Tragedy* and the old *Hamlet*, his influence on popular drama was strongly established. There is little agreement on what this was, except that the five-act division common in European plays derives from him. The impression that Seneca was responsible for the 'tragedy of blood' in Elizabethan England is misleading; many of the dramatic excesses of that period would have made him 'shudder with genuine aesthetic horror'. He supplied the ghost, the revenge motive, and temporary insanity, but in other respects the worst that can be held against him is that he may have provided an excuse for introducing horrors from popular Italian drama and from English crime. Eliot passes rapidly over the influence of Senecan language on Elizabethan dramatists to stress technicalities of style which they owed to Seneca, in addition to declamatory qualities, and the development of blank verse cadences after the pre-Marlowe period of 'monotone' and of that grotesque 'Ercles bombast' which looks like Seneca in caricature. After such an evolution, the chief influence on blank verse was Shakespeare's. Attention is given also to 'Senecal' drama, which was written in opposition to popular sensational plays, first of all by scholars assembled by Sidney's sister the Countess of Pembroke, and later by Fulke Greville, Daniel, and Alexander; in every way they are more restrained than Seneca. On the qualities of Senecan thought in Elizabethan drama, Eliot hardly gets under way; most of what he says is expanded in 'Shakespeare and the Stoicism of Seneca'.

This rather uncertain exploratory essay begins with sceptical comments on modern impressions of Shakespeare the man. Eliot notices too how he has been explained by reference to Montaigne and Machiavelli, and proposes to 'disinfect the Senecan Shakespeare before he appears'. He believes that Shakespeare read from Seneca's tragedies at school, and was familiar with the Senecan influence in Elizabethan drama, especially in Kyd. It is limited in Shakespeare's plays to the 'self-consciousness and self-dramatization' of some of his heroes at tragic crises, especially when they are dying. He is convinced that Othello, just before he commits suicide, is *cheering himself up* by this kind of rhetoric (as Eliot defined it in *The Sacred Wood*), his primary aim being to deceive himself rather than the spectator. In describing such well-timed action as *bovarysme*, Eliot attempts a realistic, but not very cogent, explanation of a stage convention. As stoicism is a kind of 'cheering oneself up' in a hostile world, it is apparently a logical step from this to Roman stoicism (the reverse of Christian humility, we are told) in Elizabethan drama. On the question of influences, after positing that Shakespeare or Dante *as a poet* thinks, but Swinburne and Tennyson as poets do not think, Eliot expects us to believe that neither Shakespeare nor Dante 'did any real thinking'. The difference between them is that Dante had 'one coherent system of thought' to support his poetry. It does not follow that he was a Thomist any more than that Shakespeare accepted the Renaissance scepticism that appears in his plays. Eliot's doubt whether 'belief proper' affects poetic thinking conforms to his theory of the impersonality of art, but it does not preclude the possibility that philosophical or religious thought derived from reading or experience becomes an integral part of the creative mind; with Eliot's poetry there is ample evidence that it usually did. His generalization of Shakespeare's 'struggle – which alone constitutes life for a poet – to transmute his personal and private agonies into something rich and strange, something universal and impersonal' is rooted in his own experience; it applies even more to *Ash-Wednesday* than to *The Waste Land*.

The surprising thing is not that Eliot was unable to pursue the ambitious project announced in 'Four Elizabethan Dramatists' but that he had time to write as much as he did on drama in the Elizabethan and Jacobean period. His essay on Thomas Middleton (1927) and four reviews in *The Times Literary Supplement* from 1930 to 1934 are further evidence of devotion to this enormous subject. Little is known of Middleton, the readiest of collaborators except Rowley, and the most inconsistent performer; all his plays are a mixture of tedious and lively drama. Though associated with six or seven important plays, he has no personality or point of view; his best tragedies and his best comedies seem to be the work of two different men. *The Changeling* is inferior in poetry and dramatic technique to the best of Webster, but in 'the moral essence of tragedy' it is surpassed only by Shakespeare. The tragedy of Beatrice is universal; it happens 'every day and perpetually'. The 'unmoral nature' is 'suddenly trapped in the inexorable toils of morality'; Beatrice 'becomes moral only by becoming damned'. The tragedy lies deepest in *'habituation* to sin'; it is comparable to Macbeth's 'habituation to crime'. Most important of all, Middleton's language is equal to the tragedy. The same kind of permanence emerges from conventional evil in the 'picture-palace Italian melodrama' of *Women Beware Women*; Bianca is the type of woman who is motivated purely by vanity. Middleton understood women better than did any of his contemporaries except Shakespeare; the best of his comedies, *The Roaring Girl*, presents a finer woman than can be found in any of their plays. He is a 'steady impersonal passionless' observer of human nature; his comedy marks a transitional phase when London tradesmen wished to belong to the gentry. It has its realism, but it is a comedy of individuals, like the later comedy of Dickens; it produced one great play which more than any other Elizabethan comedy 'realizes a free and noble womanhood'. Eliot's enthusiasm for the best of Middleton reduces him finally to the epithet 'great'; it speaks for Middleton as dramatist, recorder, and poet. To illustrate his mastery in versification, Eliot quotes the passage beginning with the line (echoed in 'Gerontion') 'I that am of your blood was taken from you'.

Tourneur remains a mystery. The two plays with which he is credited, *The Revenger's Tragedy* and *The Atheist's Tragedy*, differ as much from each other as they do from all other Elizabethan plays. Eliot offers valuable observations on both in support of the view that the second, though largely inferior, more conventional, and yet offensively tasteless, could have been written later than *The Revenger's Tragedy*. The excessive cynicism and disgust of the latter suggest immaturity; its horrible, intense, unique vision of life could express the shocked reaction of a sensitive youth gifted with words. Hatred of life sets it apart from all other Elizabethan plays except *Hamlet*; nor is it like *Gulliver's Travels*, for the latter makes us feel how loathsome humanity is, while Tourneur makes us think 'how terrible' it must be to loathe human beings to that extent. You cannot condemn the human race merely by presenting people as 'consistent and monotonous maniacs of gluttony and lust'. The verse is as rapid as Webster's is slow; it gains by sudden abruptness and frequent changes of tempo. The characters may be grotesquely distorted, but they are appropriate to each other, and therefore the play has its own reality. Tourneur excels in the requisites of a dramatist; he is a master of plot-construction, stage effects, and of language and versification. His genius is revealed in *The Revenger's Tragedy*, where the appropriate words and rhythms express a horror of life which is unequalled in his period or any other.

The essay on Thomas Heywood, a seventeenth-century 'literary Jack of all trades', is for a long period enmeshed in problems of authorship. Consequential attributions make little difference to Eliot's assessment of him, for he is outstanding in little. His sensibility is that of the common man in common life: he produces 'no supernatural music from behind the wings'. Nor is there any 'reality of moral synthesis'. His not very poetic versification reaches a high dramatic level at its best, however. He shows some skill in plot-contruction but, having little sense of humour, is handicapped in underplots, and tries to compensate with bawdiness. Eliot thinks the plot of *The English Traveller* Heywood's best, but it needed a Stendhal to make the most of it. Sympathetic delicacy in this play and *A Woman Killed with Kindness* is superior to that of his contemporaries, but, as the author's interest is sentimental, and not moral, it allies him with nineteenth-century writers of popular sentiment rather than with great dramatists; he is more successful in the pathetic than in the tragic.

In order to place John Ford, Eliot found it convenient in 1932 to classify Elizabethan and Jacobean dramatists into three groups: those who would have been great had Shakespeare never lived (Marlowe, Jonson, Chapman); those who made their own contribution after Shakespeare (Middleton, Webster, Tourneur); and those who exploited Shakespeare (Beaumont, Fletcher, and Shirley in his tragedies). He views Shakespeare as a writer of continuous development, the full meaning of any one of his plays being assessable only in the light of the whole. The extent to which writers attain such a unity is a measure of greatness, he adds. The first of Ford's important plays, *The Lover's Melancholy*, has many echoes of Shakespeare's last plays, but its recognition scenes are devoid of those symbolical overtones which we associate with Perdita, Marina, and Miranda, who all have a kind of beauty the secret of which is beyond Shakespeare's earlier heroines. Eliot suggests that a dramatic poet cannot create characters of such living beauty unless they dramatize somehow 'an action or struggle for harmony in the soul of the poet'; (he could reflect on 'Marina' when he wrote thus). In this respect *'Tis Pity She's a Whore*, based on an Italian tale of incest, fails; it is well constructed, and the versification and poetry reach a high level; the subject is taken seriously, without any of 'the prurient flirting with impropriety' which gives a meretricious cast to Beaumont and Fletcher's *King and No King*; but it lacks the 'general significance and emotional depth' which such an action requires. *The Broken Heart* and *Perkin Warbeck* are superior, the latter being undoubtedly Ford's best work.

Eliot does not accept Havelock Ellis's view that Ford's mind is modern and psychological, nearer to Stendhal and Flaubert than to Shakespeare. It would be truer to say that Shakespeare is nearer to Stendhal and Flaubert than to Ford. Stendhal, Flaubert, and Balzac study the individual in particular social surroundings, but the Elizabethan and Jacobean dramatists accepted their age, and could concentrate on characteristics of humanity regardless of period. For them our criterion is Shakespeare, and his works are *one* poem, unified by 'one significant, consistent, and developing personality'. Marlowe comes next in this respect. (Descending the scale, Eliot comes to the single play, and – as he does in 'Thomas Heywood' – indicates a willingness to think Middleton wrote *The Revenger's Tragedy*.) In all these dramatists there is 'the essential, as well as the superficies, of poetry'; they give the pattern or undertone of 'the personal emotion, the personal drama and struggle' which no biography can supply. Ford's drama is superficial, dependent on stock responses; it is the lack of the deeper personal qualities which makes the plays of Ford, Beaumont, Fletcher, Shirley, Otway, and (later still) Shelley incline to 'mere sensationalism'. (More than once Eliot has seemed to be returning to some aspect of his impersonality-of-art theory, but here there can be no doubt that he has shifted substantially from the extreme position he originally took.)

In the last essay of this group (written in 1934) Eliot spends much time on John Marston's demerits (which seem incredibly bad), and accepts with reservation the view that *The Malcontent* is his best play; its virtue lies in its lack of the 'grosser faults' expected of its author. Eliot's main interest is in Marston's peculiar quality, a factor which helps to sharpen our appreciation of his fellow dramatists, and may also serve to distinguish poetic drama from prosaic drama. This is a 'kind of doubleness in the action' which reminds Eliot of Dostoevsky, some of whose characters live simultaneously on a familiar, recognisable plane and on another 'plane of reality' from which we are excluded. He believes that Marston belongs to the writers of genius by virtue of this power to give a sense of 'something behind' which has greater reality than his characters and their actions. For this reason he would like to think, as its author appears to have thought, that *The Wonder of Women (The Tragedy of Sophonisba)* is Marston's best play. Its tone differentiates it not only from other dramatists of the period but also from his other plays; it imparts an 'underlying serenity' to a tumultuous action marked by ferocity and horror, and creates behind this pattern another pattern 'into which the characters deliberately involve themselves', the sort of pattern, Eliot adds, anticipating 'Burnt Norton', which is perceived in life only at 'rare moments of inattention and detachment, drowsing in sunlight'. The ancient world thought it indicative of Fate; it is 'subtilized by Christianity into mazes of delicate theology; and reduced again by the modern world into crudities of psychological or economic necessity'. The essay ends with a thought which seems incompatible with one urged in 'John Ford': Marston's play should be judged not by Shakespearian, but by 'Senecal', standards, and soon after reading Corneille and Racine, with whom he has greater affinities.

14

Poems, including
Ash-Wednesday

All but the last of the five sections of 'The Hollow Men' were published in the winter of 1924–5, the first in *Commerce* (Paris), the second and fourth in *The Criterion*, and all three of these in *The Dial*. Together with 'Eyes that last I saw in tears', and 'The wind sprang up at four o'clock', the third section ('This is the dead land') appeared under the title of 'Doris's Dream Songs' in November 1924. Early images of wind, dry grass, rats' feet, and broken glass indicate the link with *The Waste Land*, but the poem as a whole is more forward-looking, and most of it seems to have been written after the publication of that work. Some time elapsed before Eliot realized that the four parts, together with a fifth ('*Here we go round the prickly pear*'), were best presented as a sequence, and as such 'The Hollow Men' appeared in *Poems* (1925).

The germ of the poem, nevertheless, is found in one of the visionary poems Eliot wrote before *The Waste Land* was substantially under way. Part of 'Song' ('The golden foot I may not kiss') was completed in the minatory personal vision of 'The wind sprang up at four o'clock', a pendant to 'The Hollow Men', the subject of both being 'death's dream kingdom'. In this poem the sound of bells swinging between spiritual life and death is occluded by the wind, and Tartar horsemen show their hostility on the far side of a blackened Acherontic river. Like the Arnoldian echo in 'Song', an Arnoldian image, from 'Sohrab and Rustum', emphasizes the exclusion which is surrealistically mourned by the sweating face of the river. The golden vision of 'Song', not its image, reappears in 'Eyes that last I saw in tears'; the mourning of the river is now imaged in eyes that were last seen in tears at the sufferer's exclusion, separation, or division. Now he is afflicted because the eyes appear without pity; they will not reappear unless he reaches the entrance to 'death's other kingdom'. This prospect gives him no reassurance; he is afraid of another rejection. Once again the eyes will outlast the tears, then disappear as if in mockery of him. Usually of Dantean rather than of Crucifixional significance, they betoken spiritual grace or light eternal. Such is the love in the eyes of Beatrice (*La Vita Nuova*, xxi) which Dante sees again after his Lethean immersion in the Earthly Paradise (*Purgatorio*, xxxi). The eyes and their religious symbolism are central to 'The Hollow Men'.

The straw figure mentioned by Jessie Weston in *From Ritual to Romance* (v), as representative of the 'Old Man' or 'defunct Vegetation Spirit', probably suggested the 'Old Guy' of Guy Fawkes's Night, but the supreme hollow image, which may have originated in Virgil's concept of souls in Purgatory hanging *empty in the wind*, owes much to Conrad. The epigraph, which is translated from the physical meaning of its context to the spiritual, refers to Kurtz, who was 'hollow at the core', unaware of the horror of his ways until he was at the brink of death. The people of 'The Hollow Men' are not violent souls like the 'hollow sham' Kurtz, but stuffed, neither alive nor dead, reminiscent of those souls gathered by the Acheron river beneath the starless sky of Dante's Ante-Hell. They do not appear in human form but in disguises, as if they were scarecrows in a field, behaving like the wind, with no fixity of purpose or direction. Their force is paralysed; their gestures are motionless. Phrases in this particular context ('Shape without form, shade without colour') seem to echo Marlow's description of Kurtz: 'greyness without form', a 'shadow' or shade.

As in *The Waste Land*, seeing is crucially significant. There, looking into the heart of light, the eyes fail; here, in a world where death has undone so many, the eyes of the hollow men are sightless unless the eyes of the other kingdom reappear. God's kingdom is a dim dream, a hazy peripheral notion; it rarely, if ever, enters our conscious daily lives and transactions. Some people pray for its coming; those whose eyes have been opened, who have crossed to 'death's other Kingdom' with direct, unevasive eyes, think of us as the hollow men. For most of us the eyes of the dream kingdom ('Thy kingdom come') do not appear; at best – and the ecstasy of this experience finds its voice in rarefied lyrical beauty – we have 'Sunlight on a broken column' (a broken Coriolanus, the Prince of Aquitaine by his ruined tower) or, more remote and solemn than 'a fading star', voices in the singing wind of God's grace, utterly different from our desert voices, which are meaningless as 'wind in dry grass' or the feet of rats running over shattered glass in our dry cellarage. The higher dream of an earthly paradise, recalling the 'melody which pervades the luminous air' of Dante's (*Purgatorio*, xxix.22–3) seems more unrealizable than the perception of God which is fading. (The star has a similar significance in Laforgue's 'Au Large', and God is the single star of *Paradiso*, xxxi.28.) Our representative hollow man shrinks back at the thought of the personal effort required for salvation.

The cactus land of the third section renews the desert symbolism of *The Waste Land*, and refers to the dead formality of worship in a world from which God is disappearing; the idea is similar to that presented by the vision of Prague in George Eliot's *The Lifted Veil*. The question is whether the same spiritual deadness will be found when, yearning for the true life, the 'other Kingdom', one fails to find it in a Church which has decayed: lips ready to kiss 'Form prayers to broken stone'. There are no eyes, the poet continues disconsolately, in this hollow valley; the broken stone of the Church is like the 'broken jaw' of 'our lost kingdoms'. The last image may suggest a relic indicative of life which is now dead; it may mean that the Church has lost the power of communicating the world of the spirit, an interpretation which is supported perhaps in the juxtaposed non-communicativeness of those who gather gropingly by the river they seek to cross. Unless the single star and the Rose of the *Paradiso* appear, there is no hope for hollow men.

That the one hope is the Incarnation, the spirit of God informing Man through Christ, can be clarified only through reference to Dante. 'There is the Rose, where the living Word was made flesh', Beatrice tells Dante with reference to the garden which flowers beneath Christ's rays. This rose expanded in the eternal peace when God's love was rekindled in the Virgin Mary's womb; its 'multifoliate' character is seen by Dante when he finally gazes at the eternal Light, and sees in its depths how all the pages of the universe are bound together in one volume (*Paradiso*, xxiii.70–4; xxxiii.1–9, 82–93). Eliot is already on the road which leads to the conclusion of *Four Quartets*.

The valley of 'The Hollow Men' is the valley of the shadow of spiritual death, with an echo of the twenty-third psalm. This paralysing shadow falls between the idea, the hope, the effort and their attainment. It falls between the 'essence', which is the spirit of God, and the 'descent', which is Incarnation. We must submit to His will: 'For Thine is the kingdom'. The broken repetitive lines at the end, in which this affirmation from the Lord's Prayer is hesitated, communicate a weakened, unsustainable, but unstilled hope that 'the power and the glory' will be inherited. The prickly-pear version of a happy nursery rhyme expresses disillusionment with the world (for lack of direction leads only to 'round and round', Harry says in *The Family Reunion*). The hollow men may be like the Old Guy; their civilization ends, not with a celebratory bang, but with a cry like that of a child, like that perhaps of Tennyson in *In Memoriam* (liv, lv), where he stretches out 'lame hands of faith', and gropes, and feels he is 'An infant crying in the night'. Far more than in *The Waste Land*, Eliot's subject is becoming insubstantial, and the extent to which the poet can communicate it through key words and images (his 'feelings'), or in objective correlatives, assumes increasing interest.

'Journey of the Magi' (1927) opens with lines from a sermon on the Incarnation by Lancelot Andrewes, Bishop of Winchester, who died in 1626. The essay Eliot wrote on him for the tercentenary of his death takes pride of place with one on John Bramhall, another seventeenth-century divine, in *For Lancelot Andrewes* (1928), a miscellaneous collection of essays reflecting the convictions and interests which made Eliot a convert to Anglo-Catholicism in 1927. He thought the sermons of Lancelot Andrewes ranked with the best prose of their time or of any period, and that, if the Church of England, which was created in the reign of Elizabeth, was worthy of the age of Shakespeare and Jonson, it was due to Hooker and Andrewes, in whom we find a European breadth of culture, old and new. Andrewes is the first of the great preachers in the 'English Catholic Church'. The outstanding qualities of his sermons, which are restricted to what he regarded as the essentials of dogma, are ordonnance or structural discipline, precision and simplicity of language, and 'relevant intensity'. Eliot admired his genius for taking a word and making a world out of it, his gift for 'flashing phrases', above all his immersion in thought and expression, the relevance of the intensity which makes him more pure than the spell-binder Donne, who is less mystical and traditional, but dangerous only to those who are fascinated by personality, and oblivious of higher places than Donne's in the spiritual hierarchy.

Eliot's account of the journey of the magi (the wise men: Matthew, ii.1–11) begins with the statement 'A cold coming [they] had of it . . .'. Such idiomatic succinctness came from Andrewes, as may be seen from the passage which provided the opening of the poem:

> It was no summer progress. A cold coming they had of it at this time of the year, just the worst time of the year to take a journey, and specially a long journey in. The ways deep, the weather sharp, the days short, the sun farthest off, *in solstitio brumali*, 'the very dead of winter'.

The poem impresses by the subtle changes in its rhythmic movement. Although it is true that most lines are four-stressed, such a description is too simple and crude to reflect their variety; there are many intermediate stresses, especially in longer lines; and stresses, whether dominant or subordinate, differ considerably in weight and length. The extraordinary effectiveness with which the reader's attention is dramatically fixed in the final paragraph by pauses which break an emphatic repetition germinated from the 'Set you down this' of the speech which convinced Eliot, about the time he wrote the poem, that Othello was giving himself a rhetorical fillip just before his suicide.

The poem contains more descriptive elements than is customary with Eliot; to some extent, general rather than specific, this was due to the stimulus of St-John Perse's *Anabase*, which he had begun to translate. Some of the imagery came from the inner world which drew from the whole of Eliot's sensitively recording life. In the final chapter of *The Use of Poetry and the Use of Criticism*, he asks,

> Why, for all of us, out of all that we have heard, seen, felt, in

a lifetime, do certain images recur, charged with emotion, rather than others? The song of one bird, the leap of one fish, at a particular place and time, the scent of one flower, an old woman on a German mountain path, six ruffians seen through an open window playing cards at night at a small French railway junction where there was a water-mill: such memories may have a symbolic value, but of what we cannot tell, for they come to represent the depths of feeling into which we cannot peer.

On the hard journey towards Incarnation, the magi, like the poetic persona of *Ash-Wednesday*, regret the loss of worldly pleasure, but they have escaped the winter of spiritual death; the oblivious snow of *The Waste Land* has melted, and they reach a warm valley of life, with running water. The three trees, and the dicing for silver, prefigure the Crucifixion; the tavern with vine leaves over the lintel (a reminder of the Passover; cf. Exodus, xii) hints at the Paschal Lamb who declared, 'I am the vine, ye are the branches'; the white horse signifies the Word of God (Revela---- --- 11 13) and it is aging. The meaning of these signs is   ie Birth is so painful and difficult   y return to their old 'dispensatior   ation of the grace of God' (Ephes   clutch their worldly gods, and a   g. Back in the 'lost kingdoms' (rrator longs for the death which

The subj   Song for Simeon', a meditative lyric the subdued wave ch befits an old man who feels the feather-like wind of death on the back of his hand. Having seen the newly born Jesus, the Word made flesh but unable to speak a word (as in Lancelot Andrewes and 'Gerontion'), he wishes to depart this life in peace (Luke, ii.25ff.). The Roman hyacinths suggest that the stubborn winter will come to an end but, as in 'Journey of the Magi', Birth is associated with Death and the Crucifixion on Calvary; indirectly, with the Stations of the Cross in Catholic worship, and with the desolation of the chosen (Mark, xiii.14). Simeon's wish to die has metaphorical overtones which go back to the epigraph of *The Waste Land*; his resigned acceptance that the 'ultimate vision' is not for him speaks for the poet of *Ash-Wednesday*.

The philosophical nature of 'Animula' (1929) is confirmed by
the title and by the quotation from Dante (*Purgatorio*, xvi.85–8)
in the opening line. Whatever its autobiographical reminiscence,
Eliot contrasts the happiness of infancy with the heavy burden –
almost Wordsworthian – of the soul as it grows up. The
question of 'is' and 'seems' is raised in the 'Animula Vagula'
chapter of *Marius the Epicurean*, the title of which comes from the
emperor Hadrian's address to his soul; the 'doctrine of motion'
having seemed to make 'all fixed knowledge impossible', Pater's
young philosopher had come to believe that 'the momentary,
sensible apprehension of the individual was the only standard
of what is or is not, and each one the measure of all things to
himself'. The context of the Dantean quotation (a passage that
may provide a key to Eliot's use of the tower image at the end
of *The Waste Land*) relates to free-will, describing how the soul,
happy at birth, continues to seek pleasure unless it has learned
the distinction between right and wrong (the imperatives of
'may and may not, desire and control', or the Damyata of *The
Waste Land*). In contrast with the soul which issues from the
hand of God, the soul that is the product of time is selfish,
deformed, and Prufrockian; it makes more explicit the young
man's failure in the hyacinth-garden of 'The Burial of the
Dead':

> Unable to fare forward or retreat,
> Fearing the warm reality, the offered good,
> Denying the importunity of the blood.

It remains that of the hollow man until death. The concluding
prayer is for representative types of the western world; 'Floret'
suggests a less aggressive type from a much earlier era, slain
between the yew trees (like the victim of *The Hound of the
Baskervilles*; we learn that Eliot dreamt of yew-trees, and of a
boarhound among yew-trees[41]). The prayer ends with a line
from the Roman Catholic 'Hail Mary', the final word changed
from 'death' to 'birth', the promise of which comes in 'Marina'.
    Such liturgical phrases occur in *Ash-Wednesday*, which was
published in 1930, several months before 'Marina'. Three of its
sections had already appeared, the second as 'Salutation' in
1927, the first as 'Perch'io non spero' in 1928, the third as 'Som

de l'escalina' in 1929. Paragraph after paragraph in the first is hinged on the introductory 'Because I do not hope' or its corresponding clause. The faltering which twice marks the opening hardens into the certainty of 'Because I know', on which the expression of hopelessness without despair is built. The key to this poem, the beginning of the epistle for Ash-Wednesday, 'Turn ye even unto me, saith the Lord', assumed added significance for Eliot from Lancelot Andrewes' repeated use of 'turn' in his Ash-Wednesday sermon 'Of Repentance', especially from his insistence that repentance depends not just on turning to God but on the necessity to turn *again* and look back on our sins; the intention needs to be based on recognition and contrition. The biblical metaphor (Andrewes' sermon has Joel, ii.12–13 for its text) reminded Eliot of the opening of Cavalcanti's eleventh ballata 'Perch'io non spero di tornar già mai', which he echoes; just as Cavalcanti was in exile when addressing his poem to his lady, so Eliot is spiritually exiled. His recognition that worldly ambition occludes spiritual grace makes him refer in 'Desiring this man's gift and that man's scope' to Shakespeare's twenty-ninth sonnet on one who troubles 'deaf heaven' with 'bootless cries'. In asking why the old eagle should stretch its wings he alludes, as he was to do in *The Family Reunion*, and as Dante and St John of the Cross had done (*Purgatorio*, ix; *The Dark Night of the Soul*, II.xiii.11), to the spiritual regeneration which became symbolized in an old belief that the aged eagle flies up to the circle of fire, from which, after its feathers are burned away, it falls blinded into a fountain of water, where its youth is renewed. Eliot takes comfort from having renounced worldliness; the power of customary rule has vanished. On the other hand he has no hope or assurance that the positive experience will ever return; such power and glory is uncertain or transient. Since he is unlikely to know spiritual illumination again, it is fruitless to mourn; he accepts the limitations of time and place. The rebirth which is not for him is associated with the trees, flowers, and streams of Dante's Earthly Paradise, and it is the blessed face and voice of Matilda, the genius of this Eden, which he renounces. In submitting thus to God's will, rather than agonizing over matters which give him no peace, he has reason to rejoice. His wings cannot lift him; they can only beat air which is drier than his will. He would like to care without the anxiety of self-regard (cf. Philippians, iv.6–7), remain passive ('sit still') and receptive, waiting, even without hope. The poem concludes with the ending of the 'Hail Mary' prayer.

The first part of the second section is lighter, quickened by rhythms which accord with the uplift of hope; the dried bones sing. A more positive phase in the progress of a soul is marked by a significant change of symbolism: the desert and dry bones of *The Waste Land* and 'The Hollow Men' (waiting for rain) now express the asceticism of one who has turned away from the world; as in *The Dark Night of the Soul* (i.xi.1), the bones are dried up by the thirst for God. The main thought of the second section is based on Old Testament passages, the first (I Kings, xix.1–8) on the bringing of comfort to Elijah when, in exile (as it were) in the wilderness, he wishes to die as he rests under a juniper tree; the second (Ezekiel, xxxvii.1–14) on the valley of dry bones which come to life. The whiteness of the leopards indicates that they perform God's will; they feed on liver, brain, and heart, once regarded, in Shakespeare's words (*Twelfth Night*, i.i.37–8), as the 'sovran thrones' of the passions, judgment, and the sentiments. Seeking a higher form of life, the ascetic receives hope from a Lady whose role is like that of Dante's Matilda, causing his dry bones to shine. When the 'I' who is 'dissembled' (a neologism antonymous to 'assembled') renounces his worldly self (Jonah's gourd which sprang up and perished in a night symbolizes the ephemerality of earthly things), his remains recover, though there is no rebirth; the white bones must 'atone to forgetfulness'. Ezekiel's anticipation is relevant, nonetheless: 'Prophesy unto the wind . . . , Thus saith the Lord God; Come from the four winds, O breath, and breathe upon these slain, that they may live.'

In dimeters, and with the burden of the grasshopper, indicating death to this life (Ecclesiastes, xii.1–7, 'burden' suggesting the low-key Elizabethan accompaniment of undersong), the bones address Mary the mother and virgin ('Torn and most whole'); in her womb was rekindled the Love under whose warmth the Rose unfolded in the eternal peace. In this context (*Paradiso*, xxxiii.1–21) can be seen the link between the first two sections of *Ash-Wednesday*: he who would have grace and resorts not to her 'seeks to fly without wings', Dante writes. In her human and divine role, Mary embodies such contraries as 'Exhausted and life-giving'; the process is continuous. As the

Rose, she is also the Garden of Paradise where all torment of love ends in peace. Under a tree 'in the cool of the day' (a reminder of the loss of Eden: Genesis, iii.8), with 'the blessing of sand' (the dense-desiccation of 'Burnt Norton'), the bones are both scattered and united. Neither division nor unity matters in this initiation towards a state which Eliot compares with the rebirth of a nation (cf. Ezekiel, xxxvii.14; xlv.1, as a prologue to the vision of the new Jerusalem and the holy waters, and its termination in xlvii.21). The whole symbolism of this poem could be considered as an elaboration of the prophecy in Isaiah that the desert shall rejoice and blossom as the rose.

It is fortunate that the title 'Som de l'escalina' was withdrawn from the third section, for, despite the progress indicated, it is misleading; the summit does not appear to be in sight, and the spiral stairway has no precise reference to Dante's *Purgatorio*. The reminder of Satan's success in Eden near the end of the previous poem is timely, for the poet's persona finds himself struggling with 'the devil of the stairs', who gets the better of his judgment with either untoward hope or despair.[42] As he moves upward he sees these faces twisting and turning below him. His self-disgust gives the dark turning stairway a repulsive appearance; he thinks of the old Adam, 'corrupt according to the deceitful lusts' (Ephesians, iv.22), and is horrified, as if he were looking into the gaping jaws of an old shark. The slotted window at the first turning of the third stair bellies out like the fruit of the fig, and probably has the same uterine connotation as it had for D. H. Lawrence in *Birds, Beasts and Flowers*. The scene it reveals of the colourfully dressed, broadbacked figure with the 'antique' flute in a maytime meadow may be intended to recall Marlowe's 'antic hay'; it reminds the climber of lilac and sweet brown hair blown over his face. The distraction of the flute and an access of 'strength beyond hope and despair' give mental 'stops and steps' which correspond to his movements on the third stair. The simple repetition which indicates the receding of worldly allurement illustrates how almost by sound alone psychological effects are felicitously achieved, just as they are, earlier, on a larger scale, by striking denotative imagery. The final lines, from the lips of the centurion at Capernaum (Matthew, viii.5–8) show humility and trust: 'but speak the word only, and [thy] servant shall be healed'.

The fourth section is prospectively transitional, ending in

'after this our exile' (from the Anthem of our Lady), after the
yearning recurrence of 'Redeem the time' (cf. Ephesians, v.16).
Another key expression is 'between': in 'the years that walk
between', more emphatically in the repeated 'Who walked
between' at the opening. The anonymous Lady is an
intermediary between the human and the divine, as Matilda is
before Dante meets Beatrice in the Earthly Paradise. Dante sees
Matilda beyond a rivulet, culling flower after flower in this
divine forest. Eliot alludes to her in the ambivalence of between
violet and violet, and again between 'The various ranks of
varied green'; the violet and green, like the white and blue (the
Virgin's colour) are more significant as spiritual symbols: violet
indicates penitence (and is the liturgical colour throughout
Lent); white and green represent faith and hope. The Lady in
white and blue is carefree; she knows the 'eternal dolour' of
Hell (*Inferno*, iii.2) but is withdrawn from experience of it by the
eternal peace of God's love. As Matilda, she is associated with
streams which preserve eternal spring in the Earthly Paradise;
she is the Lady of the second part of *Ash-Wednesday* whose
beneficence redeems the desert. With her walk the new years,
and Eliot links the change they bring with the quality of his
verse, as he does in *Four Quartets*. The 'higher dream' redeems
the early poetry, in which the vision, sought or seen, had not
been read. The flute of the garden god (Priapus to the Romans)
is no longer heard (he seems to be no more than a sculptured
form), while the 'gilded hearse', signifying the burial of 'the
pomps and vanity of this wicked world', is drawn away heavily
(the verse suggests) by unicorns (the symbol of purity) bedecked
with jewels, which have the heavenly significance associated
with them in Revelation. A quickening of the verse with the
springing-up of the fountain (which, in the Earthly Paradise
with its flowers and birdsong, is continuously supplied by God,
and divides into Lethe and Eunoë, streams which respectively
remove the memory of sin and impart new life) confirms the
hope that the higher dream will be redeemed; it is a token of
the Incarnation, of the Word that will be heard when the wind
shakes 'a thousand whispers from the yew'. The whispers
confirm an awareness of God; the perpetual verdure of the yew
is a symbol of resurrection and immortality, as it was for Sir
Thomas Browne.

Bold verbal and semantic reiteration (of a kind Eliot would

at one time have been quick to condemn), for the sake of sound in the opening lines of the fifth section, reaches a memorable climax in the word-play of 'Against the Word the unstilled world still whirled About the centre of the silent Word.' The repetition, based first on Lancelot Andrewes, then on expressions in the introductory verses of St John's gospel, is enriched when the 'world'-'whirled' pun of Sir John Davies' *Orchestra* is inwound, to anticipate 'the still point of the turning world' in 'Coriolan' and 'Burnt Norton'. God's 'controversy' with his people is that the world still whirls against the Word of light: 'O my people, what have I done unto thee?' In the Catholic mass for Good Friday these words occur as if spoken by Jesus on the cross, and the most haunting line of Eliot's second paragraph, 'No place of grace for those who avoid the face', was probably written with this in mind. Those who walk in darkness (cf. John, viii.12) have neither time nor peace for religious contemplation. The repetition of opposites between the world and the Word is continued, and the question is whether the Lady who is veiled in white and blue will pray for those who, being in the dilemma ('torn on the horn', the *argumentum cornutum*) of having to choose between these alternatives, are like 'children at the gate', unable, in the words of 'Animula', to 'fare forward or retreat'. The gate is probably the 'strait gate' of Matthew, vii.13–14: 'Enter ye in at the strait gate . . . which leadeth unto life. . . .' The image of children may have come from 'The Collar' by George Herbert, a poem which dramatizes the dilemma projected by Eliot, and ends with submission:

> But as I rav'd and grew more fierce and wilde
> At every word,
> Me thoughts I heard one calling, *Child!*
> And I reply'd, *My Lord.*

The waverers have reached a point in the 'last desert', near the sea and between rocks blue as the sea (Mary's colour; 'Mary', like 'Marina', suggests lady of *mare*, the sea). Such is their dilemma, it is as if the desert is in the garden (of Earthly Paradise) and the garden in the desert, with the 'withered apple-seed' of sin (which drove our first parents from the garden) in the process of being rejected.

There is no resolution of the poet's spiritual crisis; he still wavers. The change from the opening of *Ash-Wednesday*, from 'Because' to the introductory 'Although' of the last section, stresses the dilemma; spiritually his position has hardly changed. He wishes not to wish things but to 'sit still', 'to care and not to care' (cf. I Peter, v.7: 'Casting all your care upon him; for he careth for you'), recognising that 'Our peace is in His will' (the *sea* to which all things move: *Paradiso*, iii.85–6). It is a time of suspense between dying and birth (between death to the world and spiritual regeneration) or between birth and dying, profit and loss (a phrase from 'Death by Water'), a twilight period which is 'dreamcrossed'. In this place between blue rocks, where one yew-tree relates to the dying life, the other to the nascent, and both to 'resurrection', three dreams cross; they belong respectively to the transit period, the life which is past, and the new, as yet unattained, life. The last is indicated in the white sails *flying* seaward, 'unbroken wings' suggesting the eagle's renewed strength. The call of the past causes the spirit to rebel; 'the lost heart stiffens and rejoices' in the thought of past happiness, which Eliot associates with holidays in New England, with lilac, voices of the sea, golden-rod, birds, the tang of the sea, and the saltness of sandy soil. So heart and senses are diverted to earthly, 'empty forms' (which come from Sleep's ivory gate in Virgil). ('Bless me father' and 'Suffer me not to be separated' are familiar in Catholic worship; 'And let my cry come unto Thee' is a common response in Church prayer, from the hundred-and-first psalm.) The poet's prayer is to the Lady (the veiled sister) and the Virgin Mary, to whom the 'spirit of the river' and the 'spirit of the sea' seem to be in apposition. The Lady (like Matilda, and Lethe and Eunoë) is related to the river of life, as Mary, mother of the divine, is to the sea; and the waters of the river that 'go down into the desert' are healed when they are 'brought forth into the sea' (Ezekiel, xlvii.8).

The starting-point for 'Marina' may have been a passage in *Mon coeur mis à nu*, where Baudelaire imagines vessels in harbour asking 'Quand partons-nous vers le bonheur?' The poetry of flight originating in this paragraph, Eliot writes in his essay on Baudelaire (which, like 'Marina', was published in September 1930), is 'a dim recognition of the direction of beatitude'. Baudelaire's idea is single; 'Marina' is complex. Eliot was

particularly influenced by the recognition scene in *Pericles*, the
'paradisal radiance' of which was renewed for him on reading
G. Wilson Knight's 'Myth and Miracle' (1929);[43] it was the
finest of all those in Shakespeare's last plays. It could be argued
that Eliot's symbolism arises from a few lines in this scene
(v.i.191–5): Pericles has reached the shores of his mortality,
and is given new life by reunion with his daughter Marina, who
was born at sea:

> Lest this great sea of joys rushing upon me
> O'erbear the shores of my mortality,
> And drown me with their sweetness. O, come hither,
> Thou that beget'st him that did thee beget;
> Thou that wast born at sea . . . .

Earlier in the scene Marina has said that she does not belong to
any shores. Eliot's New England shores, which are vividly
evoked in picture, sound, and scent, mark the transit-point
between the old self and the new. The epigraph from Seneca's
Herculens Furens (translated in Thomas Newton's edition 'What
place is this? what region? or of the world what coast?'), when
Hercules emerges from the hell of madness in which he has
mistakenly killed his wife and children, has its recurrent parallel
in the poem. It bears on the Pericles story, and is inextricably
related to the torment of Eliot's marriage, to an access of
religious hope, and to the certitude that relief is not of this
world, the thought of which provokes a change of key, a rather
pulpit-thumping passage, salvaged by fine imagery and
phraseology to present generalities with poetic definition. The
symbolical seashore renders insubstantial the world of death
represented by predatory business, vanity, complacency, and
sensuality. 'By this grace dissolved in place What is this
face . . . ?' recalls 'No place of grace for those who avoid the face'
in *Ash-Wednesday*. The grace which is expressed in Marina is
presented as it occurs both to an old, physically failing man
and to the yearner for salvation. It is near and far, crescent and
evanescent, raising the question whether it is given or lent; it is
conveyed in terms of whispers, 'small laughter' (the first hint in
Eliot of children's laughter with this import), and the meeting
of all the waters – Dante's sea of God's will, to which all things
move, and the voice of God (Revelation, i.15; xiv.2). It is heard

near the shore in the call of the woodthrush through the fog. Pericles' timbers are decrepit; his ship has suffered the hellish extremes of ice and fire (*Inferno*, iii.85–7). After confused recollections of his former erring self ('unknowing, half-conscious, unknown, my own'), he returns to the subject of the sea-change, and becomes more evidently the poet's persona. He resigns his old life for one beyond this timekept world; his hope is in new ships, the new voyage of *la vita nuova*. The musical dreamlike beauty of the Pericles scene has become the inspiration of an artistically rounded poem which makes the indefinable real through a range of imagery, reaches almost ecstatic intensity, and exerts exceptional appeal through dramatically punctuated and lyrically varied rhythms.

Another Ariel poem, 'Triumphal March', which appeared in October 1931, and 'Difficulties of a Statesman', published late the same year, were intended as part of a 'Cyril' sequence; Eliot told G. Wilson Knight he was engaged on a poem inspired by Beethoven's *Coriolan*. His unfinished 'Coriolan' turns to the outer contemporary world, satirizing lack of statesmanship in the western democracies when first signs of Germany's preparations for war were evident. Eliot had probably read Ludendorff's *The Coming War* (1931), which contains the statistics he gives of weapons, machines, and equipment surrendered by the Germans at the end of the 1914–18 war. Coriolanus, a great Roman patriot who had defeated the Volscians, scorned to seek the favour of the populace; Eliot grew tired of the inefficiency of democratic governments who, in times of crisis, chose to shelve responsibility and postpone decisions by setting up commissions and *ad hoc* committees. The First World War, it was said, was the war to end all wars, and Eliot's thoughts on the practical futility of so much work by proliferating deliberative councils may be gauged by his commission set up to confer with another commission on the subject of 'perpetual' peace.

Fantastic though the procession in 'Triumphal march' is, it is not too long for the spectators, whose comments comprise the greater part of the poem. There are touches of Aristophanic relief: while stools and sausages are available, people don't mind waiting. The crowd is excited by the flags, the eagles, and the trumpets (which Eliot had failed to find at an earlier period, when he imagined multitudes weeping over scones and crumpets). The crumpets return with the trumpets, in an aside which registers Eliot's assessment of people's religion: 'And Easter Day, we didn't get to the country, So we took young Cyril to church. And they rang the bell And he said right out loud, *crumpets*', being reminded of the itinerant muffin-man. This use of illiterate and idiomatic speech in poetry is hardly successful, but it has seldom been more daring. In his quotation to the effect that perceiving is the 'natural waking life of our Ego', Eliot mischievously alludes to the view expressed by Edmund Husserl in *Ideas* that the average man thinks of perception as 'the empty looking of an empty "Ego" towards the object'.

The question 'Is he coming?', and the references to the temple and the sacrifice, after his passing, suggest overtones of the Passover festival and the Crucifixion, which are reinforced by the juxtaposition of 'the still point of the turning world'. Eliot's hero is indifferent to the pomp and hero-worship; as the sequel shows more fully, his humanity has deeper springs. The Jovian oakleaves and eagles recall the triumphal processions, and the deification by the populace, of victorious generals in ancient Rome. The heavy materialism of worldly power, denoted by imagery weighted down with 'stone' to give the massed processional beat, is closely associated with dust. The ending passes from the vulgar comedy of not throwing away the sausage ('It'll come in handy') to the polite smoker's request for a light. The Light which Eliot seeks is barred out, as when *les soldats faisaient la haie.* It is blotted out with *ILS LA FAISAIENT.* The quotation is taken from a description of a State occasion in Charles Maurras's *L'Avenir de l'Intelligence*.[44]

'Difficulties of a Statesman' opens with 'CRY what shall I cry? All flesh is grass' from Isaiah (xl.6). As in 'East Coker', those who have won worldly honours (here they are more cosmopolitan) monopolize this category. Commissions, committees, and sub-committees pullulate, while guards neglect their duties, and frogs croak, in the marshes. (The frogs foretell the coming storm: *Georgics*, i.378. The Mantuan apostrophe may deliberately echo the address of Sordello, a Coriolanus-like figure, to Virgil in the *Purgatorio*, vi.61–75; Eliot quotes it in his 1929 essay on Dante: 'O Mantuan, I am Sordello of thy very soil.') The voice speaks for Coriolanus and the poet: the former addresses his mother; the poet, the Holy Mother (the wild clematis is called 'Virgin's Bower'). Each yearns for the wisdom that comes from the still point of the turning world; the poet associates it with the dove (the Spirit of God, or the Holy Ghost: Matthew, iii.16; Luke, iii.22), the sheltering palm of the desert, and running water. 'O hidden' does not express a wish to take refuge; it vibrates quietly with the desire for awareness of God's will. Through the dust or in the croaking night, hints of the coming storm are felt, and the only demand is for an investigating committee. The repeated 'RESIGN' which ends the poem works on two planes, like so much in Eliot's verse; it is a protest against mundane futility in high places, and an insistence on the need to make the kind of resignation which Pericles hopefully foresees at the end of 'Marina'.

As the situation in western Europe deteriorated, Eliot lost faith in political measures; satire lost its appeal with the growth of his foreboding, and it is no wonder that the 'Cyril' sequence was allowed to lapse. The discontinuation of 'Coriolan' manifests Eliot's first serious presentiment that his efforts to maintain an exchange of west-European views in *The Criterion* were doomed to fail. When, after this decline, England and France, menaced by Hitlerite militarism, made, in the words of Shakespeare's *Coriolanus* (v.iii.191), 'convenient peace' at Munich, Eliot, like many of his compatriots, felt humiliated.

15

Essays and Lectures

i BAUDELAIRE AND DANTE

Eliot's first essay on Baudelaire, which was included in *For Lancelot Andrewes*, after appearing in May 1927, was a critical review of Arthur Symons' translations of Baudelaire. It has as much to say on Symons as on Baudelaire, and is particularly critical of his transformation, rather than translation, of Baudelaire, a rendering in terms of religious aestheticism, ritual, and confession which recalls Pater, and is as incongruous with Eliot's own period (he adds with some chronological confusion) as with that of Shaw, Wells, Strachey, and Hemingway. Using 'violet' pejoratively (instead of with approval, as in *The Waste Land*), Eliot illustrates how Symons, using 'counters of habitual and lazy sentiment', envelops the definition of Baudelaire in the 'Swinburnian violet-coloured London fog' of the eighteen-nineties. He had assumed that Baudelaire's poetry was devoted to the passions, and was affected by heredity and nervous temperament. 'If a writer sees truly', Eliot answers, making less of his conditional clause than he ought, 'his heredity and nerves do not matter' — a statement that must seem inconsistent with other, more striking, assertions he made on the relationship between poetry and the writer's nerves. Symons, he continues, suffered from the childish attitude toward religion of the 'nineties: for the disciples of Swinburne, sin was good fun as a subject; Wilde was a 'child-actor'. To Baudelaire on the other hand, evil, vice, and sin were real. Symons' translation was excellent for his generation, but one is now needed to show how much Baudelaire resembled Racine. Unlike Swinburne, he did not waste a word; he was, Eliot concludes, born out of his time both as a classicist and as a Christian, and he acquired humility, the supreme Christian virtue, and the most difficult to achieve.

The second essay, which appeared in 1930 as the introduction to Isherwood's translation of *Journaux Intimes*, is more general than Eliot initially suggests; it stresses the importance of Baudelaire's prose works, studies his poetry, and holds considerable interest as a mirror of Eliot himself. As a result of Swinburne's extravagant presentation, and the view that *Les Fleurs du Mal* was the work of an artist for the sake of art (which nobody can be, Eliot adds), Baudelaire had been misunderstood; he is, Eliot contends, a later, more limited, Goethe, though it is priggishly unreal to speak of his unhealthiness, as opposed to Goethe's health. Most of his prose is as important as most of Goethe's; we can see from it that Baudelaire was no Satanist, but one who discovered Christianity for himself, and asserted its necessity. Study of his own suffering made him reject the natural and human in a wordly sense, 'in favour of Heaven and Hell'. Though technically more skilful than Gautier, he had less sense of form; he is more intent on 'a form of life'. In a romantic age a poet can be classical only in tendency, and the counter-romanticism of Baudelaire's stock imagery has not always worn well, though his use of the city for background and image has acted as a release for other poets. He is 'the greatest exemplar in *modern* poetry', his verse and language being the nearest to a 'complete renovation' that we have known. Equally admirable is his sincerity, though he was unable to disengage himself completely from the 'romantic detritus' of Byronism and Satanism; when his sorrow takes refuge in romantic flights of nostalgia, he is vague compared with Dante. Unable to make the Dantean ascent from the natural to the spiritual, Baudelaire discovered that the difference between human and animal sexual relationships is the consciousness of good and evil; he realized that the sexual act is 'more dignified, less boring' as evil than as the 'natural, "life-giving", cheery automatism of the modern world'. From this Eliot concludes that it is better 'to do evil than to do nothing'; Baudelaire was 'man enough for damnation', and we can pray for his repose. Eliot implies that awareness of human fallibility is healthier than belief in human perfectibility; he indulges, nonetheless, a propensity for bravado and arresting statement, buttressed no doubt by the ample attestation of Dante's Ante-Hell, anticlimactically coupled with what must appear as the ingenuous detachment or bland assurance of a convert. He sees *La Vita Nuova* and *La Divina Commedia* as the complement or antidote to *Journaux Intimes*, and finds grandeur in Baudelaire's view that the progress of civilization depends on the reduction of original sin.

Eliot's first essay on Dante, a 1920 review which was included in *The Sacred Wood*, is restricted to the question whether great poetry is incompatible with philosophy. Among the ancient philosophical poets, Lucretius is eminent; his authentic direction is toward an 'ordered vision' of human life, which is expressed with vigorous poetic imagery and acuteness of observation; his philosophy, however, did not generate a sufficient width and variety of feeling to create a successful whole. In Dante's *La Divina Commedia* the absorption of mythology and theology has created complete unification of allegory, didactic ends, and emotional significance. To differentiate between them, as critics are apt to do, introduces a bias which misrepresents the poetry. In discussing an example of this kind of misrepresentation, Eliot clarifies his admiration of Brunetto Latini: in Dante's *Inferno* souls are not deadened, as they usually are in life, and among them he seems to be 'the one who gains and not he who loses' (xv.124). It is the emotional structure within Dante's framework which needs to be understood; it is the most comprehensive and the most 'ordered scale of human emotions' ever devised. By comparison with Shakespeare's, they are simple and unanalysed, but they are finally assessable only in relation to the whole, including the philosophical, an integrated vision which is perfected only in the last canto of the *Paradiso*.

'Dante', published in 1929 in 'The Poets on the Poets' series, and dedicated to Charles Maurras, is a personal introduction to *La Divina Commedia* and *La Vita Nuova*. Eliot himself prefers to come to poetry without any introduction, and is convinced, as readers of his own must be, that genuine poetry is communicated before it is understood. For him the last canto of *La Divina Commedia* attains the highest point ever reached by poetry, and the greatness of the whole work is such that one can only hope to be adequate to it at the end of life. On the writing of poetry more can be learned from Dante, Eliot thought, than from any English poet. He has learned from the *Inferno* that the greatest poetry can be written with the maximum economy of words, and with the utmost 'austerity in the use of metaphor, simile, verbal beauty, and elegance'; from the *Purgatorio*, that philosophy can be made poetical; and, from the *Paradiso*, that rarefied states of beatitude can be the subject of great poetry. Dante's philosophy or theology does not need to be accepted; if his poetry is read as poetry, it commands 'poetic *assent*'; both belief and disbelief are suspended. In a long note on this subject, he qualifies this view by stating that full appreciation of poetry is most likely when the reader shares the beliefs which inspire the poet; *pure* literary criticism and poetry are abstractions, and 'both in creation and enjoyment much always enters which is, from the point of view of "Art", irrelevant'. On the question of love, Eliot is more unconvincing than in the essay on Baudelaire; his statement may cast light on his first marriage, and on some of his poetry. He maintains that the sentiment surrounding love ignores the fact that it can be 'explained and made reasonable' only by the 'higher love' (the context indicates the love of God), without which it is no more than the coupling of animals.

In saying that Dante is 'the most *universal*' of modern poets, Eliot implies that he is 'first a European'. His lucidity is due to a number of factors: he was trained in the common tongue of medieval Latin, and adopted the kind of allegory which was familiar in western Europe; predominantly a visual artist, he uses simple language, and few metaphors compared with Shakespeare. His major work cannot be understood in parts without an appreciation of the whole, but the reader is advised first to concentrate on episodes. Of those in the *Inferno* which impressed Eliot most at first reading, two stand out, the meeting of Brunetto Latini and Dante (xv) and the last voyage of Ulysses (xxvi); in both Eliot notes the element of *surprise* which Poe thought essential to poetry. He cannot refrain from comparing Tennyson's 'Ulysses' adversely; its Virgilianism is too poetical, and the work falls flat, containing nothing more than can be recognised by the 'average Englisman, with a feeling for verbal beauty'. Dante's Hell is a state which can be thought of, and perhaps even experienced, only 'by the projection of sensory images', and therefore, Eliot concludes, the resurrection of the body has a deeper meaning than is usually understood; he implies, as his poetry does, that this is also a state. His prejudice against Milton is revived in a most interesting form; Dante's Satan (xxxiv) may seem grotesque, especially if we have in mind 'the curly-haired Byronic hero' of *Paradise Lost.*

Only after reading *La Divina Commedia* and re-reading the *Inferno* can the *Purgatorio* be appreciated, for 'Damnation and even blessedness arc more exciting than purgation.' Four of its episodes were of particular interest to Eliot, one containing the line echoed in *The Waste Land,* 'Siena made me, Maremma unmade me'; two recount moving scenes, when Sordello meets his fellow Mantuan Virgil (vi), and when Statius learns from Dante that he is in the presence of the author of the *Aeneid* (xxi); the last, ending with 'Poi s'ascose nel foco che gli affina', illustrates how souls in Purgatory suffer willingly. When we reach the Earthly Paradise, we are already in the world of the *Paradiso.* Eliot confesses that he had difficulties to overcome before he was reconciled to its pageantry, the first arising from his antipathy to Pre-Raphaelite imagery, the second from the distaste engendered by the nineteenth century for anything optimistic. It took him a long time to realize that the states of spiritual purgation and beatitude at the end of the *Purgatorio* and in the *Paradiso* are much further removed than the *Inferno* from what his contemporary world could regard as optimism. He says little on the *Paradiso,* holding that it is neither episodic nor monotonous, and that nowhere has such rare experience been more concretely presented, in imagery of light which is typical of mystical literature (and not without influence in 'Burnt Norton'). Eliot finds 'the greatest *width* of human passion' in Shakespeare, but the greatest 'altitude' and 'depth' in Dante. *La Vita Nuova,* which is best appreciated after *La Divina Commedia,* belongs to the literature of vision; its philosophy springs from Catholic disillusionment with the world. To pass 'through the looking-glass' into its world, which for Eliot is as reasonable as ours, is as difficult as spiritual rebirth. The acceptance of its medieval forms is more important than belief, but it may lead to the point where the New Life begins.

In his introduction to G. Wilson Knight's *The Wheel of Fire* (1930) Eliot defines his position more clearly on the question of poetry and philosophy. He does not retract his former statement that Dante made 'great poetry' out of 'a great philosophy of life', and that Shakespeare made 'equally great poetry' out of a philosophy of life that was 'inferior and muddled'; he asserts that Dante's poetry is the richer for the philosophy, and

Shakespeare's the poorer by a 'rag-bag philosophy'. He confesses his preference for poetry with a clear philosophical system, especially if it is Christian and Catholic, always provided that it has the kind of high poetic pattern beyond verbal beauty which he finds extensively, and most elaborately and inscrutably, in Shakespeare's plays. The irony is that readers attempt to impose a philosophy and moral aims on Shakespeare, and are indifferent to the philosophy of Dante. 'So we kick against those who wish to guide us, and insist upon being guided by those who only aim to show us a vision, a dream if you like, which is beyond good and evil in the common sense.'

In 'What Dante Means to Me', a talk given at the Italian Institute, London, in 1950, Eliot, after telling how he began to read Dante, turns to the influence of poets on his own poetry. Baudelaire and Laforgue made him realize that it was the poet's business to make poetry from 'the unexplored resources of the unpoetical' (an aim which Hardy set himself as early as 1877). The appreciation of the masters, such as Shakespeare, Dante, Homer, and Virgil, is the task of a lifetime; when Eliot was young he was more at ease with the lesser Elizabethan dramatists than with Shakespeare. The deepest and most lasting influence on his poetry was Dante and, in illustration of it, he dwells especially on his problem of imitative verse-form in 'Little Gidding', before reciting a lengthy passage of *terze rima* from *The Triumph of Life* (chosen for its comment on Rousseau, which he refers to incidentally); he thought Dante's influence on Shelley more remarkable than on any other English poet. He draws three conclusions from Dante's example. The first is that the highest achievement possible for a poet is the passing on of language as a 'more highly developed, more refined, and more precise' instrument than it was before he used it; the master of language is its servant, the most painstaking 'practitioner of the *craft*'. The second is the importance of emotional range; English religious poets are specialists compared with Dante, who expresses all that man can experience, from 'depravity's despair' to the 'beatific vision'. The two points are virtually one, for to communicate such width of experience demands an extensive range of resources. Finally, as Dante is the most European of European writers, the lessons of his craft and of his 'exploration of sensibility' can be an inspiration to many.

ii HUMANISM AND CHRISTIANITY

At a time when weak and dishonest statesmanship allowed western Europe to drift into war, Eliot could write in *Murder in the Cathedral* that 'Destiny waits in the hand of God, not in the hands of statesmen.' A more accurate view is the law of consequences which George Eliot saw in history as much as in the scientific world. The view that human affairs, individual or international, are in the hands of men was opposed by Eliot more and more openly from 1927. An essay on Machiavelli, which he withdrew from publication after its appearance in *For Lancelot Andrewes*, is significantly based on complete sympathy with Machiavelli's rejection of 'the myth of human goodness' which liberal thinkers substitute for 'belief in Divine Grace'. The 'John Bramhall' essay is directed against Hobbesian determinism, which excluded free-will, and was a forerunner of Marxist materialism; free-will is axiomatic with Dante and Eliot, and Bramhall's opposition to Hobbes is relevant to the present (1927), a 'period of debility' when few men have the strength to follow the *via media*. For lazy minds there is only apathy or the extremes of fascism and communism. A review at the end of the year on the philosopher F. H. Bradley is devised to attack the humanism of Matthew Arnold. The perfection of Bradley's style, an index of his passionate intellectual intensity, receives its due. His banter reminds Eliot of Arnold, from whom he proceeds to Mill and Utilitarianism, which Bradley succeeded in undermining far more successfully than Arnold did. Bradley had the wisdom of scepticism and 'uncynical disillusion', which are useful aids in the cultivation of religious understanding; and this he employed to wreck Arnold's contention that the will of God is 'our best self, or right reason', to which we should turn for guidance. Eliot finds the answer he seeks in Bradley, that man needs to submit his whole self to the divine will.

The debate gathers momentum, and becomes more confused, in 'The Humanism of Irving Babbitt' (1928) and 'Second Thoughts about Humanism' (1929), the first prompted by Babbitt's *Democracy and Leadership*, the second by the wish to correct impressions, through particular reference to *American Criticism*, the work of Norman Foerster, one of Babbitt's disciples. The argument becomes complicated, many small points being raised and refuted as if they resolved the larger issues. Eliot is too narrowly dogmatic to spread much light: you must be, he says, 'either a naturalist or a supernaturalist'. 'Man is man because he can recognize supernatural realities, not because he can invent them.' Remove from the word 'human' all that man has derived from belief in the supernatural, and he is reduced to the level of an animal. Eliot makes no allowance for the transmission of values and ideals, the wisdom learnt from experience, in the evolution of civilizations. His opposition to such views is expressed in ridicule of 'romantic visions of perfectibility', as if humanism could still imply such eighteenth-century ideas. Turning in the last resort to Hulme and Original Sin adds nothing to his argument.

He maintains that humanism is either 'an alternative' to religion or 'ancillary' to it. The 'inner check' which democracy increasingly demands of individuals is insufficient for Eliot, who sees the threat of chaos in 'private notions'. He refers to Comtism, but makes no mention of its crusade against self-seeking in favour of altruism, which was undoubtedly the product of Christianity, though widely operative today outside Churches. Eliot doubts whether civilization can survive without religion, or religion without a Church, but does not stop to consider whether humanism, with its emphasis on education, on science for enlightenment and welfare, and on humanitarian action and justice, can modernize the Church, and give new vitality to religion. He dismisses Babbitt's ideas as a by-product of 'Protestant theology in its last agonies', but concedes that humanism is valuable as 'a mediating and corrective ingredient in a positive civilization founded on definite belief'; the 'pure' humanist will not 'set up humanism as a substitute for philosophy and religion'. The pure humanist may have a commendable philosophy and religion of his own, it should be added. Writing in *The Criterion* of October 1933 (on Irving Babbitt's death), Eliot indicated that such a possibility disturbed his thinking; humanism, he wrote, cannot survive without the existence of people who believe in 'the Christian supernatural order' and its operation in the world.

'Arnold and Pater' (1930) is less controversial but characteristically dismissive. It contains an assessment of *Marius the Epicurean* which ends with the assurance that it did not influence 'a single first-rate mind' after its generation. Pater, it is conceded, only Hellenizes, whereas Arnold alternately Hellenizes and Hebraicizes. Arnold is considered to be deceptively persuasive; his 'culture' appears so reasonable and enlightened that his indifference to all theological and ecclesiastical differences may pass unnoticed. His books on Christianity insist that the Christian 'emotions' can be retained without the belief; from them it might be deduced that religion is either morals or art. Eliot's strength and extravagance of feeling are indicated in his conclusion that the full effect of Arnold's philosophy would be the substitution of culture for religion, and the laying waste of religion 'in an anarchy of feeling'; Arnold is guilty of 'intellectual Epicureanism'. Eliot's tetchiness when he accuses him of 'loose jargon' arises from Arnold's belief that the essential for Christians is not the Incarnation but 'the imitation of Christ'; he does not refer the reader to Arnold's sonnet 'Anti-Desperation', which reveals how positive religion could be in a humanist and humanitarian world. He refers sardonically to Arnold's prophecy and Pater's gospel, and is certain that the 'degradation' of philosophy and religion which the former 'skilfully initiated' was 'competently continued' by Pater, who turned his emotional and moral self towards art. 'Art for art's sake' was fathered by Arnold's 'culture', Eliot continues; it becomes 'religious art' and eventually 'aesthetic religion' when religion is somnolent. The theory of art for art's sake is valid only as 'an exhortation to the artist to stick to his job', as Flaubert and Henry James did.

'Thoughts after Lambeth' (1931), a commentary on the Report of the 1930 Conference of that 'oddest of institutions', the Church of England, begins in a sprightly style which cannot be sustained when some of its leading recommendations are considered. The popular press had fastened attention, not on the most important parts of the report, the Christian doctrine of God, but on its most insipid subjects. On youth and vocation it seemed to indicate that the bishops had been listening to 'ordinary popular drivel'; the 'great intellectual stirring among the rising generation' that is noted is nothing but 'journalistic hyperbole', for the proportion capable of being intellectually stirred to a high degree in any generation, anywhere, is small. Eliot believes that prejudice against religion had declined, but is dismayed to read the trope that youth has 'struck its tents and is on the march'. Everybody, according to the press, is on the march; whatever the destination, the one thing not to do is to 'sit still'. Even if it has no more than 'the spirit of a tomtit or the brain of a goose', youth could hardly rally to two such depressing supporters of the secular Life Force creed as Bertrand Russell and Aldous Huxley. There are many preachers of what may be called the 'enervate *gospel of happiness*'; the new freedom creates a 'meagre impoverished emotional life'. There can be no such thing as mere morality, Eliot insists, adding with characteristically absolute finality that the real conflict is not between various opinions of morality but between theism and atheism. There must be a great deal between these extremes which can generate a progressive and spiritual outlook, and the question is whether Christian morals can survive without the whole of the traditional Christian faith. Eliot thinks it cannot, and writes ironically of the 'new respectability' which has relieved the Church of its burden, and has its pious pilgrims, who would once have been considered 'intellectual vagrants', all 'on the march' along the road that leads 'from nowhere to nowhere'.

The word 'generation' reminds him that some of his more commendatory critics had said that *The Waste Land* expressed 'the disillusionment of a generation'; his answer is that he may unintentionally have expressed their own 'illusion of being disillusioned'. His position now seems different, a reviewer of *For Lancelot Andrewes* having greeted it with a 'flattering obituary notice', treating him as a lost sheep, if not as a lost leader. The thought of his absence from the 'roll-call of the new saints' inspires Eliot to some interesting comments on Middleton Murry, humanism and its fugleman Norman Foerster, the press, the Huxley brothers, and Freud. Without religion the whole race, including the man who believes in an outing by car and a round of golf on Sunday, would die of boredom.

On birth-control he is, without jettisoning any of his spiritual imperatives, progressive in outlook, raising critical questions for the Catholic Church as well as the Anglican. He knows that social, political, and local divisions make the union of English Churches very difficult, but thinks that for historical reasons the Church of England has a special responsibility towards the Methodists. His strict views on theology and transubstantiation make him object to the admission of dissenters to the Holy Communion service, and he regards reunion with the Eastern and Baltic Churches as more important than union at home. The Church, he thinks, is gradually becoming 'the Catholic Church of England'; only through it can England be converted to Christianity 'in any appreciable degree'. Its disagreements are an indication of life, and qualify it to initiate steps towards the reunion of the Christian Churches, the 1930 Conference marking an important step in that direction. The attempt to form a secular civilization will fail, but we need to await its collapse with great patience, 'meanwhile redeeming the time: so that the Faith may be preserved alive through the dark ages before us'.

In 'Catholicism and the International Order' (1933) Eliot asserts that the heretic, whatever his political complexion, is unlike the Catholic in having 'low ideals and great expectations'. Without moral conversion no great improvement is possible, for most people are morally idle and evasive. Without a clear moral and religious standpoint, literary criticism is not complete, he argues in 'Religion and Literature' (1934), where he admits a readiness to fulminate at length against those who admire the Bible purely as literature; it is unfortunate too that disregard for religious values makes readers assume that religious poetry is minor poetry. The context in which Eliot refers to George Eliot, Meredith, and Hardy shows that his disapproval hinges on their non-acceptance of Christian dogmatism; he excepts Joyce from most modern novelists, who regard Christianity as an anachronism. We can gain from such authors if we see clearly how they looked at life, and how they differ from us; the most insidious corruption comes from the less-demanding popular authors who are read for pleasure. Modern literature, in its failure to realize 'the primacy of the supernatural over the natural life', is tainted with secularism. 'Modern Education and the Classics', a lecture given during his 1932–3 period at Harvard University, is notable for Eliot's attack on the liberal policy of assuming that any one subject for academic study is educationally equal to another, and for his assertion that no one is well educated until he has studied something for which he has no aptitude. More significant is his venturing to advocate a revival of monasticism for the maintenance of a Christian education, a thought which he presented more fully in *The Idea of a Christian Society*.

This work, the subject of three lectures given at Corpus

Christi College, Cambridge, in March 1939, was written with the fear of the war which became the Second World War in mind, and published not many weeks after its outbreak. Western civilization was faced with the alternative of Christianity or paganism, Eliot wrote, but his discourse suffers so much from nice qualificatory discriminations such as are confessed in 'Lines for Cuscuscaraway and Mirza Murad Ali Beg' that rarely until the final pages does it warm to the urgency of its convictions. His main interest is in promoting attitudes for the creation of a Christian society; such a change would affect industry and commerce. In England, which was primarily the subject of his analysis, the liberalism of 'free exploitation' had passed, but the country was in the doldrums, incapable, Eliot held, of criticizing with dignity the politics and economics of non-democratic states until it had set its own house in order. The real objection to fascism, he thought, was its paganism; the English were too pagan to recognise this truth. The more industrialized a country, the more materialistic its outlook becomes; its people increasingly lose sense of tradition, turn against religion, and develop mass-mindedness. However well-off they are, they will be prone to mob action; 'totalitarian democracy' is not out of the question.

Eliot sees the danger of 'unlimited demagogy', and of the debasement of art and culture for commercial ends. There can be no political stability or coherence without a political philosophy, 'not of a party, but of the nation'. Education therefore is more important than a system of government. Influenced by the views of Jacques Maritain, Eliot recommends the setting-up of a Community of Christians, drawn from the laity as well as from the clergy, to ensure the increase and maintenance of Christian values as far as possible in a free society. The Christian society which he advocates could be created only through the Church of England, which would be the final authority on dogma, faith, and morals. It would work with the Community of Christians, and be subject to its criticism, even as it must be free to criticize the State. The idea of a Christian society implies one Church, representing the nation, which would have allegiances to State and Church.

As it is, 'only fear or jealousy of foreign success can alarm us about the health of our own nation', and the result may be nothing better than 'sanctimonious nationalism'. What distinguishes a Christian society from a pagan is not enthusiasm but dogma; it is a 'very dangerous inversion' if, 'instead of showing the necessity of Christian morality from the truth of Christianity', the Christian faith is defended because it supports moral standards.

In democracies the opposition of a sluggish majority will always slow down reform; 'the Kingdom of Christ on earth will never be realised', but 'is always being realised'.[45] Like Lawrence, Eliot sees the 'deformation of humanity' caused by 'unregulated' industrialism; reckless 'exploitation of the earth', for which future generations will pay, is an offence against God and nature. For long enough we have seen nothing more important than the values of a 'mechanised, commercialised, urbanised way of life'; we should do well 'to face the permanent conditions upon which God allows us to live upon this planet'. Only by discipline and effort can 'material knowledge and power' be gained without loss of 'spiritual knowledge and power'. We need to recover a sense of 'religious fear' in order to recover 'religious hope'. Democracy at present lacks positive force, and staggers from compromise to compromise. The Munich agreement of September 1938, resulting in the betrayal of Czechoslovakia by Britain and France for their own ends, brought not only a sense of humiliation but 'a doubt of the validity of a civilisation'. While events have continued to reinforce Eliot's diagnosis, they have done nothing to suggest that his proposals are practical or that they afford a solution. It seems rather that much wider reforms than he recommended are necessary to create a healthy, progressive democracy.

iii LECTURES IN AMERICA, 1932–1933

Eliot's Charles Eliot Norton lectures at Harvard, published as *The Use of Poetry and the Use of Criticism*, begin with a note of flattery to a man in whose honour the lectures were instituted, and for whose abilities the speaker's respect was seriously qualified by the thought, already stated in 'Arnold and Pater', that Norton was largely responsible for American humanism. Eliot notes his foresight in a letter of 1869 which refers to a dark future for Europe; he is impressed too by the importance Norton attached to literature, if not dogma, as a criterion of civilization. He himself holds that poetry represents a people's 'highest point of consciousness', and emphasizes the value of critical discussion in the experience of poetry. With much on criticism and its history that is neither new nor exciting, his introduction seems unduly long. He wishes more attention were given to the use of language in verse, 'the good or bad breeding' of poets, pointing out that Wordsworth and Coleridge revolted not only against a poetic tradition but also against a social order. He is convinced that there is a close relation between the best poetry and the best criticism of any particular age, and that the study of criticism may help to formulate conclusions on what is permanent in poetry. An interesting, rather autobiographical, note on the development of taste in the appreciation of poetry raises the question whether English literature should be included in the academic curriculum.

The 'Apology for the Countess of Pembroke' is an odd amalgam on Elizabethan criticism with reference to dramatic form and verse-technique. The survey shows no new research, especially where it is expected, on the Countess and her literary group. From the critical controversy of Campion and Daniel (on whether poetry needs rhyme) to Sidney's essay, from drama to the Aristotelian unities, with comments on *Hamlet* and Joyce's *Ulysses*, it reaches blank verse. Here Spenser's influence is highly praised, and even Milton is elevated to greatness. The later Elizabethan critics produce little above the level of dullness. A remark on the unities is significant as a pointer to Eliot's dramatic development: a play which observes them as far as possible is to that extent superior to one in which their artistic potentialities are not fully realized.

Still relying on Saintsbury's *History of Criticism*, and quoting useful passages on which to fasten commentary, Eliot manages a telling survey from Jonson to Johnson in 'The Age of Dryden'. He regards the Elizabethan era as the greatest age of English poetry, and is particularly pleased with Jonson's third requisite in a poet, which is '*Imitation*, to be able to convert the substances, or riches of another poet, to his own use.' 'Invention', the 'first happiness of the poet's imagination' for Dryden, is convincingly interpreted as 'the sudden irruption of the germ of a new poem, possibly merely as a state of feeling'. On the question of fancy, Dryden is found more satisfactory than Coleridge; for him the imagination was the total process of poetic creation including fancy. Addison throws no light on this question; unlike Dryden's, his remarks, as Johnson implied, were not so much for the writer as for 'those that read only to talk'. Addison was a 'popular lecturer', a 'bourgeois literary dictator' during an age of 'formalistic slumber'. Johnson, superior to Gray and Collins in sensibility and moral sentiment, was isolated, but, unlike later critics, could treat poetry as poetry, and not as something else.

Eliot is a better judge of Wordsworth's criticism than of his poetry. When he hazarded the cheap witticism that Wordsworth 'went droning on the still sad music of infirmity', he ignorantly parroted the view of critics who had never troubled to discover just how much poetry of distinction Wordsworth wrote from, say, 1803 to 1832. He makes allowance for the fact that *Biographia Literaria* was written years after the decline of Coleridge's poetic genius; he had been 'visited' by the Muse and was a 'haunted man' thereafter. Wordsworth's famous preface was written in his 'youth', and Eliot – it would need a special study to resolve this question – considers his influence on Coleridge greater than Coleridge's on him. He makes great play of the 'social passions' of the two poets, and thinks (without considering the evidence) that Wordsworth influenced Coleridge in this respect; it is doubtful, however, whether such passion has any bearing on 'Resolution and Independence'. Eliot is right in asserting that Wordsworth's revolutionary faith was more vital to him than it (he must mean Coleridge's) was to Coleridge, and it is refreshing to find a poet and critic asking what all the fuss is about with reference to Wordsworth's *essential* views on poetic diction; to say, as he does, that the two poets made common cause on this is to ignore *Biographia*. On Coleridge's distinction between fancy and imagination Eliot writes from experience: it does not seem wise, he concludes, to take memory into account in the analysis of fancy, and ignore it completely in discussing the imagination; there is much he admires in Coleridge's definition of the imagination, but to learn from it, he insists, one needs first to forget what he says on fancy.

The 'Shelley and Keats' lecture relates chiefly to the question of poetry and beliefs. Arnold's conclusion that Wordsworth's greatness as a poet is independent of his opinions is unacceptable; he is 'part of history', whereas Landor is 'only a magnificent by-product'. Eliot finds Shelley's views adolescent and repellent, and what he says on Shelley's poems indicates quite clearly that his own prejudices affect his judgment, though he comes back to the Rousseau passage in *The Triumph of Life* to illustrate the precision which he prefers in imagery, and appreciates Shelley's unusual gift for passionately apprehending abstract ideas. His conclusion is that a philosophy or view of life is no barrier in poetry when it is 'coherent, mature, and founded on the facts of experience'. It is a mistake to think of poetry in terms of pure enjoyment, as if it could be dissociated from life. Goethe 'dabbled in both philosophy and poetry and made no great success of either'. Keats, of whom Eliot says little, had a kind of greatness like Shakespeare's; of this his odes are sufficient proof, and there is hardly a statement on poetry in his letters which is not true; he lacked theories, but he did not withdraw from life, and had a philosophic mind.

Eliot finds Arnold to some extent the most satisfactory writer of his age, for Carlyle, Ruskin, Tennyson, and Browning were deficient in wisdom. Yet he was 'an undergraduate' in philosophy and theology, and a Philistine in religion. His poetry is academic 'in the best sense'; 'after associating with the riff-raff of the early part of the century' (which seems to refer to Wordsworth and Coleridge, Shelley and Keats), it is pleasing to be 'in the company of a man *qui sait se conduire*', even though Arnold's patronizing attitude to Burns makes him conclude that it is advantageous for the poet 'to deal with a beautiful world'. For Eliot, whose sympathies are with Baudelaire, Conrad, and Dante, this is not the essential: 'it is to be able to see beneath both beauty and ugliness; to see the boredom, and the horror, and the glory'. Arnold suffers in the eyes of a poet-critic who prefers the impersonal form of presentation: his verse has no technical interest, and his criticism tells us little about poetry from a writer's angle; he was an educator, and chose subjects for the expression of moral views. In criticism as in poetry he was dependent and academic; he lacked the originality to see the past in the new perspectives that are requisite for every generation. Eliot's play with the dictum that 'Poetry is at bottom a criticism of life' is based on an excess of literal-mindedness, though his later difficulty with Arnold's references to 'simple primary affections' and 'nature' in Wordsworth makes one wonder whether he is sincere or facetious. He is rather more assuring when he stresses the inconsistency of the 'criticism of life' theory and Arnold's contention that Wordsworth's philosophy is an illusion, though poetry with no explicit philosophical views often succeeds in presenting an Arnoldian criticism of life. In the attempt to find a substitute for religion in poetry, Eliot continues, Arnold confuses poetry and morals, sometimes with deplorable critical results, notably in his condemnation of Chaucer for lack of high seriousness. He knew more about what he expected of poetry than he knew about the nature of poetry. His own verse lacked what Eliot calls the 'auditory imagination', a 'feeling for syllable and rhythm' which invigorates every word.

In 'The Modern Mind' Eliot devotes much of his time to I. A. Richards' Arnoldian view that poetry can save us when religious belief is dead. Jacques Maritain disagrees, finding the influence of the devil in contemporary literature most significant; Eliot warns us that he will take up this subject in another book. He has tried to show how development and change in poetry, and in the criticism of it, have been due to external historical factors; different critical assumptions arise at different periods. It is difficult for anyone, even its author, to say what a poem precisely means, and Eliot is astonished that Richards could find 'a complete severance between poetry and *all* beliefs' in *The Waste Land*. He concludes that contemporary critics make 'particular responses to particular situations', and that 'the criticism of no one man and of no one age can be expected to embrace the whole nature of poetry or exhaust all of its uses'.

His 'Conclusion' is the most interesting, and probably the most important, part of the lectures. It offers most on the subject Eliot knows better than anyone else – himself: on the genesis of poetry, usually when he was out of health; on the rising of imagery, 'like Anadyomene from the sea', saturated with indefinable feeling; on his own recurring images; on his wish for a non-literate audience, in the theatre; on the layers of significance in poetic drama like Shakespeare's; on the two scenes Eliot wrote experimentally for a verse play; and on the poet's desire to have 'some direct social utility', the theatre being the best place for it. The urge to write plays, instead of theorizing about poetry, is indubitably clamant.

The implications of Eliot's second introduction to *The Sacred Wood* seem to be revealed in their extremest form in the sub-title of *After Strange Gods* (1934),[46] the three Page-Barbour

Lectures given at the University of Virginia in the spring of 1933; the work is regarded as 'A Primer of Modern Heresy'. When he told Virginia Woolf the previous September that he was 'no longer so sure that there was a science of criticism',[47] he was understating his position. In his preface of January 1934 he describes his lectures as a thesis which was not undertaken as literary criticism; if acrimony had arisen (as he suggests), he is not very repentant. In a society 'worm-eaten with Liberalism', a person with strong convictions can do no other than 'state a point of view and leave it at that'. He must have had many second thoughts, for the book was never republished.

Perhaps he calculated that the University of Virginia was a suitable place to air his views; he describes it as a 'gracious' institution in which 'some vestiges of a traditional education seem to survive'. Less industrialized than the New England he had seen when returning in the fall from the glory of maple, beech, and birch among the evergreens of Vermont, and less subject therefore to the influx of foreign races, Virginia offered a better chance for 'the re-establishment of a native culture'. For tradition to be stable and progressive, one needs a society which is not economically depressed, racially mixed, or exposed to Jewish free-thinking; to preserve a sense of community there must be a balance between town and country, industry and agriculture. After defining tradition and orthodoxy, which is more conscious and personal, Eliot suggests some analogy between orthodoxy and heterodoxy (or heresy), with their wider connotations, and classicism and romanticism. In answer to critics who see inconsistencies between his poetry and criticism, he argues that prose reflections relate to ideals, whereas poetry must deal with the actual. Only a poet of the very highest order could be classical in the present age, when awareness of the meaning of education is minimal, and lack of tradition encourages a writer to exploit his individuality and cultivate heterodoxy.

For illustration, Eliot turns to three short stories, one by Katherine Mansfield which seems to prove nothing, one to establish lack of moral or social sense in the relations of Lawrence's men and women, and another to show the contrasting orthodoxy of Joyce. Turning to the decay of Protestantism, Eliot stumbles badly in attributing the conduct of her 'sons' to Mrs Lawrence's lack of firm Christian principles.

He proceeds to Irving Babbitt, Confucianism, and Indian philosophy, two years of which had left him in 'a state of enlightened mystification'. Speaking of Pound, a greater libertarian than Babbitt, Eliot remarks that, when the idea of Original Sin and of moral struggle disappears, people in literature become less real and disturbing, as happened with the society consigned to Hell in the *Cantos*. Literary criticism cannot be excluded from his thesis, and it is effectively applied to Yeats, who as early as sixteen, he thought, adopted the Arnoldian doctrine that poetry can replace religion, and, after recourse to various forms of supernaturalism, reached greatness 'against the greatest odds'. Hopkins is an exception, but he is a devotional poet, not a religious writer like Baudelaire, Villon, or Joyce; and he has little to offer in the struggle against liberalism. Eliot's aim has been to illustrate 'the crippling effect upon men of letters, of not having been born and brought up in the environment of a living and central tradition'.

Before turning to 'diabolic influence', he points out that it can hardly appear as blasphemy in modern literature, since only believers can blaspheme. The first sign of heresy in nineteenth-century novelists came with George Eliot, who belongs to the same tribe as all the 'serious and eccentric moralists' who followed her. Concentrating on Hardy and Lawrence, Eliot makes some pertinent remarks which suggest he knew more about Lawrence. In both he sees evil forces at work in the presentation of cruelty, but his main target is Hardy's short story 'Barbara of the House of Grebe', in which he finds 'a world of pure Evil'. Lawrence had no guidance but 'the Inner Light, the most untrustworthy and deceitful guide that ever offered itself to wandering humanity'. Hardy betrayed a 'morbid emotion', and Lawrence's imagination was that of a spiritually sick man; his fiction appeals to the sick. To some extent Eliot is right in each respect: without embarking on the Lawrence issues, which are too complicated, we can agree that Hardy's writing was sometimes morbid. Eliot generalizes, however. There is a larger world of evil in *King Lear* than in Hardy's story, but it is doubtful whether Eliot would have seen it as evidence of demonic powers in Shakespeare. He is biased and intolerant; biased by religious inflexibility, and handicapped sometimes by not knowing enough about his subject. George Eliot and Hardy are much less self-centred than he; they are more alive to good and evil in the world at large. The pity and horror stirred by Hardy's story originate from a sense of 'charity' which is entirely Christian, and so genuine and habitual that it is communicated widely throughout his works. George Eliot's altruism was also inspired by Christianity; and her kind of scientific humanism may offer more hope for the future than Eliot's ancient orthodoxy. There are many religions inspired by the same spirit for good, whatever their formulations and extrinsic differences. A footnote to the seventh Norton lecture, indicating that Eliot was not opposed in principle to the Roman Catholic or communist idea of an index of prohibited books, is significant. Art can be debased by evil, but if there is to be a proscription, the question is on what principles. Surely more fair-minded judgment is possible than Eliot's in his third Page-Barbour Lecture. His bias and standpoint are clear in the 'consequently' of the comparison he draws between Meredith and Hopkins: the former offers 'a rather cheap and shallow' philosophy of life, but Hopkins 'has the dignity of the Church behind him, and is consequently in closer contact with reality'. There is a logicality in this which cannot be final; it expresses the intransigence of a rash, immature form of zealotry. New truths are perceived, and 'reality' changes; any orthodoxy must change to keep in touch with it.

16

Drama: to *Murder in the Cathedral*

It is often assumed that Eliot's central interest in Elizabethan drama was the development of his own poetic style; 'The Possibility of a Poetic Drama' (1920) suggests that he had wider aims. Advocating drama based on popular entertainment techniques, he anticipates the conviction of his obituary essay on Marie Lloyd (December 1922) that the music-hall, with the audience-participation of the only kind of people capable of a full and genuine response, afforded the best opportunity for live drama. One of his major incentives in the study of poetic drama during its peak in England was the hope that it would give him hints on means by which drama could be revived as a form of art.

One aspect of 'Four Elizabethan Dramatists' (1924) is his reaction against realism on the contemporary stage, and it recurs in 'A Dialogue on Dramatic Poetry' (1928), a discursive discussion of drama past and present which indicates the trend of his thought. The formal element which drama needs is seen in the best Russian ballet, where the performer is subdued by strict training to the art in which he works; it could be said that drama, which sprang from liturgy, should return to it, though it can be no substitute for religion. For intensity we need poetic drama; Shakespeare's most dramatic scenes are his most poetic. If it is argued that the dramatist's task is made more difficult by the confusion in modern social and moral standards, it should be remembered that great poetic drama was produced in the Elizabethan and Jacobean period, another age of chaos.

The dramatic unities are important; they lead to concentration, and we need shorter, more intensive plays.

The two scenes of a verse play which Eliot referred to at the end of his Norton lectures were the Sweeney fragments, which he probably wrote in 1926.[48] Their rapidly fluent conversational exchanges in animated verse-beat accordant to characterization and action, together with the jazzed-up rhythm of song, and a chorus prompted by Gilbert and Sullivan's *Iolanthe*, suggest fascinating possibilities for short dramatic sketches to drum accompaniment. The title and epigraphs hint at a struggle for spiritual rebirth, but the tone of this experiment in 'Aristophanic Melodrama' seems too much like parody for a serious subject; that being so, it is not surprising that the Eliot of 1927 and later pursued it no further. The name 'Pereira' (after a famous pharmacologist), the egg, the coffin, and the repeated knocking, may be pointers to a death which is rebirth; and the Sweeney story of a man who murdered a girl, and did not know whether he was alive and she was dead, or vice-versa, may have all the seriousness of Conrad's 'Outpost of Progress', the ending of which provided this challenging thought. The climax reaches an orgy of rhythm, but the theme turns it into a veritable *danse macabre*; the South Sea pleasures are Dead Sea fruit. Eliot had in mind one character who could communicate with a sensitive and intelligent minority in the audience, while the 'visionless' remainder of his *dramatis personae* appealed to the majority. There was hope, it seemed, for Sweeney after he had discovered the emptiness of life with nothing but birth, copulation, and death; but Eliot must have realized that Sweeney and his entourage, with Mrs Porter the Queen of Hearts to the diviners, were not an appropriate channel for his theme, just as he had rejected a similar temptation, after experimenting with Sweeney's friend Doris as dream-purveyor on this side of 'death's other kingdom'. The *idea* was revived in *The Family Reunion* of 1939; how far Eliot had shifted in the long interval may be gauged by the staggering contrast of the two plays in their settings.

Whatever its rhythmical prowess, there is little in 'Sweeney Agonistes', or his subsequent drama, to suggest that Eliot's vision could have stirred a music-hall audience or any but a minority group. In any event, his experiment came at a time when, as H. M. Tomlinson makes plain in 'Beauty and the Beast', the music-hall was doomed to displacement by the cinema, and a living community response to the artist surrendered to the impersonality of the screen, with audiences herded physically together but 'separate in heart'.

The first real opportunity to write poetry for drama came to Eliot soon after his return from America, when he was invited to prepare the dialogues and choruses for *The Rock*, a pageant which had already been planned and designed in accordance with the promotion of a London church-building programme. He was advised by Martin Browne, and revised accordingly, discussion leading to the substitution of a scene which was suggested by Eliot. *The Rock* (1934) presents important stages in the history of the Church in London, interwoven with scenes connected with the building of a church in the present; all this, almost entirely in prose, is combined with general choruses in verse, at the opening and the end, and at intervals throughout. The missionary zeal of Bishop Blomfield, who saw the need to build schools as well as churches, probably reminded Eliot of his grandfather's work in St Louis. Scenes from the past merge thematically with the contemporary action; that of Rahere and his builders is especially significant, for their undaunted spirit in working 'to the glory of God and for His people' gives renewed impetus to the modern builders, who remember his faith in visible and invisible helpers when their church nears completion. The subject of church decoration, or art and worship, links the three strands of present, past, and chorus, just before the craftsmen of the present are seen working rhythmically to complete their church.

The play is in two parts; the Rock which is revealed at the end of the first in answer to a workman's prayer, when a plutocratic quarrel arises over the golden calf of power, appears as Saint Peter at the end of the play (cf. Matthew, xvi.18). When he enters at the beginning he is led by a boy, an allusion perhaps to the scriptural 'Whosoever shall not receive the kingdom of God as a little child, he shall not enter therein.' The key message of the Rock anticipates Becket's resolution of his temptations: '*Make perfect your will*', he says, and 'take no thought of the harvest, But only of proper sowing'. Not all the choruses are included in *Collected Poems*, and the full or true significance of some of those which are presented is not clear out of context. There are entertaining and satirical scenes, and a song which seems appropriate to Gilbert and Sullivan. It is true that Eliot was given assistance in cockney expression and thought, but the liveliness of the comic parts is well sustained, and the whole is a balanced work which suggests the free play of a mind fast recovering from distress and happily absorbed in creative work. This was largely true, for his work on *The Rock* came when he thought he had exhausted his 'meagre poetic gifts', as he hints at the end of the Norton lectures, in his reference to the ghost of Coleridge beckoning to him from the shadows.

Ethelbert, the leader and most loquacious of the builders, is unusually informed. He talks about Major Douglas and Social Credit, one of Pound's obsessions. Occasionally he speaks for Eliot: if people give up religion, they will turn to other things such as politics, and then they will 'get into a 'ell of a muddle'. He holds his own with an agitator, 'a *lung* worker' who thinks religion a 'degradin' and outworn superstition', cites Darwin and the Rationalist Press, and harps on sweated labour. Ethelbert's pride in building a wall evokes a scene from Nehemiah, when 'the people had a mind to work' (iv.6), and 'built as men must build With the sword in one hand and the trowel in the other'. A living Church, Eliot is saying, depends on active-mindedness and vigilance, and he designates its main enemies in the sequel. The agitator returns with a crowd of people whom he addresses as comrades, unlikely to be dupes of capitalism. They will follow the Russian example, and turn churches into workers' clubs, pleasure-domes, and restaurants where you can get all the cups of coffee you want for a halfpenny, and sausage and mash for twopence. He urges sabotage of the church that is being built. Redshirts and Blackshirts march in, each band promising utopia; plutocrats follow. They are all materialists, and the plutocratic speaker with his specious political adroitness is a forerunner of the knights at the end of *Murder in the Cathedral*. This was the one scene Eliot contributed to *The Rock* as spectacle. The Chorus concludes that no help will come from political parties and interests, whose souls are choked in 'the old winding sheets of place and power' or 'the new winding sheets of mass-made thought'. The unemployed are brought in, and not forgotten; from first to last the builders' call is 'A Church for us all and work for us all and God's world for us all even unto this last'. The inclusion of the last three words (from the parable of the workers in the vineyard, Matthew, xx.14) shows that Eliot fully supported Ruskin's call for 'social affection', or the application of Christian principles, in industrial relations.

In the choruses Eliot enunciates a truth repeated in *The Idea of a Christian Society* that 'the Temple is forever building, forever to be destroyed, forever to be restored', and reveals an emergent image which is more familiar in *Four Quartets*. At a 'predetermined' moment, not of time, but in time, 'transecting, bisecting the world of time', came the Word; but since then people have turned to other gods such as Reason, Money and Power, Life, and Race; the Church is disowned, and (reverting to images at the end of *The Waste Land*) the tower is overthrown, and the bells are upturned. The Rock urges that we always live at an intersection-point of time and eternity. The question of devoting art to the glory of God leads Eliot to think of that struggle for 'the perfect order of speech' and 'the beauty of incantation' which he associates with the search for holiness in *Four Quartets*; the 'life of music' comes from 'a sea of sound', from 'the slimy mud of words', 'the sleet and hail of verbal imprecisions', approximations of thought and feeling, and words substituted for thought and feeling. Such creation should be brought to the service of God, for we are spirit and body; the visible and invisible meet in man.

The best of the choruses are those which are least specifically related to the events; of general contemporary interest, they are primarily directed to the audience or reader, and are tauter and more regular in rhythm. They are hortatory in spirit and often in tone; there is nothing new in their wisdom, but it is often well expressed. Endless invention brings 'knowledge of motion, but not of stillness'; we have 'Knowledge of words, and ignorance of the Word'. One thing does not change in a world of change, says the Rock, and this is the struggle between Good and Evil; we neglect the desert that is not only 'around the corner' but 'squeezed in the tube train next to you'; the good man is a builder, 'if he build what is good'. The question of building is recurrent: 'We build in vain unless the LORD build with us'; has the corner-stone (Ephesians, ii.20) been forgotten in discussing the 'right relations of men' but not men's relations to God? Imperialism and neglect in our own country (the law of consequences) are not overlooked. 'There is no life that is not in community, And no community not lived in praise of God',

Eliot insists, before turning to common evidence of its modern dissolution. Without God, man is the victim of his own conceit and inventions; there is the eternal Law, and you 'set up commissions', writes the author of 'Coriolan';

> Much is your reading, but not the Word of GOD,
> Much is your building, but not the House of GOD.
> Will you build me a house of plaster, with corrugated roofing,
> To be filled with a litter of Sunday newspapers?

A contrast is drawn between unemployment with industrial dereliction and the 'decent godless people' whose only monument will be 'the asphalt road And a thousand lost golf balls'. Whatever the accomplishments and enthusiasms of the age, there can be no denying 'the Stranger': 'Life you may evade, but Death you shall not.' The Stranger is the Rock; he is the Watcher, the 'God-shaken, in whom is the truth inborn'. In the final chorus, part of which is based on the *Gloria in Excelsis* ('We praise thee . . . we worship thee, we glorify thee, we give thanks to thee for thy great glory'), the call is for the Light which is invisible, which 'fractures through unquiet water' towards our 'submarine' gaze. The light is 'dappled' with shadow, and our 'bodily vision' is made only for 'little lights'. The dimness of this light points forward to 'Burnt Norton'. Whatever the quality of *The Rock*, and however dogmatic Eliot's theology may be, one must concede that he presents a devastating 'criticism of life' which is so profoundly true of the western world that it has lost none of its significance. The explicitness of Eliot's play, even where it is more prosaic, is particularly valuable for the illumination it casts on his more intensive poetry, both earlier and later; its contemporaneity gives greater and more lasting reality to his thought.

As Eliot's verse-rhythm depends on stress, with changes in length of line from chorus to chorus as well as within choruses, he was able to achieve considerable variation of movement. He realized that, as the Chorus spoke with one voice, their speech, syntax, and thought had to be direct and uncomplicated. To the extent that they spoke for him, they were not dramatic. In *Murder in the Cathedral* (1935) he had to identify with the women of Canterbury, express their feelings, and through them the feelings of many of his contemporaries. Yet, as he tells us in

'The Three Voices of Poetry', his dramatic scope in the entire play was limited, for he had only one principal character, and the conflict is largely internalized. To add life to this kind of play, verse-variation is essential, and it was for this reason that Eliot rejected the iambic blank-verse tradition of nineteenth-century drama in favour of stress rhythm. One style he adopted in *Murder in the Cathedral* is that of *Everyman*; it is an approximation to speech, and has sufficient rhyme and alliteration to sharpen attention. There is no monotony in Eliot's play; in line-length, manner, rhythm, and tone, it changes frequently to offset the relative lack of external action.

Eliot's style had gained, as it continued to do, from his early realization of a playwright's role. He never forgot the lessons he soon learned from his producer Martin Browne, and from conscientious attendance at rehearsals. He discussed staging and textual problems, enjoying collaboration with the actors, and discovering in this way obscurities, difficulties, and superfluities which led to frequent revision. Drama, he saw, is a performing-art, not something merely to be read, or completely composed in one's study; it is, he insisted, a group venture.

Keeping close to the unities, Eliot was faced with the problem of how to introduce historical background; the solution came when Rupert Doone suggested the tempters, after a convention in medieval drama; through them and their flashbacks Eliot was able to approximate a Greek form of tragedy. Of the other conventions used, one is ancient, the Chorus keeping close to that of Aeschylus; one is liturgical, as may be seen in the two choruses which synchronize with the singing in Latin of the *Dies Irae* when murder is imminent, and of the *Te Deum* at the conclusion; another is new, from Shaw's *Saint Joan*, when murderers of the remote past address the audience in extenuation of their crime, as if they were twentieth-century politicians. At the centre, between part I and part II, is Becket's Christmas-morning sermon; the keynote is that of the Rock, making perfect the will. Becket's conclusion, that the true martyr is 'the instrument of God, who has lost his will in the will of God', brings us to the still point at the centre of the wheel of life and action which has brought Becket to his crisis.

In design *Murder in the Cathedral* has a unity and simplicity which are characteristic of classical art; the universality of its theme strengthens this impression. However, there are twentieth-century overtones, particularly evident at the opening, which impart deeper resonances to the chorus. The women of Canterbury present ordinary people in the England of 1170, but their fears sometimes merge with those of Eliot's contemporaries, as spectators of German militarist expansion and the threat to peace; they are 'forced to bear witness':

> /Destiny waits in the hand of God, not in the hands of
>   statesmen
> Who do, some well, some ill, planning and guessing,
> Having their aims which turn in their hands in the
>   pattern of time.

The question of peace or war which arises when news comes of Becket's return to England was hinted at in the original title ('Fear in the Way'; the more sensationally specific 'Murder in the Cathedral' was recommended by Martin Browne's wife, and gratefully accepted). It is winter, and the question arises, how many think of true service in God's cause, or, like Peter (Mark, xiv.53ff.), warm themselves before the fire of life and deny the Master.

The question for Becket is whether he should turn aside from God's will to avoid conflict with the King. The tempters (his temptations externalized) are the most interesting subordinate figures in part I. The first is pleasure, recalled from the distant past; the courtesy of his style is marked by the light, tripping rhymes 'ceremony' – 'acrimony', 'gravity' – 'levity', when he enters and withdraws; resistance hardens the temper of his speech. The second temptation is to become Chancellor again, to serve God by protecting the poor and setting down the mighty (Luke, i.52); the questions beginning with 'Who shall have it?' (from Conan Doyle's short story 'The Musgrave Ritual', and whimsically related perhaps to the detective question of the fourth knight, 'Who killed the Archbishop?') declare Becket's interest, as does the emphasis of his repeated rejection; to give up his office, with power from the Pope to bind or loose, for temporal power, is beneath him. The third temptation is to use the Church, with the Pope's blessing, in alliance with the barons, against the King; Becket rejects the idea of treachery, especially with men whom he once regarded with Coriolanian scorn (ruling them like 'an eagle over doves').

The fourth tempter is unexpected; he is subtle, and speaks elliptically. Knowing that the King will not change towards him, Becket is advised to 'Fare forward to the end', keep his supreme power to bind or loose, and think of glory after death, surpassing that of kings, when he is honoured as a saint and martyr. Becket admits he has already thought of this, and when he is reminded that both the earthly fame and the shrine of a martyr saint are subject to damage and decay, asks if he can obtain a lasting crown. He is told that he has already contemplated eternal grandeur among the saints in heaven as a reward for martyrdom. The fourth tempter reflects the imperfection of his will, his wish for self-glory. Released from his devils, Becket can now think clearly. He recognises that his last temptation is 'the greatest treason: To do the right deed for the wrong reason'. He recalls youthful pleasure in music and philosophy, lilac and bullfinch, tilting, chess-strategy (to be taken literally here), 'love in the garden', and singing; he reflects on the worldly ambition that was fulfilled when his youthful energies were spent; and he concludes that a servant of God can sin more greatly than one who serves a king. He is thinking of political taint. Finally, in lines directed at every individual in the audience, with reference to their world, he speaks for his author in driving home the law of history, that every type of sin will be visited upon later generations. In an age when many accepted the shallow rational optimism of Shaw or Wells, Eliot believed that 'war among men defiles this world, but death in the Lord renews it'.

The four tempters of part I are balanced by the four knights of part II. These murderers are not individualized; they are factual and businesslike; in loyalty to class and king they speak with one voice, as they do in the crudely pointed verse of contempt for Becket the tradesman's son, the Cheapside brat, the creature that crept out of London dirt and, swollen with the blood of pride, crawled on the King like a louse on one's shirt. Brusque exchanges, Becket responding in like manner at one point, are studded with firm and pointed rhymes; when the knights return maddened with wine, the unity of their final arrogance is emphasized in sledge-hammer demands with sharp '-ated' verse-endings. After the murder, when they address the audience in polite prose, they are clearly differentiated in a double role which satirizes modern upper-class politicians and provides some parallelism with the tempters and with Becket himself when he has overcome them. The first knight acts as chairman, ostensibly in the cause of *fair play* and respect for the underdog. The second, after repeating the chairman's clichés, flatters his audience, and turns to Becket's opportunity to create a union which would have meant the subordination of 'the pretensions of the Church to the welfare of the State'; his regret for the necessity of violence strikes a note which is all too familiar from political humbugs in a mass-media age. The third, like the speaker from the barons, argues that the knights' motivation was disinterested; they put country first, and took on a 'pretty stiff job'; Becket put up a 'good show', and the third knight is 'awfully sorry' about what happened. Like the fourth tempter, the fourth knight is concerned with Becket's inner self: he was a 'monster of egotism', determined on death by martyrdom, and guilty of suicide while of unsound mind. This echoes Becket himself, when he addresses the audience at the end of part I.

The three priests are distinctively characterized. The first, an observer who remembers him as Chancellor, realizes that Becket believes in subjection to none but God, and despises any form of power that derives from temporal devolution; knowing what the King is, he has reason to fear for the Archbishop and the Church. The second is a confident supporter of the Archbishop; he feels that the Church can lean on him as on a rock, and has no patience with the women of Canterbury when they give way to apprehensions; they are foolish babblers who continue 'croaking like frogs in the treetops'. The third is philosophical. When he talks of the wheel which has been still for seven years, he is thinking of Becket's fate: for good or ill, let it turn, for 'who knows the end of good or evil?' In saying that each day is a day to 'fear from or hope from', that the critical moment is always here and now, and that at this juncture (when the murderous knights make their first appearance) the 'eternal design' may be revealed in the sordid, he speaks like Krishna. The speech occurs at the end of a liturgical scene, just before the first appearance of the knights. This scene completes a movement first heard when Becket in his sermon draws attention to the consecutiveness of the days which celebrate the birth of Christ and the martyrdom of Saint Stephen. The fears which follow in the opening chorus of part II relate to Becket and to war, which could have had little but contemporary significance for the audience. Then, in succession, the priests enter, bearing, to intermittent strains of song, the banners which indicate the passing of the three days, each a holy day, between Christmas Day and the day of the Archbishop's death. The banners display Saint Stephen, Saint John, and the Holy Innocents; and martyrdom and the murder of innocents are another expression of a recurring duality of theme. At the end it is the third priest whose faith in the Church remains strong; while men are prepared to die for it, it will remain supreme. His indictment of the knights, the enemies of the Church, is inspired; he predicts that they will tread 'one endless round' in the attempt to justify themselves, 'Pacing for ever in the hell of make-believe Which never is belief'.

The image of the wheel, introduced by Becket and repeated by his *alter ego*, the fourth tempter, when he leaves, is related to 'the still point of the turning world'. Becket's higher self knows that 'Our peace is in His will'; it is the point of his sermon. Eliot's image, from the Brahma-Wheel of the *Upanishads*, presents the world of time which revolves around, and is always related to, God eternal at the still point of the centre. Man's action is part of an infinitely larger process to which he must consent; action, therefore, is suffered, and what is suffered determines action. Only the fool, 'fixed in his folly', thinks he can turn the wheel on which he is turned. The world has always been stricken or threatened with war, Becket declares, but there is a peace which is not of this world. Subsequently he experiences 'a wink of heaven, a whisper'. The critical decision is not his; it is taken 'out of time', and he consents to it with his whole being. He gives his life to 'the Law of God above the Law of Man'.

The women of Canterbury express themselves on, and between, two planes. At the higher level they have intuitions of the truth with reference to both this world and the next: 'Destiny waits in the hand of God, not in the hands of statesmen', and '[here have we] no continuing city' (Hebrews, xiii.14). At the lower level they think of the common round of events in their lives: harvesting, keeping the feasts, gathering fuel for winter, births, deaths, marriages, and scandals, girls disappearing mysteriously, 'and some not able to'. This ordinariness of experience is expressed in shorter, more regular, and rather unexciting lines, in the chorus beginning with 'no continuing city', a thought suggested when the third priest hints at death ('. . . grinders cease . . . daughters of music . . . brought low': Ecclesiastes, xii.1–7). Longer, more flexible lines express higher thoughts and a range of feelings. The suggestion of death reminds the Chorus of the Archbishop's return, and their fears are voiced, quickening in repetition: 'O late late late, late is the time, late too late, and rotten the year; Evil the wind, and bitter the sea, and grey the sky, grey grey grey.' Their fears are sustained in this last repetition; they wish Thomas would return to France, before bringing death to Canterbury, and doom on their world. It is relief to dwell on the relative uneventfulness of their lives during his seven years' absence. Then the old fear returns, and the verse by and large becomes more rhythmically extended as it rises to an anguished climax. The minor artistry of Eliot's variations is illustrated at this point when the second priest tells them how foolish they are. The same kind of duality in the functioning of choral verse is found near the end of part I, when the Chorus thinks first of the common misfortunes they have suffered, without loss of hope, then of the new terror that assails them, as the Lords of Hell seem to gather like animals in darkness.

The Chorus is the most important voice in *Murder in the Cathedral*. Closely integrated with the action, unlike the principal choruses in *The Rock*, it sets the emotional tone from first to last. Sometimes the women of Canterbury speak with a twofold significance, relative to an ancient tragedy and a looming twentieth-century disaster. In part II, which is confined to the day of the Archbishop's murder, they are soon tense with feeling, passing from fear to horror when the knights threaten action. Their whole being seems infected with death; it affects all their senses; they feel the earth heaving at nightfall; they taste corruption in life, and life in corruption; they smell death in flowers, and in the dish, 'incense in the latrine', and 'the sewer in the incense'. They know that everywhere, in sea, earth, and air, life preys on life; 'light coiling downwards' has revealed 'the horror of the ape'. In measured verse they generalize on the web of fate which is 'woven like a pattern of living worms' in 'our veins our bowels or skulls', in 'plottings of potentates' and 'consultations of powers'. The women of Canterbury can do nothing; they must consent; they are mastered and violated by the corruptible, the 'spiritual flesh of nature' or the 'animal powers of spirit'. This, Becket tells them, is their share of a burden which is eternal.

After he has been dragged away, in verses which correspond to the *Dies Irae* in form at the beginning, and in both form and sentiment at the end, they express the horror that is the greater for being still, the Void behind the Judgment which is behind the 'white flat face' of Death. In this empty land there is nothing to distract one from the hell of seeing oneself 'foully united forever, nothing with nothing', a state which begins with absolute spiritual death, and never dies. With the murder of Becket, the Chorus is lost in a stony land of barren boughs that bleed when broken. The old ordinary life is recalled, but this horror is 'out of life' and time, 'An instant eternity of evil and wrong'. Their cry goes up, 'Clear the air! clean the sky! wash the wind! . . . Wash the stone, wash the bone, wash the brain, wash the soul . . . !' There is one time for the stage action, and another for the imagination; several intervals must be assumed in the closing stages of the play. The faith of the third priest that the Church has triumphed through Becket's example is communicated to the Chorus. Their *Te Deum* shows a renewal of faith in life (the life that preys on life), acknowledges indebtedness to the martyrs who, like Christ, have sacrificed their blood, and implores forgiveness. *Murder in the Cathedral* is a comedy in the Dantean sense which justifies the ways of God to man. The women of Canterbury acknowledge themselves as 'type of the common man', and they sometimes speak for common humanity. More often, particularly in part II, they express feelings which are beyond ordinary expression. They show insights, both psychological and spiritual, which are Eliot's alone; the shaft of sunlight which gives them higher revelation is like that of Plato, up which one could look to heaven and see its link with earth.[49] Their range of feeling, from fear and horror to final triumph and humility, is tremendous; they create the deeper intensities of the play, and constitute one of the finest achievements of their kind in all poetic drama.

17

Four Quartets and Other Poems

Five 'landscape' poems recall visits made by Eliot during 1933 in America and Great Britain. They are impressionistic, illustrating the truth of the couplet with which Crabbe opens 'The Lover's Journey':

> It is the Soul that sees: the outward eyes
> Present the object, but the Mind descries.

The first two, 'New Hampshire' and 'Virginia', form a contrast, one conveying the quick, lively movements of birds in an orchard, the other, mainly through arrested monosyllables and retarding rhyme, the slow flow of a river in heat and silence. Together they express something personal which probably relates to Eliot's foundered marriage. This seems to be confirmed by the voices of children in the orchard; in 'Ode', an allusively baffling poem on nuptial disillusionment (a typescript of which is headed 'Ode on Independence Day, July 4th, 1918'), they are remembered singing among the fruit-trees. 'Twenty years and the spring is over' seems to recall the time before Eliot left America to settle in England; between blossom-time and fruit-time may imply a kind of pre-lapsarian happiness. Grief gives him no rest, and the poet wishes the birds would cover him as they did the babes in the wood. Whether the redness of the river in 'Virginia' is intended to have hellish overtones (cf. *Inferno*, xiv.77–8) is uncertain, but the 'Living, living, Never moving' suggests hell, as do the 'Iron thoughts' that come with the poet and go with him.

'Usk' and 'Rannoch, by Glencoe' are based on impressions formed during Eliot's holiday with Morley. The contrast here is in landscape associations, the Welsh being enriched with superstition, legends (including the Arthurian), and haunts of holiness. (Henry Vaughan was born and died at Newton-on-Usk; 'Gently dip . . .' is from *The Old Wives' Tale*, an Elizabethan comedy by George Peele.) The 'green air' of the valley, reminiscent of Marvell's 'The Garden', suggests life; the imagery of 'Rannoch, by Glencoe', death. Time destroys and time preserves, Eliot writes in 'The Dry Salvages': by Glencoe the air is thin, and the road winds in 'Listlessness of ancient war'; the rift remains long after death; there is no 'concurrence of bone'. 'Cape Ann' is devoted to the song and flight of birds, but the final lines seem to assume a symbolic aspect: the urge to resign the land, with all that is delectable to the senses, to its 'true owner', the 'tough' seagull, suggests a link with the endings of *Ash-Wednesday* and 'Marina', and a hint of 'The Dry Salvages'.

Four Quartets was not originally conceived as a whole. Until the outbreak of the Second World War Eliot's literary concentration had continued to be on poetic drama. 'Burnt Norton', written in 1935, could be regarded as a by-product of *Murder in the Cathedral*; *The Family Reunion* was first performed and published in March 1939. There could be no revival of the London theatre until after the war, and Eliot, with time only for shorter works, wrote the three extensions of 'Burnt Norton' from 1940 to 1942, the idea of *Four Quartets* (1943) as a whole coming to him when he was working on 'East Coker'. Each poem is related to one of the four elements (air, earth, water, fire), but the claim that they have a similar relationship to the seasons can hardly be substantiated. Much time has been spent, not very convincingly, in attempts to establish analogies between Eliot's 'quartets' and the later ones of Beethoven. The poet limited the comparison to one point only, the amalgamation of a number of themes;[50] and the form of each constituent poem bears as much resemblance to *The Waste Land* as it does to a Beethoven quartet. The fourth part in each, for example, like 'Death by Water', is brief and religious in import. 'Burnt Norton' set the pattern for its successors. Each second section has two movements, the first of which relates to this world and 'the spiritual flesh of nature', or the 'animal powers of spirit', of

Murder in the Cathedral; this sameness of theme is more apparent in 'Burnt Norton' and 'East Coker'. One theme, which made its first appearance in *The Rock*, is based on an implicit analogy between the pursuit of perfection in poetic expression or art and the pursuit of holiness; it is not found in 'The Dry Salvages'.

Among the lines excluded from *Murder in the Cathedral* and used in 'Burnt Norton' was a passage on time first intended to be spoken just before Becket, after the exit of the second tempter, comments on temporal power. Its reasoning, enervated by 'perhaps' and 'If', does not provide a propitious opening for a poem. The irredeemability of the past and of the present, which are a radical part of the future, is clarified in *The Family Reunion* and 'The Dry Salvages'. The rose-garden and images of the approach to it, above the dry pool, are based on Eliot's memories of his visit to Burnt Norton, but the subject of *Four Quartets* is time and the timeless, and, as its conclusion confirms, the rose-garden hints at the Rose of Dante's *Paradiso*, the multifoliate rose of 'The Hollow Men', the 'single Rose' which is the Garden of *Ash-Wednesday* (II). After the winter symbolism of *Murder in the Cathedral*, a passage from Evelyn Underhill's *Mysticism* is apposite: 'For them [the mystics] the winter is over; the time of the singing of birds is come. From the deeps of the dewy garden, Life – new, unquenchable, and ever lovely – comes to meet them with the dawn.'

Many origins have been cited to account for the garden symbolism of *Four Quartets*. The birds and children's voices in 'New Hampshire' are recalled at the end of 'Little Gidding', where the image of children in the apple-tree is an emblem of the recovered innocence which is sought. Elizabeth Barrett Browning's 'The Lost Bower', a poem included in one of Eliot's London courses, associates childhood, roses, apple-blossom, birds, and music unheard but felt, with 'the Timeless' and 'God's Eden-land unknown'. The poem is quoted by Kipling in the short story 'They' (*Traffics and Discoveries*). In this the children are unseen presences; the repeated emphasis of 'they' for other unseen presences in the 'Burnt Norton' garden is hardly fortuitous, and Eliot's indebtedness (which he acknowledged, after forgetting it) is confirmed in the words of the mysterious guardian of the House Beautiful: 'And the passages all empty. . . . And how could I ever bear the garden door shut?'. The image of the passage which is not followed towards the door which is not opened into the rose-garden shows that Eliot had *Alice in Wonderland* also in mind.[51] All such references are subordinated to his prime source, the garden of Earthly Paradise in the closing cantos of the *Purgatorio*. His subject is not the 'footfalls' of memory or the faded leaves of the rose-bowl but echoes in the garden of the present. With Emily Hale at Burnt Norton, Eliot experienced a passing vision of the timeless; the experience is conveyed in the invisible presences, the unheard music to which the bird responds, the light like water in the pool, and the lotos which rose as the surface 'glittered out of heart of light'. The water 'out of sunlight' which fills the pool is like the water at 'the still point of the turning world' in 'Triumphal Arch'; the lotos is a Buddhist symbol for the experience of the divine in conjunction with the natural.

The imagery in the cryptic opening lines of the second section (where originally the axle-tree was muddily associated with thunder and sapphires) derives from the 'Tonnerre et rubis aux moyeux' and the 'boue et rubis' of Mallarmé's sonnets 'M'introduire dans ton histoire' and 'Le Tombeau de Charles Baudelaire'. The triumph of spirit through the body in the first is seen as a chariot which becomes the fiery sun before it sets in the empurpled sky. Eliot, mindful of Original Sin, presents an axle-tree clotted with garlic and sapphires as it lies in mud. Man has possibilities for evil and good; like the 'hellish sweet scent in the woodpath' of *Murder in the Cathedral*, the garlic hints at corruption, whereas the sapphires indicate heaven and God's glory (Ezekiel, i.26). Soul and body are one, and there is life in the blood and senses which makes us capable of atonement (resolving conflict and becoming one with the universe), as if, after rising from the earthly, mud-bound axle-tree, we were moving in light above a living tree that moves, and were looking down on the soggy ground where animal life pursues its course as part of the universal law.[52] (The 'figured leaf' of *In Memoriam*, xliii, derives from a passage near the opening of the second part of *Religio Medici*, where Sir Thomas Browne, referring to 'outward figures' in plants, states that God's finger has left an inscription on all his works.) From this more natural aspect of life, Eliot turns to the more spiritual. Yeats's poetry (cf. 'Those Dancing Days' and 'The Dancer at Cruachan and Cro-Patrick') may have revived an image he became familiar with in Evelyn Underhill's *Mysticism*: 'But when we *do* behold Him, says *Plotinus*, then we are no longer discordant, but "form a truly divine dance about Him; in the which dance the soul beholds the Fountain of life".' Release from the action and suffering discussed by Becket gives spiritual elevation (*Erhebung*) with 'a grace of sense', like a white light which is 'still and moving' because the timeless, the still point at the centre of the turning wheel, or 'the moment in the rose-garden', is perceived in the course of time's duration,[53] the new world through the old, with 'partial ecstasy' inevitably accompanied by 'partial horror'. The point from which the light radiates is God (*Paradiso*, xxviii.16), the Love which never moves but is the source of all movement. Only in the timeless, beyond the world of past and future, can we be completely conscious.

The later movements of 'Burnt Norton' add very little. The world of time gives neither daylight suggestive of meaningfulness and permanence nor darkness to purify the soul. Purposeless people, driven with 'strained time-ridden faces' from distraction to distraction, are no more significant than scraps of paper blown by the cold wind that links past and future. (The seven gloomy time-swept hills of London are calculated to evoke a wistful reflection on the traditional holiness of Rome with its seven hills.) To obtain spiritual life, we must descend from this dim 'twittering' world into a world of 'internal' darkness ('Desiccation of the world of sense, Evacuation of the world of fancy, Inoperancy of the world of spirit') and wait. A lighter, freer, more poetic note is introduced in the fourth section, where some of Eliot's habitual images combine with the sunflower (from Blake) and the flashing light of the kingfisher's wing (a water-loving bird, observed at Kelham in 1935) to voice a prayer rather than a hope that communion with the light at the still point will be renewed. In the fifth section Eliot attempts a parallel between the frustrations of the spirit and those of the artist; his thought may owe something to Keats's 'Ode on a Grecian Urn': 'dost tease us out of thought As doth eternity'. Only in perfection of form or pattern, such that it seems to be eternally present like the whole of time, can the poet be free from the recalcitrance of words.[54] The freedom does not last long on earth; even Christ, and saints, could not escape voices of temptation, shadows, and chimeras, in the desert. Finally we are told that the detail of the movement towards the stillness is like the figure of the ten stairs, the ladder of contemplation in St John of the Cross (*The Dark Night of the Soul*, II.xviii): 'upon this road to go down is to go up, and to go up is to go down; for he that humbleth himself is exalted and he that exalts himself is humbled'. In this we have a repetition of the epigraph from Heraclitus, which, with a balancing one to the effect that the Word is common to all but most men act as if their insights were adequate, was to serve for *Four Quartets* as a whole. The last movement begins prosaically, turns to abstract philosophy, then to statement in imagery which rounds off the poem without adding anything new. The Platonic 'shaft of sunlight', which is found in the first chorus of *Murder in the Cathedral*, reveals eternity fleetingly, 'while the dust moves'.

There is little elevation, or apparent unity, in 'East Coker'. That may be due to the subject as well as the difficulty of expressing it, which was increased by the anxieties and disturbances of war. The last two complications are twice associated in the poem. The second section begins with seasonal disturbances in the garden, and a kind of apocalyptical vision of war in the heavens which, with its thunder simulating 'triumphal cars', recalls Mallarmé, and contrasts with the universal law of the corresponding section in 'Burnt Norton'. This 'not very satisfactory' way of 'putting it' – Eliot's live idiomatic speech underlining his criticism by force of contrast – is a 'periphrastic study in a worn-out poetical fashion' which leaves the poet in an 'intolerable wrestle With words and meanings'. The struggle makes him feel that the years of '*l'entre deux guerres*' have been 'largely wasted'. Every attempt at poetry is a completely new start, for expression at one's command comes from what has already been communicated; the new situation, and a new way of looking at things, make it inadequate. Every new beginning, therefore, is a 'raid on the inarticulate' with 'shabby equipment' which persistently fails in the 'general mess' of imprecise and uncontrolled feeling. What one hopes to overcome has been conquered throughout the ages by writers whom one cannot hope or wish to emulate. One can only struggle to recover a command of language which has been continually lost and found through the ages. The time now seems unpropitious; the endeavour is everything.

The subject of the fourth section, redemption on the Cross, shows why the poem was published for Easter; the five verses, each of five lines, are the external reminder of Christ's five wounds. Eliot, it is clear, found it difficult to manipulate thought to a regular rhyming verse-pattern. Although the idea of the earth as a hospital, a place to die in, occurs in a sermon on the Redemption by Lancelot Andrewes (and elsewhere, as in *Religio Medici*; cf. the *Paradiso*, vii.28), Eliot took his more elaborate conceit from André Gide's *Le Prométhée mal enchaîné*, where Zeus is transformed into a millionaire who gives away his wealth to endow a hospital in which a wounded surgeon and a dying nurse tend the sick.[55] Eliot's ruined millionaire is Adam; the dying nurse is the Church; the wounded surgeon is the crucifed Christ. God's love, which prevents us (is ahead of, and ready to safeguard, us) in all our doings, is linked with Purgatory and Christ's crown of thorns. The section ends in terms of transubstantiation.

The modernity of the imagery here (more fortunate in 'the enigma of the fever chart' than in the mental wires of the singing fever, an image dragged in from 'Burnt Norton' for rhyming-requirements) consorts with three similes more invitingly conveyed in the less regular rhythmic verse of the previous section. Waiting in the darkness of deprivation, without hope, reminds Eliot of the theatre, when rumblings and movements of darkness indicate the removal of scene-settings; of the stopping of an underground train between stations, when the blankness behind every passenger's expression deepens, leaving (Eliot thought) a 'growing terror of nothing to think about'; or of being under ether, 'conscious but conscious of nothing'. Another effective passage, much more regular, keeps time and rhythm in the evocation of ancient country dancing by superstitious couples whose meeting on Midsummer Eve was a token of marriage. The lines on 'daunsinge, signifying matrimonie' are from *The Boke Named the Governour* (1531) by Sir Thomas Elyot, a descendant of one of the Eliots of East Coker.

Eliot's own East Coker ancestry is alluded to at the beginning of the poem, and again at the end, where, in the form of Mary Stuart's motto, it completes a movement which may subordinate a hint of Andrew Eliot's arrival in New England waters to the poet's 'deeper communion' in 'The Dry Salvages'. The main thought of 'East Coker' is based on time and the succession of generations. It is first presented in the image of houses; 'there is a time for building' may have the wider connotation which it assumes in *The Rock* but, in alliance with generation and decay (actualized in images which recall Tennyson's 'Mariana'; can a field-mouse trot?), is reminiscent of verses in Ecclesiastes (iii.1–8) which end with 'a time of war, and a time of peace'. Eliot's impressions of the village follow, the sleep of the dahlias preceding the owl, which 'rehearses the hollow note of death' in *Murder in the Cathedral*. The couples of the age-old ceremonial dance have heavy earth-feet, and now nourish the corn; the feet which rise and fall present the long succession of life and death. Dawn points significantly to a glimpse of the sea, where the image of a wrinkling, sliding wind owes much to Tennyson's 'The Eagle'.

The continuing wrestle with words makes Eliot reflect on the wisdom that is assumed to come with age. It can have only a limited value, imposing a pattern on experience which cannot be trusted, for the pattern changes every moment, and demands continual reassessment. We are always in the middle of Dante's wood of error (*Inferno*, i.1–3); as it is written in Conan Doyle's *The Hound of the Baskervilles*, 'Life is become like that great Grimpen Mire, with little green patches everywhere into which one may sink and with no guide to point the track.' The double reference to *Samson Agonistes* in 'O dark dark dark' and 'vacant interstellar spaces' (from 'vacant interlunar cave') at the opening of the third section leads to the darkness of this world, with its men of eminence, chairmen of countless committees, financiers, and leading industrialists, all resembling those consigned to Hell by Pound. Eliot's faith in the darkness of St John of the Cross recalls old images of spiritual rebirth, together with new ones such as the scent of wild thyme hidden from view and the wild strawberry, from the memory perhaps of happiness in New England. He then paraphrases a paradoxical passage from *The Ascent of Mount Carmel* (i.xiii.11) by St John of the Cross, on the way to light through darkness, to life through dying to this world; the collocation of the Good Friday verses is, as Eliot might have said, no accident. An introduction to this lengthy paraphrase, in which he asks whether he has been repeating himself, and will do so again, implies, like his comments on knowledge and its communication, that the pattern continually changes and demands new expression. Our beginning goes back many generations, to gravestones that cannot be deciphered; there is a time therefore for the photograph album in the evening. Anticipating the Krishna passage in 'The Dry Salvages', and harking back to Ulysses, he asserts that what matters is not so much the moment of illumination but a lifetime 'burning in every moment'. 'Old men ought to be explorers', seeking 'another intensity', a 'further union', he concludes.

'The Dry Salvages' is a complicated, uneven, and rather prosy poem, in which Eliot continues to say the same thing, with some progression, mainly in maritime imagery; his most memorable images are inspired by recollections of the Mississippi at St Louis and of the sea 'voices' off Cape Ann. He does not simplify matters by referring to the god of the river and the many gods of the sea; his 'many voices' (from Tennyson) is a reminder of the Ulysses symbolism. The river is 'within us'; it is the more natural, instinctive or primitive self, forgotten and thwarted in our urbanized and industrial world, but incalculable and always to be propitiated or taken into account. It is with us at all seasons, from birth to death. The sea is life at large, 'lo gran mar dell'essere' (*Paradiso*, i.113); it is Aeonian, and includes many forms of creation; our shores provide the evidence of 'earlier and other creation', as well as of the wreckage of human endeavour. The ultimate significance of this sea is to be found in Dante's 'His will is our peace; it is that sea to which everything moves . . . .' It is all around us; on our coasts its salt is on the wild rose, and its fog, in the fir trees.

Among the many voices there is the recurrent sound of the bell rung by the groundswell 'that is and was from the beginning' (an echo of the *Gloria Patri*). This clanging bell measures a time which is not our time, not the time of women lying anxiously awake, unweaving and piecing together (another reminder of Ulysses) past and future, 'before the morning watch', when the soul turns to the Lord (cf. the Prayer Book version of Psalm cxxx.6). At this point, and again in the fourth section ('Women who have seen their sons or husbands Setting forth, and not returning'), Eliot is thinking not only of New England fishermen but also of sailors drowned in the Second World War; the drowned cannot hear 'the sea bell's Perpetual angelus'. The sea bell and the question of right endeavour are related to the Incarnation, and this is the ultimate subject of the sestina, the six six-lined verses which form the first movement of the second section. It is impossible to think of an 'oceanless' time, or of 'an ocean not littered with wastage', or of a future which is not like the past, one, that is, with no destination or arrival; the voyager can only 'fare forward' or try in the midst of failure; in dying to this world, the 'bone on the beach' (like the white bones of *Ash-Wednesday*) accepts His will. The 'one Annunciation' related to Incarnation is 'be it unto me according to thy word' (Luke, i.38), and in time of war and stress this may spell calamity.

In one of his prosiest passages Eliot argues that evolution is a popular theory which tends to make us disown the past, and reminds us of what he said in 'East Coker' on the life of many generations continuing into the present and future. Hence the 'backward look behind the assurance' of history, and the 'half-look' back towards the 'primitive terror'. Like the Mississippi with its cargo of dead negroes, cows, and chicken coops, time destroys and preserves; it preserves Original Sin, Adam's 'bitter apple and the bite'; the past may be forgotten in action as a reef is covered by sea-currents, but the agony remains like the Dry Salvages, 'the ragged rock in the restless waters'. For those who turn the wheel, it is 'a seamark To lay a course by'. The thought that the future contains the past reminds Eliot of Krishna; changing the terms, he reaches the conclusion of Heraclitus, giving it, as in 'Burnt Norton', the spiritual connotation of St John of the Cross: 'the way up is the way down' or 'the way forward is the way back'. Time cannot heal, for the inmate of the hospital is never the same; he is always moving on like passengers in a train who see the receding lines narrow together, or like those on a liner who see the furrow widen behind them. At nightfall (and here the reviving poetry reaches a peak), in timelessness, a voice audibly descants in rigging and aerial, 'Fare forward. . . . You are not those who saw the harbour Receding, or those who will disembark.' Then with a brief reference to Krishna's words to Arjuna before battle (in the *Bhagavad-Gita*), on the need to do what is right at the point of death, it insists that 'the time of death is every moment'; one should act according to the divine will, without regard for consequences or the fruits of action. Voyagers, those who reach port and those who suffer at sea, must fare forward disinterestedly, without expecting to 'fare well'. The Virgin Mary (cf. *Paradiso*, xxxiii.1) is asked to pray for those who fish, all others in ships, and those drowned at sea, whether washed ashore or sunk to the depths (Eliot told his friend William Turner Levy that the shrine he had in mind was Notre Dame de la Gard, overlooking the Mediterranean at Marseilles).

The fifth section opens with common superstitious practices by which people, whether in Asia or the Edgware Road near which Eliot once lived, try to diagnose the future, especially in time of national distress. Curiosity is usually limited to past and future. To apprehend the intersection of the timeless and time is 'an occupation for the saint'; to his customary images for such unexpected Incarnation, Eliot adds winter lightning (from 'East Coker'), the waterfall (visual impressions of which as movement and fixity impart a sense of the 'moment in and out of time', as in Wordsworth's 'Address to Kilchurn Castle'), and music heard so intensely that it passes beyond the bounds of the audible.[56] Similar release from time can come with the kind of action advocated by Krishna. For most the ideal is unrealizable, but defeat can be avoided if we maintain the effort. Eliot has the utmost difficulty in giving his subject poetic elevation, and ends with the thought that, if, with the approach of death and immortality, our new life (our 'temporal reversion') fructifies in others, we can finally be satisfied.

The Second World War confirmed the conviction Eliot expressed in the last number of *The Criterion* that severe affliction was necessary before there could be a renewal of life in western Europe; there could be no political solutions without true religion. He recalled the *flame* of monastic life (referred to in the same issue[57]) which had been kindled at Little Gidding by Nicholas Ferrar in the seventeenth century, and the brief sojourn there of the fugitive Charles I before surrendering to the Covenanters at Newark in 1646. Soon afterwards this saintly community was broken up by the Puritans; its church was restored in 1714 and again in 1853. Eliot's recollections of his own visit include the rough road, the may-blossom, the turn by the pig-sty to the 'dull façade' and Ferrar's tombstone; he associates Little Gidding with other holy places: Iona and Lindisfarne ('at the sea jaws'), Glendalough, a desert (Saint Anthony), and Padua (another Saint Anthony). Largely through the symbolism of fire, 'Little Gidding' involves much thought and conviction, not in perfection of form though in accordance with a pattern, to bring *Four Quartets* to a conclusion which may not satisfy belief but which at least commands poetical assent.

If the main subject is history, its thematic unification comes from the significance of its Pentecostal flame.

The poem begins in another time, with spring and Pentecostal fire (cf. Acts, ii.1–4) in winter, another intersection of the timeless with time, when the glancing sun 'flames the ice'. This moment of illumination, with a hint of the purgatorial, in the dark time of winter, raises the question when will summer come, 'the unimaginable Zero summer' that marks the inception of a new life of holiness. The transitory snow-blossom suggested by the thought of white-flowering may is a hint of something beyond this world. Here and at similar places we are at 'the world's end'; we are here to kneel in communion with the dead, and what they express is 'tongued with fire beyond the language of the living'. Eliot believes that the significance of their prayer and actions is seen more clearly, or in truer perspective, in the course of time.

Beginning with 'ash' and ending with 'fire', the regular stanzas which form the first movement of the second section include the four elements, partly to unify *Four Quartets*, partly to emphasize the primacy of fire in the Heraclitean strife of opposites. The conclusions, on the death respectively of air, earth, water, and fire, echo one of the axioms of Heraclitus without observing its significance, and suffer from ambiguity; the general tenor indicates the 'death' caused by the elements. Ash and dust (ashes to ashes, dust to dust) introduce the death theme; ash on the sleeve and suspension of dust in the air are memories of what Eliot himself noticed when on fire-watch duty during a London air-raid. Ash is all that is left from burnt roses; none rises refined to form the spectre of a rose, which was once regarded as a proof of immortality. The reference to burnt roses recalls 'Burnt Norton', just as that to the wainscot and mouse does 'East Coker', and that to the flood, 'The Dry Salvages'. The subject is the mortality of the physical, body and buildings; the water and sand contending for the body are dead, unlike water elsewhere in *Four Quartets* and sand in *Ash-Wednesday* (II). The destruction of forgotten religious foundations, and the thought of things undone, but of no account to the destructive elements, prepare the way for destruction by war and regrets for the past in the next movement, which cost Eliot more trouble and vexation than any passage of the same length he ever wrote, and is his greatest achievement in *Four Quartets*.

In this Eliot recalled the meeting of Dante and Brunetto
Latini, and did all he could to make his verse equal Dante's.
Knowing from experience the rhyming-difficulty presented by
the English language compared with the Italian in extended
regular verse, he introduced no rhymes but preserved the
complication of *terza rima* with its alternate rhymes by alternating
masculine and feminine endings.[58] The 'brown baked features',
one of the few phrases he used to point the parallel (cf. *Inferno*,
xv.26), are those of the 'compound' ghost who joins him in a
'dead' patrol after an air-raid (based on the recollection of one
on London, though the meeting, like the realization of the
dead in Little Gidding church, belongs to an intersection of
time and the timeless which transcends both the physical and
the temporal). The evil and destruction of aerial warfare are
conceived figuratively and darkly in terms of the Holy Spirit,
Pentecostal tongues of fire being associated with the form of the
dove, as the Spirit of God appeared when it descended upon
Jesus at his baptism. One 'plane is seen returning to base with
'flickering tongue'; the image of another as it falls in flames of
'incandescent terror' expresses the cardinal thought of the
poem, that redemption can come only from a purgatorial sense
of sin, the suffering which is the instrument of God's love.

The poet's 'dead master', like Dante's, offers him advice. The
ghost is unappeased, wandering between two worlds (an echo
of Arnold) which have become similar, both being conceived in
terms of Hell and Purgatory. There is no doubt that Eliot had
Yeats in mind, but it is impossible to judge how literally he
intended the line 'In streets I never thought I should revisit', or
what other poets were associated with Yeats in his compound
spirit; his master Dante would not have been out of place in
such a scene. Reaching the 'distant shore', the 'further shore' of
'The Dry Salvages' and the 'ripa ulterior' of Virgil (*Aeneid*,
vi.314), signifies death.

The ghost's words on change of fashion in art resemble the
sentiments of the painter Oderisi in the *Purgatorio* (xi.79ff.).
From the problem of style (purifying the language 'of the tribe'
echoes Mallarmé's 'Le Tombeau d'Edgar Poe') he proceeds to
the 'gifts reserved for age' after a lifetime of effort. The first is
Yeatsian (cf. 'The Spur'[59]); the second, impotent rage at the
folly of mankind, recalls Swift; and the last is Eliot's own

confession. He is aware of 'things ill done and done to others' harm'; no doubt he was thinking of false motivation in his writings as well as in life, particularly of persistent efforts to denigrate reputations in his criticism; he is bitterly conscious of the approbation of fools and of being awarded unmerited honour. Recovery is possible only through the refining fire 'Where you must move in measure, like a dancer', an allusion not only to the oft-quoted line on Arnaut Daniel's joyful disappearance 'nel foco che gli affina' but to the dance of those who seek union with God, as in the second section of 'Burnt Norton'. The departure of the ghost on the blowing of the horn (the 'all-clear') recalls that of Hamlet's father on the crowing of the cock.

Section III opens with terse but prosaic exposition. There are three states: attachment to self, people, and things; detachment from them; and indifference, which is like death. Together they prosper in the hedgerow, the unflowering third between the first and second, the stinging nettle and the dead nettle. The thought that memory through history can give detachment, a liberation from detail which transfigures the past and the self with it, is a key to the final philosophy of the poem. Eliot takes comfort from the words the fourteenth-century mystic Julian of Norwich thought she heard from Jesus: 'It behoved that there should be sin; but all shall be well . . . and all manner of thing shall be well.' Thinking of Little Gidding, and those involved in the strife which destroyed its community, of Charles I's arrival at nightfall, of his death, and the death of Strafford and Laud, on the scaffold, and of Milton dying peacefully in bed, he asks why we should celebrate the dead of the past more than the dying of 1942; he has no wish to revive their causes. (The expression 'ring the bell backward' comes from an ancient way of signalling distress, and is misunderstood by Eliot; his revival of the rose-spectre image alludes insignificantly to a poem of that title by Gautier but more especially, he said, to the ballet *Le Spectre de la Rose*, in which Nijinsky made his famous leap.) Those who were in conflict are now united in death; they leave us a symbol, for our inheritance comes as much from the defeated as from the victors. All is made well by 'the purification of the motive In the ground of our beseeching' (an adaptation of Julian of Norwich's statement that she was the ground of

God's beseeching). Eliot's theodicy, comfortable rather than comforting, recalls Tennyson's 'All is well' in *In Memoriam* and Hardy's comment on it in 'The Impercipient'.

As one of those communications of the dead which are 'tongued with fire', the symbol of those who fought one another in an ancient cause leads Eliot to his conclusion on the present war, in which the descending dove rends the air with fire. The Pentecostal link between fire and the gift of tongues has a connection with the opening of the fifth section of the poem, but Eliot's principal thought is that redemption from sin, error, and conflict, the fire of Hell, can come only from the fire of Purgatory. Echoing Lady Julian again, he affirms that this torment is the work of God's love,[60] and compares it to the shirt of Nessus. After enunciating his stylistic ideal, with every word 'at home', the 'complete consort dancing together', he furthers the analogy with 'Little Gidding' imagery by saying that every poem is an epitaph; one is always starting afresh, as he emphasized in 'East Coker'. Everything we do in the ground of beseeching is a step to the execution-block or to the fire, 'down the sea's throat' as in 'Death by Water', or to an illegible tombstone; 'and that is where we start'. (With this detail 'Little Gidding' recalls 'The Dry Salvages' and 'East Coker', if not 'Burnt Norton'.)

All time being eternally present, and history a known pattern based on 'timeless moments', we can die or be spiritually reborn in the lives of the past. As dying unto life is rebirth, the yew-tree and the rose are commensurate symbols. Eliot's thought is poetic; it shores up his faith, and to argue whether or not he presents a sound philosophical aspect of history is of minor importance. Quoting from *The Cloud of Unknowing*, he introduces his conclusion: the spiritual explorer aims to reach the place from which he started. Access to it is gained through the 'remembered gate' of 'Burnt Norton';[61] it is 'the source of the longest river', the voice of the 'hidden waterfall' and of the children in the apple-tree; it is the 'stillness' or timeless moment between two sea-waves. To reach it demands a state of complete simplicity, the sacrifice of everything; 'the simplicity that is in Christ' (II Corinthians, xi.3) requires that we become like little children (Matthew, xviii.3). The flames which signify the working of the Pentecostal spirit are inwoven in the 'crowned knot' (a nautical term for one that cannot be untied) of the multifoliate Rose (seen in the garden of Christ: *Paradiso*, xxiii.70ff.), which is Dante's emblem for God's love; the knot (*Paradiso*, xxxiii.91) enfolds the universe and activates the purgatorial fire, the 'torment' that draws us to Him. (For the association of God's love and fire, and the still point, see *Paradiso*, xxviii.1–45.)

The thought of losses at home, on land, and at sea, during the Second World War surfaces in the last three quartets, which Eliot regarded as patriotic poems. 'Defence of the Islands' (1940) has all the virtue of a memorable clear-cut rhythmic prose which is liturgical in character, its pauses punctuating structure in one sustained exhortation which links subject and authorial regard for the English language in their historical perspectives. 'A Note on War Poetry', included in *London Calling* (1942) at the request of the editor Storm Jameson, fits an old thought, on the impersonality of poetry which has a universal or permanent quality, to a new context. War is not life but a situation (as is indicated at the end of 'Defence of the Islands') created by forces which make the emotions of the individual mere incidents; only by conceiving intense personal experience in the abstract can it be transmuted into symbol or the universal which is inherent in great poetry. The main thought of 'To the Indians who Died in Africa' (1943) is that villagers, whether in the Midlands or the Punjab, should remember that wherever a man dies bravely in accordance with destiny is his soil, and that, whether we are aware of it or not, the value of his action at the time of his death will, as Krishna said, be judged in after years.

The demonic genius which had once insisted on poetic expression, and the gift of lyricism which revived in him at a later period, had deserted Eliot. Two of the minor war poems are more remarkable for thought than for expression. Only on three occasions, it seems, was he moved to work at verse during the last twenty years of his life. 'To Walter de la Mare', a tribute to the poet on his seventy-fifth birthday in 1948, gradually conjures up his phantasmal world, and the spell of his magic-weaving words. 'The Cultivation of Christmas Trees', published in a new series of Ariel poems in 1954, begins with prosaic economy before enlarging on its subject, the wish that the spirit of reverence and delight symbolized by the tree in childhood may never be lost, but may signify to the end the awe and great joy which came to the shepherds when the birth of Jesus was announced, and the glory of the Lord shone round about them. St Lucy signifies saving Grace for Eliot as for Dante (*Inferno*, ii.76–120; cf. *Purgatorio*, ix.55–7);[62] the ending, like that of 'Journey of the Magi' implies no second Advent but the spiritual salvation which should be our goal. Love gives a lift to 'A Dedication to my Wife', verses prefixed to Eliot's last play (1959) which hint at the Christian mysticism of 'no more twain, but one flesh'; the imagery is reduced to the extremes of climate avoided and sought by Eliot in his later years, and to roses in his oft-visited garden of happiness.

18

The Family Reunion to *The Elder Statesman*

One of Eliot's supreme dramatic aims, as he tells us in 'Poetry and Drama', was to bring poetry into the familiar world of the telephone, radio, and motor-car. He hoped that audiences would feel they could speak the same language, and acquire poetic perceptions which would help to transform the dreary round of their lives. In *The Family Reunion* (1939), his first complete stage presentation of contemporary life, his chief technical concern was the creation of verse close to speech but capable of ranging from pure poetry to the commonplace without seeming unnatural or absurd. In this, and his later plays, he is so successful that any rare oddity such as the heavily classical diction of 'batrachian' stone or the 'aphyllous branch ophidian' creates only a momentary impediment. There are times when the flow of language is too unbrokenly smooth, when we feel it would gain from the more arresting kind of dramatic intensity that is found in 'Gerontion'. In general it conforms to the standards enunciated in 'Little Gidding': 'easy commerce of the old and the new', 'neither diffident nor ostentatious', the common words being 'exact without vulgarity', and the formal, 'precise but not pedantic'. Avoiding iambic blank verse, the continued use of which would seem imitative and outdated, Eliot adopted as his norm lines of varying length, with three principal stresses and a caesura, all falling in accordance with conversational emphasis.

The other notable feature of *The Family Reunion*, reflected in departures from the verse norm, is the occasional suspension of the action, with certain characters speaking as if in a trance, revealing higher insights in moments of vision. In his essay on Marston, Eliot speaks of two planes of reality, one of the familiar world, the other of something beyond: in the ancient world this something was known as Fate, he continues, and the subtleties of Christian theology into which it was translated have been reduced to the 'crudities' of modern psychology. *The Family Reunion* is principally an inner drama, essentially psychological though presented more spiritually, in terms which are not too overtly Christian to disturb a predominantly agnostic audience, though completely consistent with Eliot's dogma. He employs verse-conventions to distinguish between two planes of unusual perception. Perceptions on the lower level are not beyond the range of ordinary persons, though their representatives in the play are arrogantly informed that they are people to whom 'nothing has happened'; those on the higher level are rare, coming only to those who have awakened to the nightmare of life, and live simultaneously on several planes. The normal conversation of the characters, whether the abnormally percipient or those who live on a common social and worldly level, is couched in what has become Eliot's standard dramatic verse.

The play observes the unities, the action being limited to the afternoon and evening of a March day at Wishwood, the home of Amy, Lady Monchensey, part I in the drawing-room after tea, part II in the library after dinner. Named possibly after Wychwood Forest near Finstock, Oxfordshire, where Eliot was baptized, this country house in the north of England suggests worldly ambition and error. The reunion is occasioned by Amy's birthday, and the drama begins with the arrival of her son and heir Harry, who is haunted by guilt. Her two sisters Ivy and Violet, and her two brothers-in-law Charles and Gerald, sometimes speak in chorus to express a vague awareness of something about to be exposed, of a past that is 'about to happen' and a future that was 'long since settled', of something outside their limited circle of understanding (an image reminiscent of the quotation from Bradley in Eliot's notes to *The Waste Land*), of 'an act of God' against which there can be no insurance. The choral expression of their inner thoughts is dramatically reinforced through the medium of lines which are either longer or shorter than Eliot's dramatic norm; occasionally, within a chorus, they change to the equivalent of individual dramatic asides. More interestingly, in shorter-lined passages, they approximate a monotonic, hypnotizing style, designed to merge the audience with them in the recognition of general truths: 'We all of us make the pretension To be the uncommon exception', 'And whether in Argos or England There are certain inflexible laws', 'Except for a limited number Of strictly practical purposes We do not know what we are doing'. (In the last of these Eliot states prosaically a view which he emphasized as early as the last section of 'Preludes'.) Gathered at Amy's bidding, they are so restricted in experience and understanding that they are almost types. Ivy, who wishes to escape the cold of Wishwood, for the warmer south, is certain the young are decadent; Violet despises the more affluent south, and is happy to help Lady Bumpus at the vicar's American Tea. Charles prefers his London club, thinks the younger generation has no stamina, but is determined to take the bull by the horns for the sake of Harry; Gerald, once a subaltern in the east, would rather let sleeping dogs lie; he is more tolerant, after finding decent chaps and good shots among the young.

Amy (Lady Monchensey), the head of the family, embodies will-power; the play opens with typical self-assertion as the parlour-maid enters to close the curtains. Like Lady Macbeth, she fears the dark; she remembers with longing the warm sun and the light taken for granted when she was young, when night was unfeared, clocks could be trusted, and 'time would not stop in the dark'. Decisiveness within her limited circle has given her persistent assurance, though its early expression is proved wrong by events: instead of being in time for dinner, her nephews Arthur and John do not come at all; Harry, who might arrive in the evening, arrives that afternoon. The best time, she decides, to cut the cake and open the presents is after dinner, but she is not there to enjoy them; her birthday is the day of her death. She has been a life-killer. She had married for the sake of the Wishwood inheritance, 'Forcing sons upon an unwilling father', who had thought of murdering her three months before Harry's birth; after seven years he had left her. Harry could remember the silence, the hushed conversation, and the averted looks that brought death to his heart when news of his father's death reached Wishwood. His mother, who had a habit of making him feel guilty, planned his marriage to Mary, a distant relative who would make a tame daughter-in-law and a 'housekeeper-companion' for her and him. For this reason he left Wishwood, and married a woman he did not love; he had wanted to kill her, and imagined that he had pushed her overboard when she was drowned in the Atlantic. Mary was convinced that Amy had willed his wife's death, and still intended Harry for her. Only indomitable will keeps his mother alive, the doctor tells him, referring to her as a machine, and warning him not to thwart her. The sins of the fathers are visited on the children; it is his destiny to leave in expiation, and Amy dies soon after hearing of his departure. The clock by which she had lived stops in the dark. No warmth of love was possible at Wishwood; it was 'always a cold place'.

The only scenes in which tenderness is felt are between Mary and Harry, and between Harry and his aunt Agatha, the former especially. These three are endowed with Eliot's higher perceptions, and it is with each of the other two, after speaking in rapt alternations of verse, that Harry sees the Eumenides. Mary and Agatha are academic, and intellectually and socially on a remarkably different level from that of the hero whose spiritual insights are seen emerging in 'Sweeney Agonistes', the first epigraph of which would be more appropriate to *The Family Reunion*: 'Orestes: *You don't see them, you don't – but* I *see them: they are hunting me down, I must move on.*' Mary and Harry are at one in the recollection of past happiness, symbolized in the lost hollow tree where they played in childhood; she seems to him like a hidden, half-heard waterfall in a forest. The thought of rebirth in a cold spring season raises them to a spiritual intensity which reaches its climax when Mary, after expressing belief in the death and sacrifice which accompany natural birth, turns to the 'terrified spirit' which is forced to be reborn, like the aged eagle to which reference is made in *Ash-Wednesday*. Recovering from this ecstasy, Harry tells her that she brings news of a door opening at the end of a long corridor, and of sunlight and singing. This experience of heaven and the timeless is cut short as he becomes aware of the Eumenides, the 'sleepless hunters' who give him no sleep. Wishwood and Mary are not for him.

Agatha, who knows the past and has won her 'dispossession', is apt to speak hierophantically from the start. The past is irredeemable; Harry's future (which is outside the scope of the play) can be built only on knowledge of the real past. When he returns to Wishwood, he will find another Harry, like the hero of Henry James's story 'The Jolly Corner', who, returning from Europe and curious about his old home, was shocked by the apparition of the self he might have been had he stayed. When she hears Amy's plans for Harry, Agatha comments on the 'interfering preparation Of that which is already prepared' by people whose blinkered awareness of what is happening is comparable to the little revealed by a pocket-torch in the surrounding darkness. Decisions, she tells Mary, will be made not by them, who are only 'watchers and waiters', but by powers beyond them. At the end of part I she speaks of the curse or evil eye on the house, and prays that the knot involving the three (Harry and his parents) will be unknotted, and the crooked made straight. It was because she felt that Harry was hers that she persuaded his father not to kill his mother before he was born; he is the consciousness of his tragic family, 'Its bird sent flying through the purgatorial flame'.

When she has told him everything, he feels he has suffered in a war of shadows or phantoms; he is liberated, as if a chain had broken and the wheel of his insane mind and all its clanking machinery had stopped. The chain, which is related to time (as for Shelley and Emily Brontë [63]), has broken for both, and spiritual release for each is expressed in alternating verse: Agatha remembers happiness for her at Wishwood, when the sun shone on the rose-garden before a black raven flew over, and then she was walking surrealistically in 'dead air', seeing only her feet, down the long corridor of a huge, empty hospital smelling of disinfectant; Harry remembers the wheel to which he was chained, the 'endless drift' of shrieking, putrescent shadows in a 'circular desert'. He is now free from the encircling ghosts, his pursuers, and is content to wait for the judgment of God: the desert is clear, 'under the judicial sun Of the final eye'. It is as if Agatha had walked through the door, and they had met in the rose-garden. They find the Eumenides have left, and Agatha takes their place, the subject of her pronouncement being the curse of Original Sin with which a child is born, and her guardian concern for Harry's fulfilment. What seems the end for him, she tells him, is only the beginning; expurgation is possible only when sin has struggled into consciousness from its 'dark instinctive birth'. He cannot return to what he was; to adapt Heraclitus, 'We do not pass twice through the same door.' He has a long journey ahead, the way of redemption, the worship in the desert of thirst and deprivation, following the Eumenides who are now his 'bright angels'.

There are resemblances between Eliot's play and the *Oresteia* of Aeschylus; in each there is a curse on the house, and the transformation of the Furies to benevolent guardians of the law in the last of Aeschylus's trilogy corresponds to the change from the Eumenides as unrelenting pursuers to the angels who are pursued when knowledge of the whole hereditary truth clears Harry's mind of phantoms. For Eliot the Eumenides are, like Thompson's hound of heaven, divine instruments in a Christian world.[64] In their differing forms, pursuing and pursued, they are an expression of the hell Harry has suffered and the purgatory and penance he must undergo. 'What we have written', says Agatha, 'is not a story of detection, Of crime and punishment, but of sin and expiation'. The tension of the drama as a whole is lessened because the past is simply revealed or explained; Amy is never tortured by it or aware of its disclosure. The ending may not seem convincing or sufficiently impressive. Whatever the cogency of Eliot's imagery for readers, Harry, after crossing the frontier and leaving this world of death, becomes a vague figure, ignorant of what lies ahead of him. The final note of the Chorus, who must do the right thing by wordly standards, is deliberately weak; but the concluding runic ritual, in which Agatha and Mary speak the words as they circle the table and blow out the candles on the birthday cake until the stage is in darkness, is hardly adequate. Its subject is the old one of the primal curse or Original Sin; the ritual suggests an incantatory charm, but it serves at the same time as a visual reminder of the Holy Week service of *Tenebrae*, with reference to darkness over the whole earth at the time of the Crucifixion (Luke, xxiii.44).

There is a strong autobiographical element in *The Family Reunion*. Opposition between Harry's wife and his mother, and the haunting sense of sin at being rid of a wife whom he had thought he could murder, may have originated from Eliot's marriage. The sunlight of a timeless moment with Mary recalls 'Burnt Norton' and a time when happiness with Emily Hale could have renewed Eliot's sense of the 'necrophily' of life with Vivienne. Harry's inner world is Eliot's: the degradation of being parted from a self which persists as a watching eye; the corridor and the hospital; the circular desert and the wheel; the rose-garden, the sunlight, and the singing. His ideas, like Agatha's, are Eliot's: the continuing self never being the same, he is not the man who knew his wife; it is not merely his conscience that is diseased but the whole world. Years later he seemed an 'insufferable prig' to Eliot, whose sympathies turned wholly to Harry's mother. Such views recall Lawrence's 'Never trust the artist. Trust the tale', for it is difficult to see how anyone, keeping to the evidence of the play, can sympathize with a mother whose unregretted domination is responsible for so much unhappiness and evil. The other weaknesses Eliot points out in 'Poetry and Drama' seem to have more foundation, though it is doubtful if the 'first act' is too long; the second suffers less from lack of room for more action than from lack of dramatic tension when the past is disclosed. The main problem created by the play affects its production: how effectively to transmit inner thoughts or higher perceptions to an audience in such a way that they appear inaudible to others on the stage. Why Eliot was opposed to the revelation of the Eumenides to the audience is not clear. The appearance of the ghost on the Elizabethan stage was a convention, not a piece of realism, but Eliot seems to have been thinking in realistic terms when he decided that the Furies should be omitted from the cast. The relevance of his comments on *Hamlet* as an 'objective correlative' to the subject and presentation of his own play are worth consideration.

Between the first production of *The Family Reunion* and that of *The Cocktail Party* in 1949, more than ten years elapsed. Eliot's poetic creativity had waned, and his deliberate avoidance of poetical imagery brings the verse of his last three plays even closer to speech than several passages in *The Family Reunion*. His second contemporary play was designed to be a West End success; the subject is serious, but it is presented for the most part as light comedy. There are no ghosts or choruses, and hardly anything which aspires to the hierophantic, though toasts at the end of the second act partake of ritual and rune; exegesis is left to a practising psychiatrist. The only unity which is observed is that of subject, and the plot is contrived much more successfully than that of *The Family Reunion* to maintain suspense and surprise, mainly through the freakish intervention of the Guardians as representatives of God's mysterious ways.

There is hardly a vestige of the religious symbolism usually employed by Eliot (though Alex's eggs may portend rebirth), so much so that Julia's reference to the 'scolding hills' and the 'valley of derision' strike an incongruous note. Whatever its technical or stage merits, the verse is so plain that it does not linger as poetry; Eliot suspected he had put it on 'a very thin diet'.

The main subject is the marriage relationship of the middle-aged Chamberlaynes. Edward's wife Lavinia has just left him because of his love-affair with Celia Coplestone, with whom young Peter Quilpe is in love. At the cocktail party which opens the play, Edward tells his guests Alex, Julia, and the drink-prone stranger who sings the song about one-eyed Riley, that his wife is staying with her aunt. These seven characters are the only ones of any importance, and they form two groups, a married and an unmarried couple in one, and a mysterious trio who prove to be their Guardians. Alex is a kind of modern Hermes, who busies himself in the kitchen on Edward's behalf, and is dramatically useful at the end in recounting Celia's fate at the hands of some primitive tribe. Julia is a seemingly silly, managing woman who contrives to lose her umbrella or spectacles, usually as a pretext for coming back to see what is going on; as she cannot see without them, and one lens is missing, she has something in common with the one-eyed Riley, who proves to be Sir Henry Harcourt-Reilly, the psychiatrist whom they assist. Nobody, it seems, until Eliot himself made the disclosure, realized that his play began with a parallel to the carousing of Heracles, the guest who did not know that his host Admetus's wife Alcestis was dead. Julia is indignant when Edward's guest leaves singing his 'One-eyed Riley' refrain: 'You've been *drinking* together! So this is the kind of friend you have When Lavinia is out of the way!' Later the unidentified guest, who predicted accurately that Lavinia would return within twenty-four hours, talks of bringing Edward's wife 'back from the dead'. Perhaps Heracles' sentiments, that since we are mortal our minds should be on mortal things, has some bearing on *The Cocktail Party*, where the higher religious part finally played by Celia is subordinated to a mundane adjustment in the marital Chamberlayne relationship.

The play opens with vacuous fashionable chatter which is never allowed to lead anywhere, and which is unfortunately rhythmically reminiscent of 'Sweeney Agonistes', until the unknown guest begins to converse with Edward about his wife's departure. The host is told that his answers are a collection of 'obsolete responses', that he can do nothing but wait, and that it will do him no harm to find himself ridiculous. He finds he cannot do without Lavinia, though he is not happy with her; his life is determined, and the idea that he can escape from it, as he had believed he could, with Celia, comes from a feeble self whose will habitually submits to his mediocrity. When the stranger tells him that we die daily to each other, he speaks, not in the Pauline, but in the Heraclitean, sense of 'The Dry Salvages'; 'at every meeting we are meeting a stranger' elucidates Agatha's 'Meeting is for strangers' in *The Family Reunion*. When Lavinia returns, she tells Edward her belief that, if she, who had been a ghost, died to him by leaving him, he might rediscover his past self. He thinks he is in hell, and must consult the specialist; he tells Reilly that he can live neither with nor without his wife. Both fail to qualify for the sanatorium because they deceive themselves; it is the honest people who really suffer. One had concealed his relations with Celia Coplestone; the other, her hopes of Peter Quilpe. Both suffer from the same kind of isolation, and must make the best of it. Only by acceptance of the past can its meaning be altered; they must renew life on the basis of the real. The cocktail party at the end of the play marks a new beginning for the Chamberlaynes.

The sanatorium is for saints. Celia, a passionate girl, does not deceive herself. Brought up conventionally not to believe in sin, she is now aware of sin and isolation. She is disillusioned with Edward, and told by Reilly that to stay in disillusion can only be illusion. Marriage can be a 'good life' in a world of violence, greed, and stupidity, he tells her, but it does not appeal to her. She can avoid the hell of 'shuffling memories and desires' (a phrase which calls up the opening of *The Waste Land*) only if she follows her higher vision; it will require the kind of faith that comes from despair. She must go to the sanatorium, but her destination will not be known until she reaches it; the choice will be hers. He blesses her, as he had done the Chamberlaynes, in the words of the dying Buddha to his disciples: 'Go in peace. And work out your salvation in diligence.' Reilly's next words, 'It is finished' (the dying words of Jesus), point to her crucifixion, but he cannot foresee it; intuition tells him that Celia is sentenced to death; he does not know what he implies when he tells her to work out her salvation in diligence.

The interval between the second act and the third (which Eliot thought rather an epilogue) represents the passing of two years. With Alex entering the kitchen and telling Julia there are no tigers in Kinkanja, the start of the play is recalled; there are preparations for another party, with a good deal of trivial conversation which is clearly juxtaposed to link monkeys in Kinkanja with monkeys in the American film industry. All this is designed to create climax, from the build-up of suspense, in two stages, the first concluding when Alex is about to impart news of Celia which creates shivers in the intuitional guardian Julia before it is announced, the second beginning with Peter Quilpe's arrival at this point, and continuing with news of his success as a film-producer, and hopes that Celia will accept the part he has in mind for her. Then follows the news of her death at the hands of the natives. So shocked were Edinburgh audiences by this that some of the details were removed: Celia, crucified near an ant-hill, had endured a martyrdom of prolonged suffering. With the propitiatory offerings that ensued, the whole still seems too like a horrible parody of the Crucifixion and the Eucharist. Peter realizes that absorption in his own career has made it impossible for him to know Celia, but is told by the Chamberlaynes, who speak from experience, that illusion has served his needs, and that self-realization is a step forward. At least he knows his *métier*, he is assured by Reilly and Julia, and has his mission. Reilly quotes from Shelley's *Prometheus Unbound* (i.191–9) on the worlds of life and death, the visible and the phantasmal, the second of which gave him the vision of Celia's death the first time he saw her. Her suffering was destined, and therefore Edward must try to detach himself from the responsibility he feels towards her; her life was not wasted, but triumphant. Those such as Quilpe and the Chamberlaynes, who live on the worldly plane, may be the better for her sacrifice. Quilpe knows that his self-interest is not worthy of her; and the one-eyed Reilly, who can depend only on hints of higher things, tells Edward and Lavinia that they must live with their memories, and see them in a new light. It is not exactly a sea-change, but something more intelligible to theatre audiences.

Character with personality emerges slowly in Eliot's plays. In those which will probably have the most lasting interest – *Murder in the Cathedral* and *The Family Reunion*, though *The Rock* has more perennial importance than the latter – his situations are chosen or created in order to express his higher convictions or vision. In the second of these plays, his first full-length presentation of a contemporary scene, the social world is wilful, impercipient, or ridiculous. In the comedies which follow characters are more and more sympathetically developed, as life on this lower plane becomes increasingly the area of Eliot's interest. Analysis of situation, particularly that involving the Chamberlaynes, takes precedence over character-presentation in *The Cocktail Party*. Reilly is the centre of interest because he is endowed with hard psychological insights; Celia's warm personality is strikingly combined with swift powers of discernment and decision; but the most fascinating character, the one who evokes the most curiosity, is the astute Julia Shuttlethwaite, who at times is wiser than the 'one-eyed Riley'. In *The Confidential Clerk*, first produced in 1953, there is greater development of character all round. The retired Eggerson (who grew from Eliot's recollections of an old clerk in his bank) is more memorable than his successor Colby; Lady Elizabeth Mulhammer, who is portrayed sometimes with a Jane Austenish verve, is more subtle than her husband Sir Claude, and Lucasta is captivatingly presented in a minor role; in her forthright way Mrs Guzzard never fails to make her mark. She is the outsider in a play where all are involved in relationships and a moral theme, but she is the indispensable *dea ex machina* in a plot where complications of identity create a puzzle which maintains suspense almost to the very end. The homogeneity and dramatic unity of *The Confidential Clerk* are steps forward in the developing process of Eliot's contemporary drama. There is no poetical revival, however, in the verse; it meets dramatic requirement with plain directness; the story contains situations and elements reminiscent of Wilde, without the sparkle.

Much more real than *The Cocktail Party*, with the extraordinary intuitions of its Guardians, and their incredibly concerted telegrams, telephone calls, and arrivals, *The Confidential Clerk* opens in an atmosphere too cosy to last long, eventually to reveal an amazing nexus of mistaken identities. Its astonishing plot originated largely from Euripides' *Ion*, where the eponymous hero is presented as a son to the childless couple Xuthus and Creusa. The oracle has led Xuthus to believe that Ion is his own bastard son; Creusa has yet to learn that he is the son she bore and abandoned after being ravished by Apollo. She hears a false foster-mother story of her husband's intrigue to conceal his son's origins, but the priestess who found Ion produces irrefutable evidence that he is Creusa's son. Ion is reluctant to exchange the peace of the temple where he has served for the responsibilities of rulership or all that wealth can offer, but he accepts Minerva's bidding, as does his mother Creusa, that Xuthus should be left to imagine he is his father. Eliot does not persist in his parallel with Euripides, preferring to complicate the issue, partly in furtherance of his theme, more perhaps for the sake of an amusing climactic *dénouement*.

The parallel is clear in the exposition before Lady Elizabeth's surprising return. She and Sir Claude are a childless couple, but he thinks he is Colby's father, and enough is said to suggest that Lucasta is his illegitimate daughter; Lady Elizabeth had a pre-marital child which cannot be traced. The time for revealing Colby's identity will depend on how much she likes him. Her memory is poor, though she has had a course of mind-control in Zurich; when she is introduced to him, she thinks she has interviewed and recommended Colby as confidential clerk to her husband in succession to Eggerson; she will share him with Sir Claude. A photograph of the 'aunt' who brought him up, and the names 'Guzzard' and 'Teddington' stir her memory, and she becomes convinced that Colby is her own lost child; when she tells her husband, he has to confess that Colby is his son, brought up by Mrs Guzzard of Teddington. Lady Elizabeth's recommendation that they should regard him as their son does not please Colby; when it is decided to interview Mrs Guzzard, she is content to let her husband think Colby is his son. In the interview Sir Claude's confidential clerk is the retired Eggerson, who conducts the inquiry. It transpires that, when the father of Lady Elizabeth's child died and payments ceased, Mrs Guzzard had allowed her neighbours, the Kaghans, to adopt the child; he had been christened, and would now be about twenty-eight. (At the time B. Kaghan, as he preferred to be known, was about to marry Lucasta; Lady Elizabeth had calculated that her son would be twenty-five, Colby's age.) Colby proves to be Mrs Guzzard's son. Sir Claude's illegitimate child had never been born; the mother, Mrs Guzzard's sister, had died during her pregnancy. When Sir Claude visited Mrs Guzzard, she had allowed him to assume that her child was his because she needed money after the death of her husband, a disappointed musician.

The more involuted the story, the sillier it becomes. Its structuring is undoubtedly one of Eliot's dramatic successes, but one couldn't expect such a writer to rest content with a plot geared merely to suspense and surprise. He presents a complicated parable. Who or what is 'the confidential clerk'? Instead of directing attention to higher and lower planes of living, Eliot has turned to the outer and inner worlds of people, particularly to the comic world of false impressions, the question of true relationships, and the more serious one of discovering the inner self and satisfying its needs, the question of choice which Reilly's patients are always left to solve for themselves. Sir Claude discovers there is much he does not know about people, including his wife and even Eggerson. Lady Elizabeth does not care for B. Kaghan, thinks him undistinguished, and Colby well-bred. She has always lived in 'a world of make-believe', and assumed that her husband preferred the hard financial world of facts. Nothing could be further from the truth; he had wished to be a potter, but had taken over a business which had been his father's passion, solely to please him, thereby changing his own life and personality. He thinks he might have been truer to his father's inspiration if he had done what he himself wanted. As it is, he is a second-rate potter, and he regards his intermittent escapes into creative art as a religious experience, just as his wife does her investigations into the life of the spirit. Eliot's views on the speciousness of the latter assumptions are well known, and Sir Claude realizes that each of his lives is 'a kind of make-believe'. He had assumed that Colby would be pleased to follow him in his business, but Colby finds that the work is changing him, and that his former self, returning at unexpected times, makes him yearn to be the disappointed organist who wished to excel in his art. He reaches the same conclusion as Sir Claude; if you have two lives which are unrelated, both are unreal, as he tells Lucasta.

The Lucasta story lights up the theme. She tells Colby that he has a sense of security, a 'secret garden' to which he can retire despite his failure to find himself in business; he has lost no more than the outer world. Unlike Eggerson, whose garden is part of his 'one single world', he is alone in his garden, he replies, and therefore it is unreal. The growth of understanding between Lucasta and Colby is expressed briefly in continuity of duologue which expresses unison on the better understanding of self consequent on beginning to know another person. Afraid that he assumed she was Sir Claude's mistress, she discloses her true relationship, and Colby is taken aback to think he might have been falling in love with his half-sister; she believes that, if people know who she is, she is more likely to become her true self. The shock she had seen on Colby's face tells her she will fare better with the foundling B. Kaghan, who has always accepted her for what she is. Before Mrs Guzzard is due, Lucasta arrives to announce their impending marriage. Kaghan had pretended to be common because Lady Elizabeth had thought him common; she gave them their parts, and they had shown they could play them. Lady Elizabeth believes that she and Sir Claude can learn to understand each other, and in so doing learn to understand other people. Lucasta's judgment of Colby shows she does not yet understand him, but she leaves with Eliot-directed comments on the changes that have taken place since they met, since 'we're always changing'. She and B. Kaghan are asked to wait until the Guzzard inquiry is over, when the parents meet their real children, all four eager to know and understand each other, through love and responsibility.

Colby has resisted make-believe throughout. He wishes he had a father to whom he could atone, as Sir Claude had been atoning to his. Sir Claude is a patron, not the father who was absent in his childhood. When one has lived without parents there is a gap that can never be filled. Instinctively he feels he would like a father whom he had never known, one who died before he was born; he knows that Mrs Guzzard is telling the truth, and feels liberated by it. He must follow his father, he reiterates; now he knows his inheritance (an echo of the ending of *Ash-Wednesday*, II). He had not known his mother in childhood, since she had been 'aunt' to him; she remains his 'aunt', just as Lady Elizabeth becomes 'Aunt Elizabeth' to Kaghan, who continues to regard Mrs Kaghan as his mother. There may be a special significance in Lady Elizabeth's words on reincarnation: it does not depend on heredity but on something 'unique . . . straight from God', which means that 'we are nearer to God than to anyone'. At the bidding of a pagan goddess, Euripides' Ion leaves the temple where he is at home, to fulfil his worldly destiny; Colby returns to a temple where he is at home, and there, like Jesus in the temple (Luke, ii.41–9), he must be about his Father's business. His future as organist and priest seems assured with Eggerson; everything points to the realization of the ideal to which Eliot's 'confidential clerk' aspires. If he were religious, he had told Lucasta (and the author's hint of Eden is clearly audible), God would walk with him in his garden, and consequently the world would become real and acceptable. Like Chaucer's Clerk of Oxenford, Colby does not seek worldly office; his wish is to discover what God would have him be, and to become His trustworthy servant. With fictional improbabilities of another kind, *The Confidential Clerk* succeeds in conveying a deeper spiritual truth (on the need to find a significant role in life) than *The Cocktail Party*; 'less complicated on the surface', it had 'much more in layers to be meditated on and thought of as meanings of life', Eliot thought.[65]

'There is a comfort in the strength of love; 'Twill make a thing endurable, which else Would overset the brain, or break the heart.' These words from Wordsworth's 'Michael' serve to express the feelings of Oedipus towards his daughters in Sophocles' *Oedipus at Colonos*, the play to which Eliot's *The Elder Statesman* bears certain resemblances in its main outline. Dedicated to his second wife, it expresses the love which had grown between them; it was first performed in August 1958, when the author was near the end of his seventieth year, but not published until the following April. Although the subject of ghosts or guilt from the past makes it a successor to *The Family Reunion*, it keeps close to the worldly plane of experience, and is more closely related to *The Confidential Clerk* in its emphasis on being true to one's self. In *Oedipus at Colonos* horrible memories of the hero's past are roused by Creon; similarly, slighter but unpleasant recollections of his early life are revived in Lord Claverton, in particular of driving over the body of an old man without reporting the incident, and of an affair with a woman he refused to marry. The visit of Polynices to his father Oedipus, and their unsolved quarrel, are reflected in the situation which develops between Lord Claverton and his son Michael. The parallel is maintained in the devotion of his daughter Monica, and in the peaceful but mysterious death of the aged hero. *The*

Elder Statesman is a sad story of psychological interest. Dramatically it is simple and straightforward like Sophocles' play; it reads rather like the dramatization of a novel.

In common with the eminent City men of 'East Coker', Lord Claverton has gone into the dark, the 'silent funeral' of vacancy. When he first appears, just before the arrival of Gomez, he is afraid of the emptiness of life; it is just as if he were alone in a waiting-room on a branch line, with the booking-office closed and the station deserted. Restored to love and tranquillity at the end, he knows that the process of dying is worth while for its revelation of what life is. Spectres of the past revive with the coming of Gomez and Mrs Carghill. The first reminds him of escapades at Oxford, and how he had changed with the changing of his name, first from Dick Ferry to Mr Richard Claverton-Ferry when he married, and finally to Lord Claverton. Gomez, formerly the Fred Culverwell who might have won a First and become a schoolmaster, had been corrupted by Ferry's expensive tastes, and sent down; later he had been committed for forgery. When his sentence was completed, his old friend had paid his passage out of the country; abroad he had changed his name and acquired a fortune by adopting the morality of his milieu. He was an isolated man, and had called to renew a friendship which would give him a sense of reality. Richard Ferry met Mrs Carghill before her first marriage, and before she became an actress; she had a physical attraction which he could not resist, and she sued him for breach of promise, a lawsuit which was settled out of court in order not to ruin his political prospects. He had 'pawed' her soul, and the touch still lingered.

According to Gomez, Lord Claverton's undergraduate son Michael had behaved rather like his father, without the latter's 'prudent devil'; he had just lost his post, and accumulated large debts. He is full of excuses, attributing his failures to his father's keenness to prolong existence through him. He would now like to live his own life and leave England. (His father, reflecting his own past, asks if he is guilty of manslaughter on the road or of being in trouble with a woman.) Mrs Carghill and Gomez can sympathize fully, and Michael accepts a post abroad with Gomez, who pays his passage and assures his father that his morals will be cared for. His sister Monica believes that homesickness will make him return (as it had made Gomez), but Lord Claverton remains doubtful.

Change of identity for better or worse is a continuing theme, from the effect of love between Monica and Charles, at the beginning and end of the play, to Gomez, Mrs Carghill, Michael, and, above all, Lord Claverton. Dick Ferry had 'died' long ago but, compared with Gomez's isolation, Claverton's life is cosy and insulated. Gomez's view that his old friend's continued pretence of success is indicative of the worst kind of failure is confirmed when Claverton confesses to Monica, the Antigone of his isolation, that his inner observant self can terrorize him. His experience makes him tell Michael that he will be greeted by his past failures when he goes abroad. He knows his own past selves are ghosts, and admits responsibility for the changes that took place in Fred Culverwell and Maisie Batterson, as he first knew Mrs Carghill, at critical stages in their lives. He thinks of Michael's happiness, recognising that his repeated efforts for his son's welfare had been misguided, and had lost him his affection. He had always wished to dominate his children, marking out a career for Michael which would perpetuate himself, and keeping Monica because her adoration strengthened his belief in his own pretences. After he has confessed everything, he is at peace; as it does with characters in all Eliot's last plays, the truth has set him free. He feels that he is 'brushed by the wing of happiness', and the spirit in which he dies brings a blessing to Monica and Charles. Badgley Court has brought the 'benignant sunshine' it promised.

Had death not released him so quickly Lord Claverton might conceivably have suffered from recurrent regrets. The happy ending makes *The Elder Statesman* a comedy in the Dantean sense, but it is serious enough despite the humour introduced by the effusive Mrs Piggott, manageress of Badgley Court, by Mrs Carghill, the ex-actress of *It's Not Too Late For You To Love Me*, and by the free-and-easy manner of Federico Gomez of San Marco. In general the verse has the virtues of prose without the substance of poetry. A notable dramatic tone is evident at the start, before the pent-up emotions of Charles and Monica are suddenly released in expressions of love. In this happy issue we have the first of several autobiographical notes which can be overheard, including Monica's fear that her father will not visit Jamaica in the winter, perhaps in Mrs Carghill's recollections of punting (Eliot and Vivienne Haigh-Wood at Oxford), possibly in Ferry's inability to understand women. The unfortunate parental wish to impose a career on a son, which is a feature of Eliot's last two plays, is obviously a subject of Eliot lineage, his own choice of career, and almost certainly his father's, incurring parental disapproval. Above all, the autobiographical accent is on the love associated with Eliot's second marriage. Charles's 'For I didn't *know* you loved me – I merely wanted to believe it' has biographical confirmation, and Monica's remarks to her father on the silent family love in the light of which everything else is seen is confirmed in the dedicatory poem 'To My Wife'. The warm declarations of love between Monica and Charles at the opening of the third act are unprecedented in Eliot. Love, which was from the beginning, comes upon them suddenly, uniting them and making them new; in their private world they are shielded against the outer world, which is seen as a destroyer of true selves throughout the play.

The love which is expressed in *The Elder Statesman* and its dedication is so much at odds with the asceticism of Eliot's earlier works and his revolt from what he had regarded as the animality of sex that one is left reflecting on the extent to which his philosophy and religion were determined by chance, in particular the circumstances of his marriage relationship with Vivienne. His last plays, especially *The Family Reunion* and *The Elder Statesman*, are closely related to his own spiritual and philosophical speculations. This self-centredness, allied to the growth of his interest in the general predicament of western civilization, militated against whatever genius he had for the creation of character. The more mature Eliot was not well endowed to cultivate the kind of '*Negative Capability*' that Keats found 'enormously' in Shakespeare, and had in mind when he thought of the empathy of the poetic character which transcends self and takes 'as much delight in conceiving an Iago as an Imogen'.[66]

Eliot's interest in the writing of the Elizabethan and Jacobean dramatists had influenced the style of his poetry for a period. Its influence on his drama had been far more negative; their over-inclusiveness and realistic bias had made him seek artistic unity or 'classical' form through the adoption of dramatic conventions. Nowhere had he used such formal discipline to better effect than in *Murder in the Cathedral*. The struggle to create harmony of effect ultimately fails in *The Family Reunion* for want of a satisfactory objective correlative. Ingenuities of plot produce a greater sense of artificiality in *The Cocktail Party* and *The Confidential Clerk* than in *The Elder Statesman*. Eliot's greatest dramatic achievement in his later years may well have been less in the substance and structure of his plays than in the development of an unobtrusive poetic medium. Its qualities are those which the poet Cowper, writing to William Unwin on 17 January 1782, admired in the poetry of Prior:

> Every man conversant with verse-writing knows, and knows by painful experience, that the familiar style is of all styles the most difficult to succeed in. To make verse speak the language of prose, without being prosaic, – to marshal the words of it in such an order as they might naturally take in falling from the lips of an extemporary speaker, yet without meanness, harmoniously, elegantly, and without seeming to displace a syllable for the sake of the rhyme [or rhythm], is one of the most arduous tasks a poet can undertake.

19

Further Prose

i CULTURE AND EDUCATION

Planning for a new progressive world after the 1939–45 war led to numerous discussions on reforms at home and programmes for international aid and enlightenment. Eliot's familiarity with these subjects arose from meetings and deliberations with religious, cultural, and educational leaders, and from knowledge of extensive projects for post-war reconstruction. His *Notes towards the Definition of Culture* (1948) is the product of reflections that began to take shape in 1943. Tending towards the abstract and philosophical, he sees principles and problems rather than their solution; the key word in his title (as it first appeared) is uncapitalized. He is more coherently constructive in the appendix of 1946 broadcast talks to Germany than elsewhere in the volume. The work could be regarded as cautionary, an attempt to ensure that politicians and zealots anticipated problems before reaching conclusions on ameliorative measures. Culture cannot be organized; its growth depends on favourable conditions, and the question is how to make varying conditions favourable.

The development of the individual, which was primarily Arnold's emphasis in *Culture and Anarchy*, depends on the culture of his group, which is related in turn to that of society at large. For Eliot culture affects the whole course of a people's life; it cannot be unified, and it needs vigilant or sceptical religion to keep it alive. As cultural groups emerge, they will influence society; unfortunately increasing specialization weakens the links between these groups, with debilitating effects on culture in general. Art, for example, is impoverished if it is dissociated

254

from religious sensibility; and religion, Eliot might have added, is weakened when it is divorced from scientific truth. As society becomes more classless, the question is how to select influential groups. Eliot envisages a pyramidal gradation of cultural levels, the highest being the most specialized, with responsibilities to society as a whole; the danger is that responsible élites will consist of individuals with professional qualifications, working like committees, with insufficient concern for general social cohesiveness and continuity.

If culture is to flourish, a country should be 'neither too united nor too divided'. As Maurras had stressed, one needs unity with diversities, loyalty to region, for example, as well as to country; differences of opinion between groups can be beneficial to a nation, and national culture can be stimulated by satellite cultures. Furthermore, a nation with class and regional divisions is more likely to be tolerant and peaceful. Attempts to create uniformity of world culture are unpractical, but such a culture should remain an ideal, for any self-contained culture, British or European, will suffer as a result of exclusiveness. Colonialism has shown the ill effects of imposing too much foreign culture on native populations. In countries where there is one religion the problem is different; cultural differences created by sectarianism are being attenuated, but any union arising from the reunion of Churches could lower the cultural level. Provided there is a common faith, conflict of ideas for the clarification and enlargement of truth is beneficial; without a common faith, the idea of uniting nations in culture is illusory.

Coming to politics, Eliot deplores the lack of contact between people of different cultural activities, and the kind of political theory which inspires students to think that the future can be settled easily according to abstract principles or dehumanized forces. For him the improvement of society rests in 'relatively minute particulars', and he wishes that politicians, instead of managing with *idées reçues*, were involved more in local issues, and subject to the surveillance of the more critically enlightened members of local communities. On the problem, which becomes intractable as politics becomes a substitute for religion, of how politicians can be led to cast off the blinkers of party prejudice, and become honest and co-operative, Eliot has nothing to offer. What he says on British imperialism is more outdated than his comment on its American form, an expansion of culture through commerce and material benefits, including that 'inflammable article the celluloid film', which may disintegrate cultures (and, as recent events in the Middle East attest, lead to the most violent revolt against its effects). Russian imperialism is more ingenious, proclaiming racial equality and giving the semblance of local self-government, while maintaining directions from Moscow and enforcing its own political culture.

Eliot's critical attention to definitions of educational aims is far too negative; he would have done better to concentrate on the kinds of education, both general and special, which are most desirable for young people of different aptitudes. His romantic argument that the majority of people in the pre-industrial era were educated sufficiently for the functions they had to perform is less convincing than his belief in the cultural importance of influences outside the schools, and in the need to harmonize all these factors. He foresees that mass culture (of which, it seems, the public can't have enough), and the assumption that education, or politics, can undertake the supreme cultural role, will contribute to a lowering of standards. Something more than instruction is required to cure 'the maladies of the modern world', but Eliot's identification of culture with religion is too inexplicit and general for basic acceptability. One fundamental question is whether Christianity can merge with science to become once more a power in the development of western civilization. Eliot's pessimism is justified by the last forty years; he sees no reason why the decline of his own age should not proceed much further; technology, commercialism, religious complaisance, and *laissez-faire* have combined to ensure that the process continues.

The broadcast talks on the unity of culture in western Europe have the merit of being much more personal. Eliot makes the dubious claim that Dante is at least as great as Shakespeare, and insists that all poets gain from foreign influences. Each component country has its own cultural heritage, but we are all indebted to the literature of Rome, Greece, and Israel. There is no frontier, however, and Eliot illustrates this by reference to the influence of Indian philosophy on his own poetry. He discusses the function of *The Criterion* in furthering unity by bringing together 'the best in new thinking and new writing' that European countries could offer, and attributes the failure of his international aims to the gradual closing of 'mental frontiers' in Europe. There is still too much interest in other countries' politics, and not enough in their cultures, he complains. No new principles emerge from his remarks on European culture, but he makes special points with tacit reference to the post-war division between eastern and western Europe. The first is that the conception of Roman law which has done so much to shape the latter was due to Christianity, without which our civilization would perish. Another is the importance of preserving other loyalties than those to the State, in universities, for example; 'our common responsibility is to preserve our common culture uncontaminated by political influences'.

Eliot did not disguise his impatience with the kind of ill-defined educational theories which began to proliferate towards the end of the war, but his published criticism was soon attacked for its inconsistencies, and he was invited to make amends in one way or another. The result was a course of lectures which he gave at the University of Chicago in 1950, with the intention of expanding them into a book, for which he never found time. They open with a digression on difficulties in word-interpretation, the minute particulars of which are more interesting than relevant as an introduction to definitions of 'education' and a discussion of educational aims. Simple definitions such as preparing a boy or girl to earn a living or enjoy a good life obviously need much qualification. In conjunction with others, they appear to create incompatibilities, and are amenable to varying interpretations. Eliot is much more concerned to raise pertinent questions than write a treatise on desirable educational aims in a democratic country. He reiterates the argument that education is the offspring of culture, not its equivalent; he insists that young people should be trained to criticize democracy, and measure it by ideal standards. He turns to the American-university elective system, the possibility of passing examinations in unrelated subjects, and of producing dilettantes or smatterers. The question of moral education is raised, and the special need for it when family and social environments are unsatisfactory. A new illiteracy has arisen, when young people forget what is taught through having no use for it, in the age of radio, cinema, and pictorial journals (all outstripped more recently by television).

We must be prepared for greater dependence on State grants in education, and ensure that this does not result in excessive State control. The problem of State schools *vis-à-vis* private schools arises from the difficulty of providing equality of opportunity, and this hypothetical equality raises the question of 'opportunity for what?' Education cannot be seriously considered apart from such matters as moral values, the creation of good democratic citizens, the need for a Church to protect us from the State, and sometimes for the State to protect us from the Church.

Eliot concludes that, as it informs less and less of our lives, religion will be replaced by belief in the State, and that, unless we can agree on basic religious truths about man, there can be no agreement on educational aims. It is not the question of religion in education which is important, but that of education in the context of religion. Eliot stresses the need for continuity, or change and preservation for the best, in culture, and also for teaching a smaller number well rather than giving everyone an inferior kind of education. Such a statement needs considerable amplification, and one is left to assume that the high quality of education which a minority can follow should not be sacrificed in accordance with an arbitrary implementation of equality of opportunity. At the higher levels of general education Eliot advocates the teaching of a world-wide view which includes what Arnold describes as 'the best that has been thought and said in the world', as well as the best that has been achieved, including the best that has been artistically created. Here, as elsewhere, Eliot emphasizes the value of a historical sense in furthering the progress of civilization. His aim has been to 'unsettle' minds rather than advance a theory, and he recognises the need for consultations between practising teachers, theoreticians, and legislators before reforms are enacted, knowing full well, as he makes clear in 'The Literature of Politics' (1955), that everything we do has unpredictable consequences.

ii ON POETRY AND DRAMA

Eliot's critical observations are most interesting when based on his own practice and experience as a writer; his more ambitious generalizations are not always convincing. In 'The Music of Poetry' (1942) he acknowledges his bias in favour of the poetry to which he was indebted as a poet, and gives a welcome assurance that the music of poetry is not independent of the meaning: Edward Lear's verse is not nonsense but 'a parody of sense'. The meaning of poetry is sometimes beyond the poet's conscious intention. He concludes that revolutions in poetry are usually a return to speech, whether presented melodiously or as spoken language in which dissonance would not be out of place. In contrast to Milton, whose 'orchestral' music repeatedly relinquishes 'social idiom', Shakespeare did more for the English language than any other poet, his final period being devoted to the musical elaboration of speech. Eliot had discovered that a poem may originate in a wordless rhythm, before evoking idea and image. He saw possibilities of theme recurrence and transitions in poetry as in music, and thought the concert hall more likely to quicken poetry than the opera house.

In 'The Social Function of Poetry', an address prepared for foreign audiences, first in London (1943), then in Paris (1945), his preliminary remarks relate chiefly to didactic or informative poetry (including satire) on moral issues or on philosophical, religious, and political subjects. The most important social function of poetry is to give pleasure; it 'enlarges our consciousness or refines our sensibility', and will appeal, in a healthy state of civilization, 'at every level of education'. The poet's immediate duty is to language; by preserving and extending it he will awaken in readers a greater consciousness of their feelings and a realization of new ones. Without poets of unusual sensibility and command of language, culture will deteriorate. As European cultures cannot flourish in isolation from each other, and poetry often conveys what is untranslatable, we need scholars who can '*feel* in another language as well as in their own' if spiritual communication between peoples is to be maintained. Eliot's worry is that the contemporary decline in religious feeling, which seemed to him more menacing than that in religious belief, may foreshadow a general deterioration in sensibility and poetry.

'What is Minor Poetry?' (1944) opens with a discussion of anthologies, one use of them being an introduction to less important poets, a subject which reminds Eliot of *The Light of Asia*, a long epic poem on Buddha by Sir Edwin Arnold which he discovered in the family library and read more than once with enthusiasm when he was a boy. His attempt to draw a distinction between major and minor poets is not very successful; it does not depend on the writing of long poems, and Eliot judges Samuel Johnson to be a major poet on the strength of 'The Vanity of Human Wishes' alone. He places George Herbert in one category and Robert Herrick in another, simply because there is a relationship between the poems of the former which illuminates each and all of them; the whole is greater than the sum of the parts. This may be an important criterion but not the most critical, for there must be many a minor poet whose work makes a coherent whole. The attempt to measure different qualities of greatness is inevitably subjective and self-defeating, and Eliot wisely decides that the only question with contemporary poets is whether they are genuine or not.

'What is a Classic?', the 1944 presidential address to the Virgil Society, is even less satisfying. Assuming that a classic can be written only in a mature civilization, that it will evince maturity of mind, manners, and language (the 'perfection of the common style'), Eliot finds these qualities most of all in Pope. In 'modern' literature his exemplar is Dante: in the ancient, Virgil. He illustrates Virgil's refinement of manners from Aeneas's not forgiving himself after being rightly snubbed by Dido in the Underworld. Eliot's generalities are too large and exclusive to be useful. He holds that a great classic poet exhausts not only a form such as the epic but also the language of his age. English poets can count themselves fortunate that they have a rich and varied language which has never been exhausted by a classic. A perfect classic expresses the 'whole genius of a people', the 'maximum possible' of their 'whole range' of feeling 'at its best'. The absolute classic exceeds such comprehensiveness in its own language, having 'equal significance in relation to a number of foreign languages'. Goethe's poetry is a classic in the first respect, but it lacks the universality of the *Aeneid*, which is at the centre of European civilization (a claim more fully substantiated in Eliot's 1951 broadcast talk 'Virgil and the Christian World'). No modern language can have the universality of Latin, and, as we 'confuse wisdom with knowledge, and knowledge with information', and 'try to solve problems of life in terms of engineering', a new kind of provincialism is spreading which makes modern classics impossible. Eliot's examination is restricted to poetry, but the comprehensiveness of his criteria wrecks the current meaning of 'a classic', making it almost non-viable. He has confused an issue, which needs redefining.

The lecture 'From Poe to Valéry', which Eliot gave at the Library of Congress, Washington, in 1948, leads to a consideration of *la poésie pure*. Poe had appealed to three French poets for different reasons: Baudelaire found his own type, *le poète maudit*, in him; Mallarmé was interested in his verse-technique; and Valéry, in his theory of poetry. Eliot detects the admission of linguistic imperfections for musical effect in Poe's poetry, and regards his poetic theory as a rationalization of his own practice. Poe's argument that a long poem is an impossibility implies that he was incapable of writing a long poem, because he would have wished to maintain a high level of intensity throughout. A long poem, Eliot adds, gains by wide variations in mood and poetic texture. Concern for the music of language rather than for substance leads ideally to *la poésie pure*; there is more than a hint of it in Poe, but Valéry made it his conscious aim, being far less interested in his subject than in the act of composition. Eliot sees the value of such exploration, but is convinced that if it becomes an end in itself it will debilitate poetry, the value and sound of which (as he has said elsewhere) depend on the sense.

'Poetry and Drama', a lecture delivered, after extensive revision, at Harvard University in November 1950, is notable for the retrospective attention Eliot gives to his own development as a playwright; he finds that he has been writing variations on the theme of poetic drama throughout his career. Although he thinks verse in drama should be such that the audience is unconscious of it, he advises against the introduction of prose, lest it divert attention from the play to the medium. He maintains nonetheless that anyone hearing *Hamlet* for the first time would not know whether it was in verse or prose; it illustrates the two aspects of great poetic drama, successful structuring for the stage being reinforced by a musical pattern which sways our emotion 'without our knowing it'. For Eliot the highest aim of poetic drama is to bring us to the border of those feelings which are expressible only in music, without leaving the everyday world of dramatic action; like Virgil, on bringing Dante to the Earthly Paradise (*Purgatorio*, xxvii.124–

42), the artist can go no further. Such moments are reached in what, for want of a better term, have been described as the lyrical 'duets' of *The Family Reunion*; another such ecstasy, less peculiar and more communicable, occurs between the lovers in the opening scene of *The Elder Statesman*.

'The Three Voices of Poetry' (1953) draws some useful but not very recondite distinctions. An implicit emphasis on speech throughout may have significance, but the definition of the first voice, that of the poet 'talking to himself' is not explicitly developed. It might raise the question of communication, whether, for example, a cryptographic poem such as 'Ode' was written purely for the poet's own satisfaction, or whether such poems should be published for interpretative indulgence which is less verifiable than solutions of allusive crossword puzzles. Eliot exploits the occasion rather unprofitably to express the view that poetry can never be written for one person only, that a good love poem is always intended for a wider audience than the person to whom it is addressed, and that the 'proper language' of love is prose. His second voice is that of the poet when he addresses an audience, as Eliot had done in the choruses of *The Rock*; in the choruses of *Murder in the Cathedral* his aim had been to use the third, the dramatic voice, in which the author identifies with his characters. Eliot doubts whether a dramatist can do this completely, believing that a character derives something from its author, and is capable of quickening latent feelings within him. The example of Browning makes him think that we usually hear the second voice in the dramatic monologue, and he draws the very dubious conclusion that this type of poetry cannot produce a character. For the creation of character action is needed, he argues, without pausing to consider whether action cannot be imagined in a dramatic monologue such as 'My Last Duchess'. He finds the term 'lyrical poetry' unsatisfactory, and declines to formulate what personal and dramatic lyrics have in common. What he says on the germination of poetry, the exorcism of his demon, and Paul Valéry's narcissistic studies of the creative mind, has its importance; it is given relevance to the first voice by Eliot's insistence that the poet's first duty is to 'achieve clarity for himself', but has little application to voices in published poetry. These voices are not exclusive; he finds the first combining with the second in non-dramatic poetry, and all three sometimes together in dramatic verse.

Appreciation of poetry is the subject most in mind throughout 'The Frontiers of Criticism' (1956). Eliot describes the best of his criticism as 'workshop criticism', since it arose from the study of poets and dramatists who had excited his interest as a practising poet. His claim that his valuations of the poets have remained 'pretty constant' must have been made with reference to them, if one excludes the contemporaries he had in mind. No doubt regret for some of his notes on *The Waste Land* led him to discuss 'the criticism of explanations by origins' with reference to *The Road to Xanadu* and an exegetical work on 'that monstrous masterpiece' *Finnegans Wake*. He assumes that danger in critical biography can be avoided by 'a trained and practising psychologist'. Background works on poems or poets do not help us to understand poetry as poetry, he maintains; more welcome, since it directs attention to poetry, is the 'lemon-squeezer school of criticism', which takes a poem and analyses it line by line without reference to the poet's background or his other words. After studying a collection of this type of criticism, Eliot needed time to recover his previous appreciation of the poems. It is dangerous to assume that just one interpretation is right, or that a valid reading tallies with what the author set out consciously to achieve. Criticism has changed: it had been subjective and impressionistic when it ought to have been interpretative; now it is 'slipping from understanding to mere explanation'. For the appreciation of poetry, the critic can 'only lead us to the door'; 'we must find our own way in it'. The function of the critic is primarily to help readers to understand and enjoy literature.

iii   EVALUATIONS AND REVALUATIONS

Eliot's antipathy to Tennyson's verse was that of the workshop critic who found Tennysonian blank verse cruder than that of a number of Shakespeare's contemporaries, and less capable of expressing the more subtle and complicated emotions dramatically. Tennyson's 'Ulysses' appealed strongly to the imaginative author of *The Waste Land*, but there is no evidence that Eliot ever realized the spiritual kinship he shared with the author of the later additions to *Idylls of the King*. The introduction he wrote for the 1936 Nelson Classics edition of a selection of Tennyson's poems, and issued later as 'In Memoriam', contains several misleading statements which no intelligent critic thoroughly conversant with Tennyson's works could have made. A footnote suggests that Eliot relied too much on Harold Nicolson's 'admirable' *Tennyson* for his views. He writes best on *In Memoriam*, but one cannot take very seriously assertions to the effect that Tennyson reached the end of his spiritual development in that poem (which he soon thought too optimistic), that he was the saddest of English poets, had nothing to hold on to but his unique gift for word music, and surrendered spiritually to become the 'surface flatterer' of his time. Nor can it be concluded that he had absolutely no gift for narrative; some of his poems show that, had he wished to pursue it, he could have excelled in that genre. It is true that the more singly he relied on it in *Idylls of the King* the more he failed in his purpose, but 'Pelleas and Ettarre' exemplifies his ability to combine narrative with powerful moral and spiritual overtones in highly imaginative and dramatic verse. In 'The Music of Poetry' Eliot speaks highly of the effect of Latin metres on some of Tennyson's poems.

A special feature in Eliot's study of Byron's poetry (1937) derives from attention paid to its inherent Scottish qualities. Scottish loyalty produces the most stirring of the Waterloo stanzas, and Calvinism accounts for Byron's posing as one of the damned, for the diabolism which, like Milton's Satan, combines Prometheanism with pride. Eliot admits the handicap of criticizing a poet with whom he had been infatuated in his schooldays, but he is still much impressed with Byron's narrational skill, judging *Childe Harold* inferior to such romances as *The Giaour*, which he studies in detail, and attributing the readability of *Don Juan* primarily to its narrative spell. Eliot finds Byron's satire of English society exhilarating, but does not rate his poetic achievement highly, and finds him most successful when he is not straining to be poetical. We expect poetry to be 'very concentrated, something distilled', he writes, criticizing the falsity of Byron, his 'schoolboy command' of language, and the lack of sensibility which resulted in his failure to develop the English language in any way. Eliot's analysis of Byron's poetry may not be complete, but it is balanced and challenging. It reveals 'a *poète contumace* in a solemn country', 'humbug and self-deception' combined with 'reckless raffish honesty', 'a vulgar patrician and a dignified toss-pot', and genuine superstition and disreputability beneath 'bogus diabolism' and the vanity of pretensions to be disreputable.

At the Abbey Theatre in June 1940, Eliot ended the first of the annual lectures in honour of W. B. Yeats with an affirmation of his historical greatness; he was one of those few poets 'whose history is the history of their own time, who are a part of the consciousness of an age which cannot be understood without them'. Having found his own poetic voice in French poetry, Eliot did not discover the younger Yeats until his own poetic course was set; it was the poetry of the later Yeats which won him over. By caring more for his art than for his reputation, Yeats had matured as few poets had done, from the skilled craftsmanship of his Celtic Pre-Raphaelite verse to an intensity of personal experience that reaches the impersonality of general truth and symbol without the sacrifice of particularity. He came at the end of a literary movement, and only one who has wrestled with language can know what persistent exertion is needed to cast off such a legacy. Yeats's achievement in his middle and later years is a magnificent example of character, of moral and intellectual strength, in a poet; his vigour and integrity may shock the elderly but will appeal to the young. At the time, a year or so after the production of his first complete modern play, Eliot was especially interested in Yeats's poetic drama. He explains why it is difficult to generate speech rhythms in blank verse, assumes that no other form could be used when Yeats wrote his early plays, and writes approvingly of the advance in his later plays which led to the 'virtual abandonment' of blank verse in *Purgatory*. Whether the lyrical choral interludes which began to appear had influenced Eliot is uncertain, but he is significantly impressed by the disappearance of poetical ornament. Eliot knew from experience what severe self-discipline had to be learnt to create the kind of beauty which is purely dramatic and often starkly simple. He was prepared to believe that there was more permanence even in Yeats's early dramatic attempts than in the plays of Shaw. Avoiding art for art's sake and art for propaganda, Yeats had shown how the artist who is wholly devoted to his art performs the greatest service he can, both for his nation and for the world.

A revival of interest in Kipling's verse during the early war period led to the publication in 1941 of a selection of his poems by Eliot. Having concluded that Kipling is 'an integral prose-and-verse writer', he surveys both his poetry and prose fiction in the introduction. The influence of Swinburne and Browning on Kipling is not what might be expected, for he wrote verse without aiming at poetry. As a ballad-writer, he enjoyed, Eliot claims, the inspiration of the music-hall. His craftsmanship is more reliable than that of greater poets, but he passes from form to form in the same idiom, which suggests no poetic urge to write about this subject rather than that; his development, unlike Yeats's, is to be found in his topics rather than in his style. He often achieves poetry, and shows a special aptitude for occasional verse, epigraph, and the hymn. His political verse reminds Eliot of Dryden, but only in style; both are masters of phrase, and both use simple rhythms with subtle variation, keeping to statement rather than to a 'musical pattern of emotional overtones'. Kipling's verse shows increasing diversity without that poetical development which Eliot had claimed to be characteristic of the major poet; as a writer of verse, however, he is great and unique.

'Johnson as Critic and Poet', two lectures given at University College, Bangor, in 1944, raises issues which were of greater concern to Eliot as a writer. Unlike Dryden, Johnson belonged to the later stages of a literary era and wrote retrospectively, instead of enunciating critical precepts for generations to come. His criticism reflects his own poetical standards, and Eliot wonders whether they will influence a future generation of writers. In the eighteenth century, when refinement of language was achieved and expected, eccentricity and bad taste were censured. The losses which accompanied such progress explain why Johnson was deaf to the music of 'Lycidas' and silent on the subtle beauties of Shakespeare's versification. Eliot's sympathy for the high regard paid to both sound and sense in the Johnsonian period is a measure of his revolt against trends in modern poetry, a tendency to incoherence, a partiality for sound and image rather than for meaning. He is disappointed to find that Johnson, though critical of Milton's pedantic use of foreign idiom, praises him as the 'master of his language to its full extent'. Johnson saw the danger of undisciplined blank verse, but could not foresee indulgence of the same kind of licence in the rhymed couplets of William Morris and others. He used blank verse in his tragedy *Irene*, for the simple reason that it is nearer to speech, but the play would have been better in heroic couplets, since Johnson thought and felt in that form. His criticism of the chorus in *Samson Agonistes* was right on dramatic grounds, but Eliot defends Milton's *poetic* use of it, and disagrees with Johnson's assumption that devotional verse cannot be poetic. The old Coriolanian hauteur gleams for a moment when he states that Akenside 'never says anything worth saying, but what is not worth saying he says well'.

Since a poet's criticism of poetry can be understood only in conjunction with the kind of poetry he writes, Eliot turns to Johnson's verse, expressing high admiration for 'The Vanity of Human Wishes', though he thought Goldsmith's 'The Deserted Village' superior. Johnson had little structural skill, and his moralizing lacked the 'divine levity' which sparkles in the satire of Dryden and Pope. The originality to which he attached importance lay in the mode of conceiving and expressing what might be regarded as commonplace; the edification he looked for is not separable from a poem, the reader's pleasure and 'instruction' being aspects of the same experience. In a period of uncertainty such as the present, we may prefer innovative individual styles, and become impatient with the wisdom of moral reflection. It is just because so much was accepted in his age that Johnson could concentrate on *literary* criticism; Eliot writes this wistfully, his one explicit comment being that reviewers often deliver 'a criticism of the hustings', judging a poem by its author's outlook. He does not dissent significantly from the view of poetic diction expressed by Johnson in 'Dryden', that words which are too familiar or remote are detrimental, contenting himself with the addition that correct diction in one age will not be the language of poetry fifty years later. He urges the benefits that would accrue from a 'common style', this limitation enabling the poet to devote his genius to greater precision, clarity, and eloquence. Only in a settled, confident age can such a style be achieved; what is particularly needed in creative composition is the critical faculty which

Johnson termed 'judgment', to save us from oddities and excesses, and ensure the maintenance of a disciplined effort to preserve our language.

Eliot's prejudice against Milton, stimulated by Pound, was that of a poet particularly antagonistic to the 'Chinese Wall' erected by the blank verse of *Paradise Lost*. His late efforts to make amends may be seen by comparing his 1936 essay and his 1947 lecture on Milton. In the first he is not content with stating that Milton exerted a worse influence than any other poet on the eighteenth century; he affirms that his influence could only be for the worse on any poet. Milton's aural gifts are admitted, but Eliot insists that his sensuousness was 'withered early by book-learning', and that there is little visual imaginativeness in Milton's poetry at any period; blindness affected his imagery considerably. Though distinguished critics have argued that Milton obtains grander imaginative effects from not including minute particulars, Eliot takes the opposite view, illustrating the value of particularity from Shakespeare, undoubtedly with Dante's practice in mind. Milton 'writes English like a dead language', his syntax being determined by musical values rather than by sense. To appreciate *Paradise Lost* to the full, it is necessary, Eliot maintains, to read it first for the sound, then for the meaning. As a general statement this can hardly convince, no part of Milton's poem presenting as much difficulty as 'Gerontion'; nor is it sensible advice, in view of Eliot's reiterated statement of the truth that the rhythms or music of poetry cannot be appreciated until its meaning is fully felt.

In 1947 Eliot sets out to show why Milton is 'a great poet and one whom poets to-day might study with profit'. He repeats his familiar argument on the danger of allowing a great writer to influence one's style until one is far enough removed or liberated to study him with artistic detachment; the influence of any writer (Milton or Shakespeare) can always be bad, but it is the injudicious imitator, not the model, who should be blamed. Eliot withdraws his long-standing charge that the 'dissociation of sensibility' which set in during the eighteenth century was due to Milton and Dryden, cautiously adding that, if such a dissociation took place, the causes are too involved and deep to be defined solely with reference to literature. He agrees largely with Johnson's strictures on Milton's language, but now sees its 'peculiar greatness'. The time may come when a writer may learn from Milton, though he is a stylistic eccentric and not a classic, since he does not raise the '*common* style' to greatness. Eliot enlarges on the appropriateness of subject to Milton's genius in *Paradise Lost* and *Samson Agonistes*, and rates very highly the imagery in which he excelled. He has learnt that Milton's rhythmical power is to be measured by the period, better still by the paragraph; and now extols the writer, whose language he had thought to be dead, for the freedom and variety of movement which animates his blank verse. A study of *Samson Agonistes*, he continues, could exemplify the virtues of metrical irregularity; and, in an age of poetic deterioration, the danger of '*servitude* to colloquial speech' might be avoided by the discovery of elaborate patterns in Milton's diction.[67] We have reached the period when poets can study Milton 'with profit to their poetry and to the English language'. Eliot's *volte-face* was occasioned as much by reaction to contemporary verse as by the humility and tolerance which came from recognition of former failings. He had always been averse to a drab conversational style, though ready to use live speech expression, in verse; he now recommends poetry which is 'at the farthest possible remove' from prose, and finds greatness in verse remote from ordinary speech.

Eliot's address on American literature and the American language, at Washington University in its centennial year 1953, consists of a number of related topics. It begins autobiographically with reference to his upbringing; he had inherited from his grandfather a reverence for religion, education, and the community, and a conviction that 'selfish aims should be subordinated to the general good'. After speaking highly, and in detail, of his education at Smith Academy, he concludes that he was lucky to be born in St Louis, rather than in Boston, New York, or London. His remarks on American literature are prefaced with a few comments on the language, more specifically on how it differs from, and increasingly affects, English. American literature is difficult to define; initially it implied English written by Americans; in retrospect, as Lawrence discovered, a new character can be seen in Fenimore Cooper's Natty Bumppo. Of the writers who represent New England, from Emerson, Longfellow, and Thoreau to Robert Frost, the greatest for Eliot is Nathaniel Hawthorne, who is best appreciated by a reader 'with Calvinism in his bones and witch-hanging on his conscience'. Authors who represent national literature have local and universal qualities. Eliot finds them in Poe, Whitman, and Mark Twain; universality comes from writing about what is completely familiar, and he has discovered it in Tchehov. With his own development clearly in mind, he points out that, once a tradition is established, a writer must turn from it, even to foreign models, if he is to develop originality; we should be on our guard against literary patriotism. Starting with 'Imagism' and the influence of Amy Lowell, Eliot sketches the development of twentieth-century American poetry into a *body* which has made its impression both in England and Europe. It is because they are different that American and English poetry can help each other, and continue a process of mutual renovation.

Eliot's confessional criticism continues in 'Goethe as the Sage', a lecture given when he was awarded the Hanseatic Goethe Prize for 1954 in May the following year. He admits that his attitude to Goethe had been 'grudging and denigratory', and now, after excluding him in 1944, elevates him to the rank of great Europeans. He does not pretend to be an authority on Goethe's writings, and is more concerned with related questions. The first is how he (Eliot) outgrew his antipathies; on this his rationale is not very convincing. His 'Catholic cast of mind', Calvinist heritage, and puritanical temperament had predisposed him against Goethe, but he realizes that his quarrel was with the Romantic movement; with this he relates the Victorians. He still finds the philosophy of Tennyson, Browning, Arnold, and Meredith 'flimsy', but can imagine them as greater poets if their view of life had been different. Accepting the inevitability that Goethe should believe as he did, he is reconciled to him. The question why Eliot has been unwilling to judge other writers with artistic detachment, irrespective of beliefs, is not raised. He amplifies on more general matters such as the permanence and universality of 'European' writers; then, after drawing obvious distinctions between what is and what is not translatable, he asks what quality survives translation, and finds it in the indefinable word 'wisdom', expatiating on the subject until he distinguishes between a poet's philosophy, which we may or may not accept, and his wisdom, which all can accept. Impressed no doubt by, among other things, the Dantean ending of *Faust*, Eliot had found that Goethe's poetry and wisdom are inseparable.

In 'To Criticize the Critic' (1961) he surveys his own criticism, and hopes other critics will follow his example. Statements no longer intelligible, errors of judgment, and evidence of arrogance or cocksureness make him hope that writers will not quote him without reference to the dates of his pronouncements. He remembers his challenging declaration of literary, political, and religious adherences in his preface to *For Lancelot Andrewes*, and would now express them differently, though they are essentially the same. (In 'The Literature of Politics', a lecture addressed to the London Conservative Union in 1955, he had announced his continued support for the political theory of Maurras, while disapproving his action as a party-leader.) Eliot attributes the success of his earlier essays to youthful dogmatism and his reaction to Georgianism. He has found that his work on the contemporaries of Shakespeare who stimulated his poetic imagination is more pleasing than his criticism of Shakespeare (in this context he mentions Webster, in addition to Marlowe, Tourneur, Middleton, and Ford). He still argues that Shakespeare is too great to have a beneficial influence on a writer, distinguishing between influence which fecundates and imitation which sterilizes. His best essays are on writers (not merely poets, for they include Lancelot Andrewes) who influenced him as a poet. His views on these remain unchanged, but they no longer excite him as they did; now he prefers Mallarmé to Laforgue, Herbert to Donne, and Shakespeare to his contemporaries. The one exception is Dante, whose directness had acted as a corrective to extravagances in other writers who stirred him creatively. Phrases such as 'objective correlative' and 'dissociation of sensibility' had served their turn, and Eliot thinks he used them as 'conceptual symbols for emotional preferences', the former indicating his bias to more mature Shakespearian plays than *Hamlet*.

He has less confidence in the criticism he has written on authors for whom he had less sympathy, Tennyson and Byron specifically. He is comforted by Johnson's antipathy to Milton, but insists that his second study of Milton was not a recantation of his first. He retracts nothing on Hardy, and finds a lack of humour in him (which suggests that he was right in concluding it would have been better if he had not written about him at all). On Lawrence he is a bundle of irresolution, and perhaps it was just as well, all aspects of the issue being considered, that he was not called upon to defend *Lady Chatterley's Lover*. The honesty Eliot displays is rare among critics, but it could never be complete; he had erred too often. Careerism had made him cultivate bias; he had dismissed authors not so much for literary as for philosophical or religious reasons; and he had blundered in his literary judgments. In *The Criterion* of July 1935 he writes off Hardy as the minor poet 'he always was'. Only a careless reader could have concluded that George Eliot degenerated after 'Amos Barton', and only a cavalier critic, apropos of minor poetry, could have referred to 'that long poem by George Eliot of which I don't remember the name'; had he known Henry James's criticism of *The Spanish Gypsy*, he might have been less dismissive. Other examples of Eliot's deliberate or perverse debasement of authors can soon be found.

20

Conclusion

All in all, as poet, critic, and dramatist, Eliot still seems to be the major figure in English literature of the twentieth century, his importance assuming greater dimensions because his work as a whole is inextricably related to the main course of our cultural tradition. More than most modern poets, he belongs to the European heritage. How great he is remains a question for the future. The life of art depends as much on the needs, outlook, and vision, of an age as on the insights of the artist, and Eliot is an important voice for a civilization confronted alarmingly with a host of moral, social, and political problems, all of which are fundamentally religious. These will have maintained his significance for some, probably with little extension of his influence in a world which is so consumed with technological communication and other mass-diversions that little time is left for reading or reflection, or for the direct contact of minds seriously engaged in the important issues of life.

Any assessment of Eliot as a writer is inevitably tentative; it must take into account his weaknesses and limitations, and to see these in clear perspective is often difficult. Especially is this true of his criticism; a large number of specialists would be needed to judge his accuracy, penetration, and sense of proportion with reference to the many authors on whom he wrote. Working under pressure in his early essays, he had not always mastered his subject or found time to express himself fully or precisely. In his more general evaluations he owed much to Matthew Arnold and Irving Babbitt; more precisely at the outset, to Rémy de Gourmont. He was always ready to adopt and develop other people's ideas, and he sometimes used them challengingly rather than wisely. For emphasis, he tended at all times to holistic statement: a writer had to be steeped in the whole European tradition; he had furthermore to be completely impersonal. (Eliot identifies culture with religion, but one can argue that social ethical standards and all lasting forms of art are rooted in serious or religious attitudes to life, without concluding that religion explains all practices and assumptions absorbed by a developing culture.) Initially, if not later, this indulgence in absolutes was a kind of theatrical flourish, or shock tactic, in a well-calculated strategy that was bound to be effective at a time when the younger generation was tired of old ideas and alert for new.

Almost inevitably such practice led to unacknowledged adjustments and shifts of viewpoint. Eliot's first promulgation of the impersonal theory of art did not carry conviction, and he soon took steps to ensure that his published views tallied with Rémy de Gourmont's aesthetic principle, the most striking feature of which was the sententiousness of its expression. Impersonality is a particular way of being personal in art; it is, one might add, the surest means of creating great poetry. To make an Arnoldian 'criticism of life' poetically, a writer does not resort to an egotistical flow, or infliction, of his thoughts or feelings, but to imagery or situation through which meaning can be imaginatively or implicitly conveyed; it is the transfused intensity of vision which gives life to such a medium. That this is not the only defensible form of poetic communication is clear from a consideration of the discourse of the composite ghost in 'Little Gidding', FitzGerald's version of the *Rubáiyát*, and even Browning's 'Rabbi Ben Ezra'. The theory of the dissociation of sensibility and intellect (an idea which developed from Rémy de Gourmont) provided a useful critical stimulus, but the completeness of its application to two consecutive eras of poetry in the seventeenth and eighteenth centuries was sufficient to destroy its general validity.

A similar failure to make necessary reservations is patent in his borrowed claim that the works of Shakespeare make a coherent whole, a single poem, knowledge of all of which is indispensable for full appreciation of any part; it is an argument he uses with greater justification in his monograph on George Herbert and his poetry. His bold contention that even the earliest of Yeats's dramatic attempts probably have greater permanence than the plays of George Bernard Shaw, simply because they are wholly conceived in artistic terms, suggests abstract reasoning rather than a genuine literary appraisal. Eliot made many amends for categorical assertions, with reference to particular authors as well as to artistic theory, and he extricated himself in various ways, the earlier resulting in some disingenuous inconsistency, the later tending to honest admission, though he was still capable of arguing a self-justificatory way round a change of attitude, notably in his second essay on Milton. Even so, his integrity in 'To Criticize the Critic' is as admirable as it is exceptional; it would be interesting to know how many have followed his example, as he urged, or what eminent critics, for that matter, have changed their views as remarkably.

The effect of prejudice on Eliot's criticism, early and late, is more serious. Impatience with the nineteenth-century poets of whom he grew weary in adolescence stiffened almost into disdain. His antipathy to Swinburne was not confined to the general criticism that his lyricism was meaningless; it can be quite as misleading in the analysis of a passage or poem. A similar blindness to meaning in Shelley suggests a pose. He prefers the company of the well-conducted Matthew Arnold to that of the Romantic poets, including Wordsworth and Keats, who belong to the 'riff-raff' or *hoi polloi* of the early nineteenth century; and he is recurrently dismissive of Victorians such as Tennyson and Meredith. Whatever may be said for his revolt from lulling Lydian poetry, his stubborn dislike of Tennyson was never overcome; his introductory essay offers proof enough that the amount of Tennyson's poetry he ever read with due critical care was limited. His remarks on George Eliot's decline almost from the outset of her career as a novelist betray an even greater impatience or ill-grounded assurance; serious as this is, it is probably surpassed in his dismissal of Hardy. Eliot had become almost inquisitorial; he had no time for authors whose views he regarded as heresy. In 1934, during his most polemical period, he told Paul Elmer More that he was no longer interested in pure literary criticism. His admission that a reader will miss much enjoyment and 'valuable experience' if he fails to seek a full understanding of the literature which calls for detachment or the suspension of disbelief came late in his life.[68] Bigotry had blinded him to the truth he had discovered in reading his favourite poet Dante, that religious or philosophical disbelief does not preclude poetic assent.

His earlier remarks on Tennyson and Milton show his inability to be critically impartial with writers whose style it was fatal to him as a poet to imitate. He is at his critical best when writing on the poetry of authors whom he emulated: on Dante, and some of the Elizabethan and Jacobean dramatists. In such essays he provides the excitement of revelatory textual insight and creative discovery, and it is regrettable that he did not find time to explore the drama of the Tudor–Stuart period more fully. It was in this area that his critical judgment as a poet was most sustained and penetrating. Criticism is the poorer that he wrote little on Webster, the dramatist whose influence on his earlier poetry is most pronounced. Furthermore, one cannot help wishing that the poet who in his maturer years became fully alive to, and wrote felicitously but briefly on, the miracle of language and symbol in Shakespeare's later plays, had chosen to write more on these and kindred subjects.

Valuable as Eliot's criticism is in the mass, it is never more memorably illuminating than when it expresses a duality of significance, when its reading of an author throws light on the poetic vision of the writer, as it does in those 'tentacular roots' which reach down to 'the deepest terrors and desires' in Jonson's 'great contemporaries'; in Marston's overtones of a world beyond, the 'something behind' which is more real than the stuff of stage-presentation; and in the boredom, horror, and sense of beatitude that are found in Baudelaire. Later essays show increasing tolerance, humility, and serenity; they are more balanced and synoptic; but growing detachment makes them more general, and less engrossed in the excitement of discovery. Some have the additional interest of their confessional amendments, but their principal attraction resides in Eliot's greater readiness to indulge in personal reflections, or in retrospective comments on his own poetry and plays. Indirectly or directly, in Eliot's essays, the personal note is deeper, and of more abiding interest, than the critical.

Some of his drama will retain a wider appeal, though it can never be popular. *Murder in the Cathedral* has more lasting interest than any other of the plays, from the universality of its central issue, the artistry of its uncomplicated presentation, and the moving imaginative resonances of its Chorus. *The Rock*, a shrewd comment on the ills of Britain for the last half century or more, will eventually be regarded as an index of a transitional age. The merits of the four plays Eliot wrote during his last creative period are less easy to assess. With the exception of *The Elder Statesman*, each undoubtedly enjoyed its *succès d'estime*, but, as with the critical essays, the personal elements within them may be the source of their most enduring appeal, taking precedence over technical qualities of style and structure. Especially is this true of *The Family Reunion*, which reflects the haunting guilt engendered by Eliot's first marriage; it applies also to *The Elder Statesman*, which dramatizes both the worldly disillusionment of a careerist and the love that came with his second marriage. Eliot's interest in humanity was too general for the creation of living characters. He concentrated more on the achievement of a dramatic verse that would not call attention to itself but pass as the conversation of life. In this he succeeded, though he is more dramatic in his early poetry, particularly in 'Gerontion', which owes much rhythmically and syntactically to some of Jonson's 'great contemporaries'.

Eliot will be remembered as a great English poet in a period of spiritual uncertainty and decline. His beliefs are grounded in philosophy, and will take their place side by side with those of the scientific philosophers who reject the nineteenth-century assumption that the laws of mechanical science apply to the whole of the universe and life. For him the growing menace of such non-religious views was evident in international history and decline. He lacks the assurance of the devotional poet, and there is nothing stereotyped about his faith. Questioning, or sceptical, as it was, and as he felt it should be, it was based on a humbling awareness of human fallibility at all levels, accounting for the blindness and lost opportunities of history, past and present, as set forth dramatically in 'Gerontion'. Whether he accepted the Incarnation of Christian orthodoxy literally as well as symbolically is uncertain, yet he repeatedly affirmed the possibility of Incarnation for the human race, an intersection of the timeless and time, of the divine and human, even though limited to moments of illumination. The working of a power beyond ourselves throughout history has created a wisdom which must be sought by meditation, prayer, and self-dicipline; we must learn to 'sit still'. Yet religion is not a matter purely for the individual. True love is an expression of it: in marriages where it does not exist there can be the horror of the void, the nothing connected with nothing of *The Waste Land*; societies without altruism or real community are vacant. There is, Eliot declares in *The Rock*, no life without community, and no true community without religion. The Church with which he is concerned is society; it must be 'forever building', for it is always decaying and subject to attack. Such a perennial state must be accepted as a law of human life with all its imperfections. As the conclusion of 'The Dry Salvages' attests, most of us must be content with sustained endeavour, hoping like Wordsworth that 'something from our hands' will 'have power To live, and act, and serve the future hour'.

Eliot's poetry, as concentrated as it is restricted in volume, covers a range of experience rarely, if ever, equalled by any other English poet but Shakespeare. From 'Preludes' onwards, for the most part, it spans both the world and communication with the 'something behind' it; it reveals spiritual death and the quest for spiritual life in a variety of forms; and, increasingly Dantean in reference and symbolism during his more mature periods, its vision extends from Hell to the Earthly Paradise of the *Purgatorio*. If, and this assumes adequacy of style, a poet's stature is assessed by Eliot's criteria (the unity and sustained development of a writer's *oeuvre*), the unusual span of his vision – width as well as height and depth – gives him a stronger claim to greatness than he found in Herbert.

Whether he is, or will remain, a major poet is another question. His verse is largely self-centred; he depended on literature rather than on life for his resources, and his inspiration failed him repeatedly, sometimes for whole periods; his last important poetry, *Four Quartets*, by which he rashly said he would stand or fall,[69] is a very uneven performance. It can occasion little surprise if many readers, wearying of philosophical expositions and some laboured verse-manipulation in this work, find more pure poetry, life, and sustenance in early, more social, dramatic poems, notably 'Prufrock', 'Portrait of a Lady', and 'Rhapsody on a Windy Night'; or more critical intelligence, intensity of vision, and originality of conception in minor pieces such as 'Sweeney Erect', 'The wind sprang up at four o'clock', and 'Triumphal Arch'. It could well be asked whether the poet in Eliot was allowed the time he needed to fulfil the promise of his pre-marriage years. Rarely did he write easily, and the intensity of his work was often the product of artifice, theft, and imitation. He lacks the human interest and lyrical power which Hardy displayed in numerous poems, and his verse rarely attains the accomplished assurance and apparent ease of Yeats. Lesser than Yeats as a poet, he nevertheless has a greater significance for the twentieth century. Unequalled as a borrower, he is paradoxically original and unique, for he belongs to no school and founded none.

Great poetry, as Eliot acknowledged in his main Dante essay, is felt and enjoyed before it is wholly understood, but it is only when it is fully understood that it can be read as it ought to be. Part of the enduring appeal of Eliot's poetry is that it offers interpretative challenges, and continually hints at new meanings which come in flashes. Its obscurity arises from the choice of imagery, more often from literary allusiveness; the two are frequently indivisible. The main defence of his allusions is their potential for the enrichment of meaning by the evocation of relevant worlds or vistas. They tend, however, to limit due appreciation to a scholarly minority. Such readers may find no need to justify the concentrated allusiveness of 'Burbank with a Baedeker: Bleistein with a Cigar' (epigraph or poem), or of the final paragraph of *The Waste Land*. The problem is not lessened either by exegetes who excel in the proliferation of possible sources or by critics who minimize their importance. One must also allow for coincidence; perhaps it is as reasonable to suppose that the 'clatter' and 'chatter' of the public house in Lower Thames Street should be associated with the kitchen 'chatter' and 'clatter' in the first chapter of *Wuthering Heights* as that the 'dry brain' of 'Gerontion' alludes to Tennyson's 'Fatima'. Even though Eliot ('Elephant') was a bookworm with a prodigious memory, he may have often repeated words and images unconsciously. When he wrote 'The Dry Salvages', did he hear the echoes of Whitman's 'When Lilacs Last in the Dooryard Bloom'd': 'dooryard' – 'tolling bell' – 'clangs' – 'perpetual'? In 'feeding A little life' at the opening of *The Waste Land*, did he realize the origin of the phrase in Thomson's 'To Our Ladies of Death'? Is the 'Given or lent' of 'Marina' a conscious recollection of Alice Meynell's 'Unto us a Son is given'?

Eliot almost invariably avoids the commonplace: it is surprising therefore to find him juxtaposing the 'kin' and 'kind' of *Hamlet* in 'Little Gidding'; his recurrent symbolical use of wind and rain in *The Family Reunion*, with the connotation given it by Shakespeare and adopted by Hardy, may have been a concession to theatre audiences. More puzzling is the transfer to Gerontion, the dying representative of the Old World, of luxuriant imagery from Henry Adams' recollections of the New. Eliot's early allusive wit may provide an incidental sparkle, but it is sometimes a form of irritating pedantry: in 'The Love Song of J. Alfred Prufrock' one may or may not be reminded of Hesiod in 'works and days' – it hardly matters; the 'eternal Footman' will set some readers wondering what relevance Bunyan's *The Heavenly Footman* can have, though Prufrock and Bunyan's runner have nothing significantly in common. It is doubtful whether this kind of self-indulgent allusiveness qualifies as wit, for it is pointless. Some of the obstacles in Eliot's later verse are much more serious. If one is unfamiliar with the literary background to the chain image which is repeatedly used in *The Family Reunion* to express the escape from time, any perplexity which it arouses must be increased by its association with the wheel. The binding-power exerted by other writers' images on Eliot can be seen in his modifications of Mallarmé's axle-tree before it came to rest in 'Burnt Norton'; but for its compulsiveness, he could have expressed himself much more lucidly. Here he wrote for his own satisfaction, in his first voice of poetry, and the meaning of this complicated knot of allusion is likely to remain uncertain.

Most of Eliot's allusions are imaginatively and intellectually stimulating, particularly those from Dante and, at least as often, from the Bible and Anglican or Anglo-Catholic forms of worship and prayer; it is unfortunate that with the waning of Christian culture so many of them have become inert or hidden. The associative richness of an image to Eliot may be illustrated from the genesis of 'a handful of dust', best known for its appearance in the first part of *The Waste Land*. He had met the phrase in Conrad's 'The Return' and 'Youth'; it almost certainly reminded him of Tennyson's use of it in *Maud* (ii.v.i); but he, and Tennyson, no doubt, had discovered it in the fourth Meditation of Donne's *Devotions*, where man himself is regarded as a sick-bed, and the question is asked what will become of his wide-ranging mind when he is shrunk and consumed into a handful of dust. 'His diseases are his own, but the physician is not; he hath them at home, but he must send for the physician.'

The idea of the earth as a hospital is common both in seventeenth-century thought and in Eliot; his first marriage must have brought it often to mind.

At the end of his Norton lecture on Wordsworth and Coleridge, Eliot emphasizes one of the qualities of a great poet, his ability to retwine 'as many straying strands of tradition as possible'. In his own poetry, he did this very considerably through literary allusion; he was imaginatively stirred most of all by literature, and quotation, borrowed images, and reference contribute vividly to the sensuous, dramatic, and even lyrical pattern of his thought. In the second half of the eighteenth century, this practice was almost axiomatic, with a difference. Johnson thought it 'a good thing' because there was 'a community of mind behind it'; classical quotation, he wrote, is 'the parole of literary men all over the world'. Some of Eliot's allusions belong to this order, but they are often ego-centred rather than communal, the key to his own interests, feelings, and values, whatever his *personae* and however dramatic his presentations. At their extreme, as in 'Ode' and the axle-tree adaptation from Mallarmé, they are sufficiently cryptographic to be regarded as private expression.

Unlike Blake, an inspired enthusiast with spiritual and imaginative certainties, Eliot as a religious writer is a seeker; he may give some readers 'the end of a golden string', but the majority will probably feel that his Ultimate is unknowable. Some will consider his experience of intersecting timelessness and time a woven fancy which would come inevitably, if rarely, to one who thought often and intensively on such intangibilities, just as Wordsworth's transient assurances of becoming a living soul hardly conscious of bodily sensation were induced, or made cognisable, by his quietist philosophy. Some would argue that Eliot's concluding 'all shall be well' is no more convincing than the 'All is well' of *In Memoriam*. Yet he cannot be dismissed conclusively; there is wisdom in his 'Teach us to sit still', as there is in Dante's 'His will is our peace'. Eliot's religious importance as a writer cannot be divorced from his years of endeavour to improve life, society, and civilization. He saw the need for leaders who have time to reflect, to cultivate wisdom, for the benefit of mankind, redeeming the time. How could its follies, its misrepresentations, its crude stumblings, and recurring disasters, be avoided without spiritual regeneration?

Eliot will be remembered perhaps as much for posing that question as for anything else. There can be no great civilization without shared beliefs or religion, and the future of religion will be directed towards the quality of human progress rather than to the other-worldly dogmatism of the past. If the faith adopted by Eliot is unacceptable to most people, it does not mean that he is essentially wrong on the larger issues that affect our future. However much it seems to be disregarded for long periods, there is incalculable truth in the conclusion of *Four Quartets*, that the fire and the Rose are one.

This truth was reaffirmed by Eliot while war was raging; history showed that this war was the price paid for the blunders, greed, neglect, and machinations of peace-time. He may not have paid attention to George Eliot's emphasis on the 'inexorable law of consequences' in human affairs, but he was apprehensively conscious of it during 'the years of *l'entre deux guerres*', as he made evident in *The Rock*: 'Of all that was done in the past, you eat the fruit, or rotten or ripe.' The only wisdom we can hope for is 'the wisdom of humility', he insisted. The world, he wrote at the end of 'Thoughts after Lambeth', was making the mistake of trying to build a new, non-Christian world; it would fail, but it would be difficult to keep Christianity alive, and preserve it for the renewal of civilization after its virtual suicide.

Eliot's evidence of the western world came first and foremost from Britain. At the opening of a series of broadcasts in March 1932,[70] he quoted Trinculo's words in *The Tempest* (iii.ii): 'The folly of this island!' As a counterbalance to his sober realism (after a long period of economic depression), the centre of the first page of his published talk was devoted to a poem of encouragement in which the young Stephen Spender looked forward exultantly to 'The beautiful generation that shall spring from our sides'. The irony of this in the light of subsequent history, pre-war and post-war in particular, underlines the truth of Eliot's diagnosis. For him the modern dilemma is the choice between Christianity and communism; his concern is not with 'the conversion of the world to Christianity, but with the organisation of the world in a Christian way'. His political comment that we must set the example at home, if we are to be critical of conditions in other countries, is as pertinent as ever; but his most fundamental and crucial conclusion is that our society has become increasingly secularized, 'until our values are at war with each other and with life itself'.

Eliot regretted that the Church was unable to attract the best minds any longer, but he seems to have attached little importance to the need for the Church to modernize its views in the light of science if it is to appeal to the young. He was convinced, however, that the failure of the Church would turn the young to politics. In Britain, where political biases are largely the legacy of sectarianism, this has meant neither the cultivation of the truth that will set people free nor the promotion of a Christian spirit of reconciliation and co-operation for the common good, but the dissemination of political prejudice, rancour, division, and hatred, with incalculable wastage of opportunities and resources. There can be no stability in politics or civil behaviour unless a country has 'an underlying political philosophy' which is national and above party, Eliot maintains in *The Idea of a Christian Society*. He does not underestimate the value of 'friction' to ensure improvements and the eradication of injustices, but he is confident that a country with a Christian tradition has principles which can be generally accepted, and prove helpful in crises, if goodwill is allowed to prevail. We are still living in a period when, as Eliot complained in *After Strange Gods*, the meaning of education is minimal.

Whatever he implied by his oxymoron 'totalitarian democracy', enough has happened recently to suggest that it indicates the kind of threat posed by leaders of political and industrial factions in a country that takes freedom for granted. Democracy was gained by Christian principles, and it will depend on them for its survival. To give them a new and credible life which keeps pace with truth will always be difficult, but not nearly as difficult as the task of reducing and minimizing the animosities inherited through centuries of injustice. Handicapped though he may appear to have been by the dogmatically outdated faith he adopted, T. S. Eliot had the insight to reflect the weakness of western society more impressively in his poetry, and more perspicaciously in his prose, than any other writer of his time. He fought, as he wrote as early as 1927, in his essay on F. H. Bradley, 'to keep something alive' rather than in expectation of triumph. His conclusion at the end of 'The Dry Salvages' is comparable to that of George Eliot at the end of *Middlemarch*: we are undefeated because we continue to strive. There can be no political integrity, and no   iocracy, unless they are animate   thought is as inherent in 'The I   Iollow Men' as it is explicit in Elic   nplated history in 'Little Gidding   ire depends on the purification of   . His greatness cannot be dissocia   ed on Christian principles in the   l promotion of civilized democrac

Notes

1. *Purgatorio*, xxvi.145, from a passage repeatedly recalled in Eliot's poems for its religious significance. The Provençal words of the poet Arnaut Daniel appeared on the title page as 'Ara Vus Prec', from a faulty Italian edition, but the mistake was spotted in time to give the correct title on the cover.
2. Eliot hints at this in his essay on Pascal; see his *Selected Essays*, third edition, London, 1951, p. 405.
3. *Purgatorio*, xxvi.115–20.
4. Aldington's lack of sympathy found expression in his skit 'Stepping Heavenward', published in *Soft Answers*, London, 1932.
5. Joseph Chiari, *T. S. Eliot: A Memoir*, London, 1982.
6. Quoted by Lyndall Gordon, *Eliot's Early Years*, Oxford and New York, 1977, p. 26, and in Richard March and Tambimuttu (eds), *T. S. Eliot*, London, 1948, pp. 21–2. See Conrad Aiken, *Ushant*, London, 1963, p. 186.
7. T. S. Eliot, *To Criticize the Critic*, London, 1965, pp. 22, 126.
8. *The Education of Henry Adams*, London, 1928, p. 34.
9. Gordon, *Eliot's Early Years*, pp. 23–4.
10. Ibid., p. 19.
11. Ibid., pp. 41–2.
12. Nor is he a hungry lion like Teufelsdröckh at 'a feast of chicken-weed' among the musical and literary dilettanti of both sexes who drink '*Aesthetic Tea*', perhaps '*Musical Coffee*', in Thomas Carlyle's *Sartor Resartus* (II.iv, v).
13. See Valerie Eliot (ed.), *The Waste Land: A Facsimile and Transcript of the Original Drafts including the Annotations of Ezra Pound*, London, 1971, pp. 90–7.
14. Pound's word for the Amy Lowell species of Imagist poetry.
15. See *Essays in Criticism*, 1953, pp. 2–5, 345–57, and, as *points de départ*, I. A. Richards, *Principles of Literary Criticism*, second edition, London and New York, 1926, pp. 293–4, and F. O. Matthiessen, *The Achievement of T. S. Eliot*, third edition, New York and London, 1958, pp. 129–30.
16. A clear echo of Ruskin, on hearing news of Rose La Touche's death: 'I wanted my Rosie *here*. In heaven I mean to go and talk to Pythagoras and Socrates and Valerius Publicola' (Peter Quennell, *John Ruskin: The Portrait of a Prophet*, London, 1949, pp. 281–2).
17. *Entertainment of Alice, Dowager-Countess of Derby.*
18. As shown by Eliot in *The Use of Poetry and the Use of Criticism*, London, 1933, p. 147.

19. For further insight into Burbank's meditations, see Spenser's *The Ruines of Time*, e.g. ll.43–63, 582–8.
20. J. H. Newman, *Apologia Pro Vita Sua*, ed. M. J. Svaglic, Oxford, 1967, p. 111.
21. See Ronald Bush, *T. S. Eliot: A Study in Character and Style*, New York and Oxford, 1983, p. 33.
22. See *The Education of Henry Adams*, p. 268 (edition as note 8 above).
23. A. C. Benson, *Edward FitzGerald* (Men of Letters), London, 1905, p. 142; for the old woman in the kitchen, see p. 29.
24. *Selected Essays*, 1932 or 1951, p. 169.
25. See Valerie Eliot (ed.), *The Waste Land*.
26. From his review of *Donne's Sermons: Selected Passages* in *The Athenaeum*, 28 November 1919. Lyndall Gordon refers to it in *Eliot's Early Years*, p. 89.
27. See F. E. Hardy, *The Life of Thomas Hardy*, London, 1962, p. 171. Hardy's note of 28 May 1885 is based on observations made while he waited near Marble Arch: 'This hum of the wheel – the roar of London! What is it composed of? Hurry, speech, laughters, moans, cries of little children.' He thinks of the people in this tragedy: 'Some wear jewels and feathers, some wear rags. All are caged birds; the only difference lies in the size of the cage.' Hardy has anticipated Eliot in both the cage image and the wheel image.
28. For another statement of Baudelaire's influence, see the third paragraph of 'What Dante Means to Me' in Eliot's *To Criticize the Critic*.
29. See the note for p. 111 in Valerie Eliot (ed.), *The Waste Land*, p. 130.
30. The 'waste land' image was probably reinforced by James Thomson's use of the 'desert' in *The City of Dreadful Night* (iv).
31. See the appendix on Eliot's poetry in the second edition of I. A. Richards, *Principles of Literary Criticism*, pp. 289–95.
32. See John Worthen's letter in *The Times Literary Supplement*, 24 May 1974.
33. See Gordon, *Eliot's Early Years*, p. 19.
34. Ibid., pp. 39–40.
35. Valerie Eliot (ed.), *The Waste Land*, p. 1.
36. *The Journals of Arnold Bennett, 1921–1928*, London, 1933, pp. 51–2.
37. Pound made the same criticism at length in his 1917 review of *Prufrock and Other Observations*; see *Literary Essays of Ezra Pound* (ed. T. S. Eliot), London, 1954, pp. 421–2.
38. This distinction is not maintained; in his later works Eliot uses 'emotion' and 'feeling' synonymously. His impersonality theory seems to incorporate his philosophical association of objects and feelings: 'I, the objective world, and my feelings about it, are an indissoluble whole', he had written.
39. See V. J. E. Cowley, *The Review of English Studies*, 1975, pp. 320–1. Eliot thought he had invented this cumbersome term, then found it had been used by an American painter; he must have met Newman's use of 'object correlative'. This expression and Eliot's use of 'objective equivalent' seem to indicate that 'objective' is adjectival to 'correlative'. Opposed to 'subjective', it implies that 'impersonality' of art which Eliot's Shakespeare had failed to achieve in *Hamlet*.
40. The significance of 'Apologie de Raimond Sebond', to which Eliot refers,

seems to have waned; it is not mentioned in his 'Shakespeare and Montaigne' review (*The Times Literary Supplement*, 24 December 1925), where he concludes that 'our imagination is tempted to brood too long' over a crisis in Shakespeare's life about which nothing is known.

41. See Helen Gardner, *The Composition of 'Four Quartets'*, London and Boston (Mass.), 1978, p. 39n.

42. For 'the demon of doubt which is inseparable from the spirit of belief', see Eliot's essay on Pascal in *Selected Essays*, 1951, p. 411.

43. See the essay, at the opening of Knight's *The Crown of Life*, London and New York, 1947. The concluding words on a parallel between the *Divine Commedia* and Shakespeare's greater plays, leading to 'the incarnation in actuality of the Divine Logos of Poetry', show a remarkable coincidence with Eliot's parallel use of Incarnation in experience and poetry (cf. *Ash-Wednesday* and *Four Quartets*). Furthermore, Knight's essay did much to convince Eliot that Shakespeare's plays present a coherent unity.

44. Matthiessen, *The Achievement of T. S. Eliot*, pp. 82–3.

45. A thought expressed by Tennyson in his Camelot; cf. 'Gareth and Lynette', ll.271–4:

> For an ye heard a music, like enow
> They are building still, seeing the city is built
> To music, therefore never built at all,
> And therefore built for ever.

46. Eliot had met the expression 'strange gods' no doubt in the Bible, and certainly in Henry James's 'The Jolly Corner' and *The Ascent of Mount Carmel*, where St John of the Cross insists that the first requirement before the ascent can be made is to cast away all strange gods.

47. Quentin Bell, *Virginia Woolf: A Biography*, vol. 2, London, 1972, p. 173.

48. He had somewhat similar drama in mind in September 1924, when he told Arnold Bennett that he wished to write 'a drama of modern life (furnished flat sort of people) in a rhythmic prose "perhaps with certain things in it accentuated by drum-beats"' (*The Journals of Arnold Bennett, 1921–1928*, p. 52). He seems to have been dissatisfied in November 1924 with his first attempt. Most of his spare time must have been taken up with preparation for the Clark Lectures at Cambridge until 1926, and it is not likely that he would have allowed the publication of experimental fragments in the kind of literature which he thought important to be deferred very long. They appeared separately in *The Criterion*, the first in October 1926, the second (as from *Wanna Go Home, Baby?*) in January 1927. 'Sweeney Agonistes' was given its first performance at the Group Theatre rooms early in 1934. Produced by Rupert Doone, it was like 'a study in the psychology of a Crippen' to Nevill Coghill, giving the impression that 'we were all Crippens at heart'. Eliot was surprised; in a discussion with Coghill at All Souls College, he adopted a characteristically modest, sitting-on-the-fence, point of view on the interpretation of the play. Richard March and Tambimuttu (eds), *T. S. Eliot*, London, 1948, pp. 82–7.

49. See the myth of Er in *The Republic*, x.613–16.

50. See the final paragraph of 'The Music of Poetry' in T. S. Eliot, *On Poetry and Poets*, London, 1957, p. 38.

51. Eliot thought also in terms of *Through the Looking-Glass*; cf. *Selected Essays*, 1932 or 1951, p. 276.

52. John Shand in 'Around "Little Gidding"' (*The Nineteenth Century*, September 1944, pp. 126–7) indicates the influence of Chapman's translation of Petrarch's second Penitential Psalm: 'sin's inveterate scars', 'hell's horrid Boar'. He also suggests (pp. 130–1) that Eliot's ideas on time at the opening of 'Burnt Norton' and elsewhere could have been influenced by what Montaigne says in his essay 'Apologie de Raimond Sebond'.

53. On this Eliot's insistence is rather platitudinous; cf. Carlyle. 'For man lives in Time ... only in the transitory Time-Symbol is the ever-motionless Eternity we stand on made manifest' (*Sartor Resartus*, ii.iii).

54. See Eliot on getting *beyond poetry*: Matthiessen, *The Achievement of T. S. Eliot*, p. 90.

55. See Gardner, *The Composition of 'Four Quartets'*, pp. 43–6.

56. See the passage referred to in note 54, on Beethoven's striving to get *beyond music* in his later works.

57. *The Criterion*, January 1939, pp. 272, 274, 371.

58. Cf. *To Criticize the Critics*, pp. 128–30.

59. For Eliot's remarks on the poem, see *On Poetry and Poets*, pp. 257–8.

60. For a memorable expression of this thought, see the Elizabethan poet Robert Southwell's 'The Burning Babe', a poem familiar to Eliot.

61. There may be an allusion to the inscription (from Genesis xxviii.17) over the entrance to the church at Little Gidding: 'This is none other but the house of God and the gate of heaven.'

62. As St Lucy's martyrdom was remembered annually on 13 December, she became associated with Christmas by children in some countries.

63. Machinery and the clock are related in *The Family Reunion*, just as Shelley's chain of Time (*Adonais*, l.234) is inseparable from Emily Brontë's description of the return of sensory awareness (which may have influenced Eliot's imagery) after mystical experience:

> Oh, dreadful is the check – intense the agony
> When the ear begins to hear and the eye begins to see;
> When the pulse begins to throb, the brain to think again,
> The soul to feel the flesh and the flesh to feel the chain!

64. E. Martin Browne, *The Making of T. S. Eliot's Plays*, Cambridge, 1969, p. 107.

65. W. T. Levy and V. Scherle, *Affectionately, T. S. Eliot*, London, 1969, p. 40.

66. Letters, 28 December 1817 and 27 October 1818.

67. Cf. Milton's 'miracles' with language: *On Poetry and Poets*, p. 63.

68. *George Herbert*, London, 1962, pp. 23–4.

69. Levy and Scherle, *Affectionately, T. S. Eliot*, p. 41.

70. See 'Christianity and Communism', *The Listener*, 16 March 1932.

Bibliography

A. Contents of Eliot's First Published Volumes of Poetry, 1917–1920

(1) *Prufrock and Other Observations*, The Egoist Ltd, Oakley House, Bloomsbury Street, London, June 1917; *twelve* poems as in *Collected Poems*, with the dedication to Jean Verdenal.

(2) *Poems*, The Hogarth Press, Hogarth House, Richmond, [London,] May 1919; *seven* poems:

Sweeney among the Nightingales
The Hippopotamus
Mr Eliot's Sunday Morning Service
Whispers of Immortality
Le spectateur [Le Directeur]
Mélange adultère de tout
Lune de miel

(3) *Ara Vos Prec*, The Ovid Press, [London,] February 1920; *twenty-four* poems:

Gerontion
Burbank with a Baedeker: Bleistein with a Cigar
Sweeney among the Nightingales
Sweeney Erect
Mr Eliot's Sunday Morning Service
Whispers of Immortality
The Hippopotamus
A Cooking Egg
Lune de miel
Dans le restaurant
Le spectateur [Le Directeur]
Mélange adultère de tout
Ode ('Tired. Subterrene laughter synchronous')
The Love Song of J. Alfred Prufrock
Portrait of a Lady
Preludes
Rhapsody on a Windy Night

Morning at the Window
Conversation galante
Aunt Helen*
Cousin Nancy
Mr Appolinax [*sic*]
The Boston Evening Transcript
La figlia che piange

B. Recommendations for the Study of T. S. Eliot

Works

POETRY AND DRAMA
The Complete Poems and Plays of T. S. Eliot, London, 1969
Valerie Eliot (ed.), *The Waste Land: A Facsimile and Transcript of the Original Drafts including the Annotations of Ezra Pound*, London, 1971

ESSAYS
The Sacred Wood, second edition, London, 1928
Selected Essays, enlarged edition, London, 1951
The Use of Poetry and the Use of Criticism, London, 1933
After Strange Gods, London, 1934
The Idea of a Christian Society, London, 1939
Notes towards the Definition of Culture, London, 1948
On Poetry and Poets, London, 1957
To Criticize the Critic (and other writings), London, 1965

Biography

Peter Ackroyd, *T. S. Eliot*, London, 1984
(For other sources see 'Acknowledgments' in the preliminary pages)

Critical Works and Essays

POETRY AND GENERAL ASPECTS
B. Rajan (ed.), *T. S. Eliot: A Study of His Writings by Several Hands*, London, 1947
Helen Gardner, *The Art of T. S. Eliot*, London, 1949
Elizabeth Drew, *T. S. Eliot: The Design of His Poetry*, London, 1950
F. O. Matthiessen, *The Achievement of T. S. Eliot*, third edition with a chapter on Eliot's later work by C. L. Barber, New York and London, 1958

---

* First published as 'Miss Helen Slingsby' in Ezra Pound's *Catholic Anthology*, 1915.

Hugh Kenner, *The Invisible Poet: T. S. Eliot*, New York, 1959
Northrop Frye, *T. S. Eliot*, Edinburgh and London, 1963
J. Hillis Miller, 'T. S. Eliot', in *Poets of Reality*, Cambridge (Mass.), and London, 1966
C. B. Cox and Arnold Hinchliffe (eds), *The Waste Land*, London, 1968
Bernard Bergonzi (ed.), *Four Quartets*, London, 1969
Graham Martin (ed.), *Eliot in Perspective*, London, 1970
Roger Kojecký, *T. S. Eliot's Social Criticism*, London, 1971
Bernard Bergonzi, *T. S. Eliot*, New York and London, 1972
John D. Margolis, *T. S. Eliot's Intellectual Development, 1922–1939*, Chicago and London, 1972
A. Walton Litz (ed.), *Eliot in His Time*, Princeton (NJ) and London, 1973
Elizabeth Schneider, *T. S. Eliot: The Pattern in the Carpet*, Berkeley (Calif.), Los Angeles, and London, 1975
Stephen Spender, *T. S. Eliot*, London, 1975
Lyndall Gordon, *Eliot's Early Years*, Oxford and New York, 1977
Nancy D. Hargrove, *Landscape as Symbol in the Poetry of T. S. Eliot*, Jackson (Miss.), 1978
Ronald Bush, *T. S. Eliot: A Study in Character and Style*, New York and Oxford, 1983

DRAMA
D. E. Jones, *The Plays of T. S. Eliot*, London, 1960
Carol H. Smith, *T. S. Eliot's Dramatic Theory and Practice*, Princeton (NJ) and London, 1963
E. Martin Browne, *The Making of T. S. Eliot's Plays*, Cambridge, 1969

LITERARY CRITICISM
David Newton-de-Molina (ed.), *The Literary Criticism of T. S. Eliot*, London, 1977
Edward Lobb, *T. S. Eliot and the Romantic Critical Tradition*, London and Boston (Mass.), 1981. Gives attention to Eliot's Clark Lectures.

Bibliography

Donald Gallup, *T. S. Eliot: A Bibliography*, London, 1969
Anne Ridler, in *English Poetry* (Select Bibliographical Guides), ed. A. E. Dyson, London, 1971. A descriptive survey of works on T. S. Eliot.

Index

T. S. ELIOT: POEMS, PLAYS, AND PROSE WORKS

304   *Index*